WELCOME

The concept of elite forces has accompanied armed conflict since the beginning of time. From the Spartan 300 and the Persian Immortals to the present, those units that have distinguished themselves beyond the rank and file share certain characteristics. Among these are sharply honed fighting skills born of intense training, inherent devotion to duty whether noble or base, and an unwavering willingness to go into harm's way.

This volume explores the formation, deployment, and combat records of elite forces during World War II, the greatest military conflict of the 20th century and perhaps of all human history. Although readers may question the inclusion or the absence of one formation or another, such a narrative would struggle to be all inclusive or to meet the criteria that must be seen in something of a subjective exercise. After all, in anyone stout-hearted enough to go into combat and possibly lose their life in service to their country, exists an essence of the elite.

Nevertheless, consider these units on their own merit, their extraordinary attributes, and their perspective on the battle. The stories of small units executing raids, reconnaissance, and search and destroy missions make pulse-pounding reading. The exploits of entire divisions that number in the thousands are indicative of strong leadership from the highest echelons of command to the individual soldier in the crucible of combat. At critical times, divisions made the difference in victory and defeat.

Employing stealth and quick strike capabilities, superior tactics and equipment, brute force and overwhelming firepower, elite forces distinguish themselves on the battlefield with incredible bravery that wins through to victory or in the fight to the last man. Therefore, the definition of "elite" really lies in the record. The reader may evaluate it, consider the circumstances, and render his or her own verdict; however, the fact that the stories of these fighting formations have stood the test of time, now 80 years or more since the difficult days of World War II, does speak volumes when elite status is weighed.

Airborne, amphibious, high flying, daring in the desert, or hacking through thick jungle, elite forces proved their worth in all theatres of World War II. They blazed a trail for conventional forces to reach the day of decision. They defended to the end, lit up the night sky with explosives, held the line for other forces to withdraw to safety, refused to give up a key crossroads, or willingly accepted missions from which others might shrink. Against long odds and with death often tugging at his elbow the elite soldier, airman, Commando, or covert operative acknowledged the risk and undertook his mission anyway.

Welcome to this exploration of the elite forces of World War II. In these pages you will find the stories of those men and women who accepted the challenge, fought with distinction, and often either prevailed or fell in the last moment of devotion.

In ancient Sparta, mothers told their warrior sons to return from battle either with their shields or on them. In other words, their rendezvous with destiny was one of victory or willingness to die. Time after time, the elite forces of World War II demonstrated their own brand of courage, spectacular success and epic failure.

They leave the lens of history to assess their experiences, and so welcome to this adventure, the saga of the elite forces of World War II.

Michael E. Haskew

Wing Commander Guy Gibson led the valiant aircrews of No. 617 Squadron RAF in the legendary Dambuster Raid. *(Public Domain collections of the Imperial War Museum Royal Air Force official photographer, Woodbine G (F/O) via Wikipedia)*

This monument commemorates Operation Chariot, the raid on St. Nazaire in which British Commandos received five Victoria Crosses. *(Creative Commons Tim Green via Wikipedia)*

The paratroopers of the US 82nd 'All American' Airborne Division engaged in multiple operations in the European theatre. *(Public Domain Signal Corps Archive via Wikipedia)*

CONTENTS

6   **Special Operations Executive**
Constituted at the order of Prime Minister Winston Churchill, the SOE's mission was to set Europe ablaze.

8   **Hugh Dalton**
Minister of Economic Warfare, Dalton was charged with organising the Special Operations Executive.

9   **Lieutenant Colonel William E. Fairbairn**
The foremost authority on hand-to-hand combat in the world, Fairbairn trained SOE and OSS personnel during World War II.

10   **Long Range Desert Group**
Deep penetration search and destroy, reconnaissance, and intelligence gathering were regular tasks of these elite personnel who became famous in the desert war.

13   **Special Air Service**
The brainchild of Lieutenant Colonel David Stirling, the SAS conducted hit-and-run raids against the Axis in North Africa and in Western Europe.

16   **Lieutenant Colonel David Stirling**
The founder of the Special Air Service (SAS) participated in numerous raids and was taken prisoner in Tunisia.

17   **Layforce**
Under its commander, Robert Laycock, Layforce laid the foundation for future Commando operations during World War II in the desert of North Africa.

19   **Lieutenant Colonel Geoffrey Keyes**
The young officer displayed tremendous courage and was killed during the abortive Operation Flipper, later receiving a posthumous Victoria Cross.

20   **The Chindits**
Carrying out deep penetration raids behind Japanese lines in Burma, the Chindits inflicted serious losses on the enemy but suffered greatly themselves.

23   **Brigadier Orde Wingate**
The charismatic leader of the Chindits created controversy and displayed tactical vision during the fighting against the Japanese in the jungles of Burma.

24   **British Army and Marine Commandos**
Highly trained and motivated British Commando forces executed daring raids against enemy targets and supported offensive actions against the Axis.

Pictured with former Prime Minister Neville Chamberlain, Winston Churchill (left) was a proponent of the formation of elite special forces during World War II. *(Creative Commons Attribution Share Alike 4.0 International License & Public Domain author unknown)*

The Kure 6th Battalion, Japanese Special Naval Landing Forces stands in ranks before its home barracks prior to the Battle of Midway in 1942. *(Public Domain Wikimedia Commons Author Unknown)*

27   **British Airborne Divisions**
The British 1st and 6th Airborne Divisions parachuted and rode gliders into combat on D-Day and in Operation Market Garden.

30   **Cockleshell Heroes**
Paddling small canoes into the harbour at Bordeaux, France, Commandos attacked German ships in the heavily defended anchorage.

32   **Popski's Private Army**
Led by Major Vladimir Peniakoff, the small but gallant Popski's Private Army served with distinction in the desert and in Italy until the end of the war.

34   **No. 617 Squadron RAF**
The famed No. 617 Squadron executed the Dambuster Raid in May 1943, dropping specially developed explosives to breach the walls of the structures.

37   **Wing Commander Guy Gibson**
The 26-year-old Gibson led No. 617 Squadron RAF during the Dambuster Raid and received the Victoria Cross.

38   **1st Special Service Brigade**
Lord Lovat led his Commando brigade ashore on D-Day, reaching the glider men who held the famed Pegasus Bridge across the Caen Canal.

40   **X-Craft Submariners**
Royal Navy midget submarines attacked the Nazi battleship Tirpitz and crippled the threat to Atlantic convoys.

43   **Special Interrogation Group**
Fluent in German and wearing enemy uniforms, the Special Interrogation Group infiltrated rear areas and conducted sabotage operations.

44   **Small Scale Raiding Force (No. 62 Commando)**
From 1941-1943, the Small Scale Raiding Force conducted raids under the direction of the Special Operations Executive.

46   **No. 10 Inter-Allied Commando**
Comprised of non-British personnel from Nazi-occupied Europe, these Commando troops were engaged in D-Day and other operations.

48   **Special Boat Service**
Using small canvas folbots and other transport, SBS personnel conducted raids and reconnaissance missions in the Mediterranean theatre.

50   **Major Anders Lassen**
The Terrible Viking was a ferocious fighter of the Special Boat Service. He earned the Victoria Cross and was killed in action in 1945.

51   **The Devil's Brigade**
The First Special Service Force, elite American and Canadian troops, executed daring missions in Italy and southern France.

54   **RAF Lysander Squadrons**
Pilots of the 'Black Lysander' squadrons of the RAF completed more than 400 clandestine missions into enemy-occupied territory in Europe and Asia.

55   **RAF Eagle Squadrons**
American pilots flew for the RAF before their country entered World War II. Squadrons Nos. 71, 121, and 133 were known as the Eagle Squadrons.

57   **Underwater Demolition Teams**
Forerunner of the US Navy SEALs, the Underwater Demolition Teams (UDT) blasted obstacles and performed reconnaissance on enemy-held beaches and coastline.

58   **The Jedburghs**
In support of D-Day and Allied operations in France and the Low Countries, the British SOE and American OSS cooperated to insert elite three-man teams into occupied territory.

60   **Doolittle Raiders**
American medium bombers, launched from the aircraft carrier Hornet, bombed the Japanese capital of Tokyo on April 18, 1942.

62   **US Marine Raiders**
Highly trained elite battalions within the Marine Corps, the Raiders were a short-lived but heavily engaged force in the Pacific theatre.

64   **Lieutenant Colonel Evans F. Carlson**
The father of the US Marine Raiders, Carlson exhibited personal bravery under enemy fire on several occasions during World War II.

65   **Major General Merritt A. Edson**
"Red Mike" Edson commanded the 1st Marine Raider Battalion and led the defence of Bloody Ridge at Guadalcanal.

66   **Office of Strategic Services**
The US Office of Strategic Services, forerunner of the modern Central Intelligence Agency (CIA), was formed in World War II to organise clandestine operations in all theatres.

68   **General William J. Donovan**
William J. "Wild Bill" Donovan formed the OSS intelligence agency and led its rapid growth throughout World War II.

69   **OSS Detachment 101**
American operatives recruited Kachin tribesmen, native to northern Burma, to conduct sabotage and reconnaissance operations against the Japanese.

An SAS Jeep and its crew are shown during an operation in France in late 1944. *(Public Domain work created by the United Kingdom Government via Wikimedia Commons)*

ELITE FORCES OF WORLD WAR II

70 Merrill's Marauders
The 5307th Composite Unit (Provisional) became famous as Merrill's Marauders, conducting deep penetrations behind Japanese lines and fighting for control of Myitkyina.

72 Black Sheep Squadron
VMF-214, the legendary Black Sheep Squadron, shot down many Japanese planes while under the command of Major Gregory "Pappy" Boyington.

73 US Army Rangers
Patterned after the British Commandos, the US Army Rangers conducted daring operations in the Mediterranean and in Europe.

75 US Airborne Divisions
The US 82nd, 101st, 11th, and 17 Airborne Divisions were engaged in major campaigns in the European and Pacific theatres.

78 Flying Tigers
The fighter pilots of the American Volunteer Group took their toll on Japanese planes in the China-Burma-India theatre.

80 French Foreign Legion
The 13e Demi-Brigade and other units of the French Foreign Legion fought in the desert, the Middle East, and Europe. At times, Free French legionnaires fought other Foreign Legion units loyal to Vichy.

81 1er Bataillon de Fusiliers Marins Commandos
French Commandos participated in numerous raids and large-scale landings during World War II in Europe.

83 Brandenburgers
The Brandenburgers preceded German Army units during offensive operations, seizing key bridges and communications centres through stealth, disguise, and the element of surprise.

An RAF Westland Lysander aircraft is outfitted as a potential gas sprayer. The Lysander carried out covert missions in Europe and Asia. *(Public Domain HM Government National Archive AVIA 15/254 – Reports on Gas Spraying Trials)*

Highly decorated Soviet sniper Vasili Zaitsev posed for this official portrait. *(Creative Commons via Wikipedia)*

85 1st Ss Leibstandarte Adolf Hitler and 12th SS Hitler Jugend
These Waffen SS divisions are representative of the ferocious and fanatical Nazi warriors that comprised the military formations.

88 German Commandos
SS and Luftwaffe commandos conducted numerous covert operations, including the rescue of Benito Mussolini from imprisonment.

92 Obersturmbannführer Otto Skorzeny
The master commando, was known as the most dangerous man in Europe.

93 Hauptsturmführer Fritz Klingenberg
Klingenberg led six SS soldiers in a stunning bluff to capture Belgrade, capital city of Yugoslavia, in the spring of 1941.

94 Fallschirmjäger
The German airborne forces were the elite of the Wehrmacht, fighting on all fronts during World War II in Europe.

97 Japanese Airborne
Both the Imperial Japanese Army and Navy fielded airborne units in World War II, but their operations were limited in scope.

98 Special Naval Landing Forces
The infantry battalions of the Imperial Japanese Navy fought tenaciously in both offensive and defensive roles across the Pacific theatre.

100 Kamikaze and Kaiten
Japanese suicide raiders struck targets in the Pacific from air and sea as the war turned against their nation.

102 Special Air Torpedo Unit
Flying the Savoia Marchetti SM-79 torpedo bomber, the squadrons of the Special Air Torpedo Unit scored numerous successes in the Mediterranean theatre.

104 10th Assault Vehicle Flotilla
Italian frogmen struck the Royal Navy in the Mediterranean with human torpedoes and motorboats.

106 Red Army Snipers
Snipers of the Soviet Red Army displayed extraordinary skill and daring on the Eastern Front as they fought the Nazi invaders.

108 Vasili Zaitsev
The most famous sniper of World War II, Vasili Zaitsev terrorised German troops and trained other snipers of the Red Army.

109 Soviet Naval Infantry
Ground units of the Soviet Navy were increased during World War II to conduct amphibious operations and fight as light infantry.

110 Ilyushin Il-2 Shturmovik Squadrons
The best ground attack aircraft of World War II was piloted by intrepid airmen who took great risks to destroy German armour on the Eastern Front.

112 13th Guards Rifle Division
The Soviet Red Army's 13th Guards Rifle Division participated in many of the major battles and campaigns of World War II on the Eastern Front.

113 Elite Forces Perspective
Elite forces brought a high-risk dimension to both Allied and Axis operations in World War II, and their legacy continues with modern special forces units worldwide.

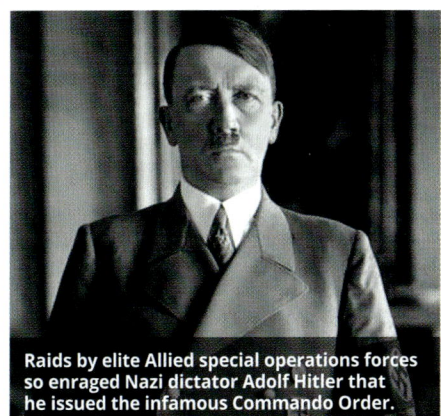

Raids by elite Allied special operations forces so enraged Nazi dictator Adolf Hitler that he issued the infamous Commando Order. *(Creative Commons Bundesarchiv Bild via Wikipedia)*

ISBN: 978 1 80282 906 8
Editor: Mike Haskew
Senior editor: Paul Sander
Senior editor, specials: Roger Mortimer
Email: roger.mortimer@keypublishing.com
Cover design: Panda Media
Main cover image: Military Images/Alamy Stock Photo
Design: SJmagic DESIGN SERVICES, India
Advertising sales manager: Brodie Baxter
Email: brodie.baxter@keypublishing.com
Tel: 01780 755131
Advertising production: Becky Antoniades
Email: Rebecca.antoniades@keypublishing.com

SUBSCRIPTION/MAIL ORDER
Key Publishing Ltd, PO Box 300,
Stamford, Lincs, PE9 1NA
Tel: 01780 480404
Subscriptions email: subs@keypublishing.com

Mail Order email: orders@keypublishing.com
Website: www.keypublishing.com/shop

PUBLISHING
Group CEO and publisher: Adrian Cox

Published by
Key Publishing Ltd, PO Box 100,
Stamford, Lincs, PE9 1XQ
Tel: 01780 755131
Website: www.keypublishing.com

PRINTING
Precision Colour Printing Ltd, Haldane, Halesfield 1, Telford, Shropshire. TF7 4QQ

DISTRIBUTION
Seymour Distribution Ltd, 2 Poultry Avenue, London, EC1A 9PU
Enquiries Line: 02074 294000.

We are unable to guarantee the bona fides of any of our advertisers. Readers are strongly recommended to take their own precautions before parting with any information or item of value, including, but not limited to money, manuscripts, photographs, or personal information in response to any advertisements within this publication.

© Key Publishing Ltd 2023 All rights reserved. No part of this magazine may be reproduced or transmitted in any form by any means, electronic or mechanical, including photocopying, recording or by any information storage and retrieval system, without prior permission in writing from the copyright owner. Multiple copying of the contents of the magazine without prior written approval is not permitted.

SPECIAL OPERATIONS EXECUTIVE

Major General Colin Gubbins succeeded Hugh Dalton as the head of the SOE. *(Public Domain via Wikimedia Commons source nikolayko.files.wordpress.com)*

Trained by the SOE, Josef Gabcik participated in Operation Anthropoid, the assassination of Reinhard Heydrich. *(Public Domain United Kingdom Government via Wikimedia Commons)*

The dismal days of the spring of 1940 weighed heavily on Prime Minister Winston Churchill. The course of World War II had gone from bad to worse. The British Expeditionary Force had been evacuated from the French port of Dunkirk under heavy pressure from the Nazi juggernaut that would march triumphantly into Paris on June 14.

Although the "Miracle of Dunkirk" was a marvel in heroism and seaborne logistics, it was hardly a triumph, and Churchill knew how important it was to strike a blow against the enemy to buoy the morale of the British people and warn Adolf Hitler that Britain, though standing alone, was still full of fight. To that end, Churchill advocated the formation of groups of stalwart, intrepid men and women who would engage in both covert and overt operations against the Germans in occupied Europe.

Responding to the prime minister's directive, elite forces were created to carry out these operations. The British Army formed the early Commando units and other hard-hitting forces, while the clandestine side of war prosecution was due for an overhaul. Churchill had also summoned Hugh Dalton, Minister of Economic Warfare, and delivered clear instructions for a comprehensive agency to coordinate and oversee covert activities.

Just eight days after the fall of Paris, Dalton recorded in his diary, "Monday 22nd June... The War Cabinet agreed this morning to my new duties. 'And now', said the P.M., 'go and set Europe ablaze.'" Ever the champion of bravery and daring in the face of the enemy, Churchill would soon be apprised of the fruits of the labour of Dalton and others. But first, there was consolidation to be accomplished.

The Electra House (Department EH), focused on propaganda, Section D of MI6, responsible for sabotage and irregular warfare initiatives, and the GS(R), coordinating engine for guerrilla warfare were under the direction of the War Office and operated in a disjointed and ineffective manner. On the day of his matter-of-fact diary entry, Dalton took charge

The SOE headquarters was located on Baker Street in London. *(Creative Commons Spudgun67 via Wikipedia)*

of the newly constituted Special Operations Executive (SOE). In the formation of the SOE, he was said to have modelled the organisation and tactics of the Irish Republican Army, a continual thorn in the British side during the 1919-1921 Irish War of Independence.

Recruiting began with renewed purpose, and SOE operatives were drawn from varied backgrounds, but each with a commitment to risk their lives in hazardous service against the Nazis. These diverse individuals underwent rigorous training at centres established across the countrysides of England and Scotland. They were instructed in hand-to-hand combat techniques, explosive usage, and methods of escape and evasion. As World War II progressed, the SOE developed a variety of schemes, specialised weapons, and well-trained personnel to conduct missions ranging from intelligence gathering, resistance coordination, and even assassination. Dalton led the SOE into 1943 and was succeeded by Major General Colin Gubbins, who had joined the group in 1940 to lead training. Gubbins had widespread contacts throughout Europe and headed the group during some of its most challenging days.

ELITE FORCES OF WORLD WAR II

SOE operatives meet local resistance members during a mission to Albania. *(Public Domain Collections of the Imperial War Museum Smiley David De C (colonel) via Wikimedia Commons)*

The damaged Mercedes convertible of Reichsprotektor Reinhard Heydrich sits in a Prague street. *(Public Domain Bundesarchiv Bild via Wikimedia Commons)*

True to Churchill's charge to "set Europe ablaze," the SOE did just that.

Many agents were parachuted or landed at clandestine airstrips in Nazi-occupied Europe to carry out their tasks, while others were trained for dangerous missions that put their own lives on the line.

Perhaps the most famous SOE sponsored operation of World War II occurred in the spring of 1942. The Czechoslovakian government in exile, led by president Eduard Benes, was well aware of the tyrannical rule of Reinhard Heydrich, SS Reichsprotektor of Bohemia and Moravia, who became known as the "Butcher of Prague" for his blood repression of the Czech people and willingness to mete out death with apparent detachment and even delight.

Benes approached the British with an assassination scheme to rid the world of the odious Heydrich, and the SOE stepped in to train and insert patriotic volunteers of the Free Czechoslovak Army to carry out Operation Anthropoid. Sergeants Josef Gabcik and Jan Kubis parachuted from a Handley-Page Halifax bomber of No. 138 Squadron RAF into Czechoslovakia on December 28, 1941, and hid out in a series of safe houses for some time, the possibility of betrayal ever present.

At length, the Anthropoid assassins made their way to Prague, and on the morning of May 27, 1942, they waited at a hairpin curve in the road that coursed alongside the Vltava River. The driver of Heydrich's big, dark green Mercedes convertible would be required to slow the car to negotiate the curve en route from the Reichprotektor's suburban home to SS headquarters at Hradcany Castle. At the opportune moment, the assassins would strike.

At the signal of two accomplices from the Czech Resistance, Gabcik stepped from the curb, pulled a Sten gun from beneath his raincoat and pulled the trigger. Click! The gun jammed, but Heydrich was startled and drew his pistol. Just then, Kubis ran forward a tossed a large grenade that detonated beneath the car's right rear wheel. Heydrich was badly wounded. He was taken to Bulkova Hospital in the filthy back of a truck. Gabcik and Kubis escaped temporarily.

Although it appeared at first that Heydrich would recover, he lapsed into a coma and died on June 4, 1942. The news of Heydrich's death shocked Reichsführer Heinrich Himmler and Hitler; both vowed revenge. The village of Lidice was razed, its men shot, women deported to the Ravensbruck concentration camp, and its children removed – many to be handed to SS families and raised as Germans. The bloody reprisals served as an abhorrent coda to Heydrich's reign of terror.

Meanwhile, Gabcik and Kubis were hunted relentlessly. Betrayed, they were cornered with a few Resistance fighters in the crypt of the Church of St. Cyril and Methodius in central Prague. After fighting valiantly, they committed suicide rather than fall into the hands of the Germans.

The SOE had struck a blow.

Throughout World War II, in every theatre of operations, the SOE became a shadowy presence. Its covert operations were conducted from Asia to the Middle East and Mediterranean, and across Europe. In November 1942, an SOE sabotage team cooperated with the Greek Resistance movement in Operation Harling to destroy the heavily defended Gorgopotamos viaduct and rail line that connected the cities of Thessaloniki and Athens, a major supply route for the Nazis. In concert with the American Office of Strategic Services (OSS), the SOE sponsored the Jedburgh initiative to assist French Resistance personnel during the days leading up to the June 6, 1944, invasion of Normandy.

However, even as this effort was underway, F-Section, the French section of the SOE, suffered a terrible loss at the hands of the Nazis. Its covert web of agents and operatives known originally as "Physician" and later as "Prosper" had been established by Francis Suttill, an SOE-trained agent, in October 1942. Hundreds of civilians were recruited to perform espionage, supply and logistics, and sabotage functions in occupied France, and by the spring of 1943, SOE operatives were active in a dozen regional departments in the country.

At the height of its operational influence, the Prosper network was compromised in June 1943, first with the arrest of a female courier and then of two Canadian SOE men. The Prosper leaders were soon taken into custody by the Gestapo, which also took control of the group's radio transmissions and sent phony messages that led to the capture and killing of many.

The men and women of the SOE earned their "elite" status during World War II, providing valuable intelligence and causing continual headaches for the Nazi counter-intelligence personnel assigned to thwart them. Many of these men and women paid with their lives, but their contribution to the Allied cause cannot be overstated. After the war, its covert work completed, the SOE was disbanded in 1946. ∎

Prime Minister Winston Churchill gave orders to establish the Special Operations Executive. *(Public Domain Library of Congress via Wikimedia Commons)*

HUGH DALTON

In the wartime coalition government of Prime Minister Winston Churchill, Hugh Dalton was a left-leaning member of the Labour Party. He had risen to prominence with his first election to Parliament in 1924, and his stature grew into the next decade as he advocated national economic planning and promoted a socialist redistribution of wealth to alleviate unemployment issues in Britain during the 1930s.

As war clouds gathered in Europe, Dalton became a prime mover in the Labour Party shift toward expenditures in bolstering national defence and military preparedness. He opposed Prime Minister Neville Chamberlain's policy of appeasement, influencing the party's political platform substantially.

Churchill appointed Dalton to the post of Secretary of Economic Warfare on May 15, 1940, just as the withdrawal of the British Expeditionary Force at Dunkirk loomed. His responsibilities included the maintenance of an economic blockade against Nazi Germany and the organisation of the Special Operations Executive (SOE), the clandestine agency that planned and executed numerous covert operations against the Axis during World War II.

In forming the SOE, Dalton was charged with Churchill's order to "set Europe ablaze." He observed, "We have got to organise movements in enemy-occupied territory comparable to the Sinn Fein movement in Ireland, to the Chinese Guerrillas now operating against Japan, to the Spanish Irregulars who played a notable part in Wellington's campaign or – one might as well admit it – to the organisations which the Nazis themselves have developed so remarkably in almost every country in the world. This 'democratic international' must use many different methods, including industrial and

Secretary of Economic Warfare Hugh Dalton became the first head of the SOE. *(Public Domain United Kingdom Government Howard Coster via Wikimedia Commons)*

military sabotage, labour agitation and strikes, continuous propaganda, terrorist acts against traitors and German leaders, boycotts and riots."

In July, just weeks after his appointment, Dalton had captured a vision for the future of the SOE. He commented, "We have on our side not only the anti-Nazi elements in Germany and Austria, not only the Czechs and the Poles, but also the whole of the democratic and liberty-loving in Norway, Denmark, Belgium, France, Holland and Italy. Moreover, in each of these countries except Italy, there will be a nationalist appeal which can be linked with the ideals of democracy and individual liberty. I am convinced that the potentialities of this war from within are really immense."

Dalton presided over the formation of the SOE for 21 critical months, and during that time SOE headquarters was established in two flats on Baker Street, London, recruiting began in earnest, and Major General Colin Gubbins, head of training and operations, set up several training sites across Britain to prepare agents for their hazardous missions. Gubbins assumed leadership of the SOE from Dalton in 1943.

On February 22, 1942, Dalton was appointed president of the Board of Trade. He served in that capacity through to the end of the war. In the post-war government of Prime Minister Clement Attlee, he served as Chancellor of the Exchequer from July 1945 to November 1947, when he was forced to resign the post amid the premature leak of sensitive budget information to the press.

Dalton returned to the government the following year and held the positions of Chancellor of the Duchy of Lancaster and Minister of Town and Country Planning. He was defeated in the National Executive Committee election of 1952, retired in 1955, and was raised to the peerage in 1959, although he took little part in the activities of the House of Lords. Dalton died on February 13, 1962, aged 74. ■

Hugh Dalton (right) and Colin Gubbins, his successor in leading the SOE, meet with Czech officers and officials. *(Public Domain Collections of the Imperial War Museum Taylor (LT), War Office official photographer via Wikimedia Commons)*

Lord Hugh Dalton responded to Winston Churchill's call for clandestine operations against the Nazis. *(Public Domain LSE Library Flickr: Lord Hugh Dalton, 1962 via Wikimedia Commons)*

ELITE FORCES OF WORLD WAR II

LIEUTENANT COLONEL WILLIAM E. FAIRBAIRN

When William E. Fairbairn was called to duty with the Special Operations Executive (SOE) in 1940, he was 55 years old. A veteran of the Royal Marines, he had served in its light infantry at the turn of the 20th century. From there, he had joined the Shanghai Municipal Police and recently retired after years of service. Shanghai was home to an extensive international population, and beginning in 1907, Fairbairn was continually patrolling rough areas of the expansive, cosmopolitan Chinese city.

Fairbairn was involved in hundreds of street brawls during his time in Shanghai and bore the scars to prove it. With the onset of World War II, his particular set of skills in hand-to-hand combat were to become invaluable in the training of elite Allied forces destined to do battle with the Axis enemy. Fairbairn was persuaded to join in SOE operative training and returned to the service with the rank of 2nd lieutenant in the British Army.

"Get tough, get down in the gutter, win at all costs," Fairbairn told the prospective SOE agents he trained. "I teach what is called gutter fighting. There is no fair play, no rules except one – kill or be killed."

With the SOE, Fairbairn earned the nickname "Dangerous Dan." He trained hundreds of operatives and was later seconded to the United States to train men of the fledgling Office of Strategic Services (OSS). Although he was quite a bit older than most of his students, Fairbairn regularly would single out the biggest and strongest in a particular group and goad him into throwing a punch. Deftly sidestepping the blow, Fairbairn would then flip the man over, face into the ground and immobilised with an arm pinned behind his back. Afterward, Dangerous Dan was always given tremendous respect.

William Fairbairn, second from left in third row, stands with OSS training staff in 1945. *(Public Domain US Govt via Wikimedia Commons)*

The Fairbairn Sykes fighting knife is an iconic weapon of close combat. *(Creative Commons via Wikipedia)*

The world's foremost authority on hand-to-hand combat, William Fairbairn trained Allied operatives. *(Public Domain National Park Service via Wikimedia Commons)*

During the course of his career, Fairbairn partnered with 2nd lieutenant Eric Sykes, another veteran of the rough and tumble Shanghai law enforcement organisation. The two developed the legendary Fairbairn Sykes fighting knife, an efficient killing instrument with a foil handle and double-edged stiletto-style blade with a fine point. The knife is still popular today and lends itself well to close-quarter combat in a variety of lethal grips. Fairbairn also designed numerous implements, weapons, and equipment used in close combat and riot control, including a police baton, protective armour vest, and a broad bladed knife called a smatchet. Some historians have speculated that he inspired the famous Q section which is notable in the James Bond spy series of books and feature films.

Through the course of World War II, Fairbairn trained elite troops of numerous Allied countries, including Britain, the US, Canada, and the Netherlands. He developed his own style of hand-to-hand fighting known as Defendu and became an expert with a pistol using his own shooting techniques. He and Sykes co-authored the 1942 book Shooting To Live With The One-Hand Gun. Fairbairn also appeared in instructional films that were used for further training by Commando and OSS forces.

After the war, Fairbairn ventured to Cyprus to train law enforcement personnel and then to Singapore, where he assisted in establishing the city's riot control unit. At the recommendation of OSS leader William "Wild Bill" Donovan, he was presented the US Legion of Merit medal. He died aged 75 in Worthing, Sussex, on June 20, 1960. ∎

Members of the Long Range Desert Group are shown aboard one of their heavy duty Chevrolet trucks traversing a sand dune. *(Public Domain Collections of the Imperial War Museums No 1 Army Film & Photographic Unit, Keating G (Capt))*

LONG RANGE DESERT GROUP

A machine gunner of the Long Range Desert Group takes aim with a truck-mounted Vickers weapon. *(Public Domain Collections of the Imperial War Museums No 1 Army Film & Photographic Unit, Graham (Lt) via Wikimedia Commons)*

Major Ralph Bagnold took advantage of the opportunity presented. When his troopship was involved in a collision in the Mediterranean Sea and docked at Alexandria for repairs, Bagnold and other personnel of the Royal Engineers were temporarily out of a job.

In Bagnold's mind, however, the wheels were turning. He had long believed that a deep penetration force, a group of elite raiders who could create havoc, gather intelligence, and provide reconnaissance behind Axis lines in North Africa, would be quite useful during World War II in the desert. A New Zealander, Bagnold had explored the expanse of the unforgiving desert between the world wars and knew it as well as any man.

When war came, he sought an audience that might be receptive to his idea, and years later he remembered, "Never in our peacetime travels had we imagined that war could ever reach the enormous empty solitudes of the inner desert, walled off by sheer distance, lack of water and impassable seas of sand dunes. Little did we dream that any of the

10 ELITE FORCES OF WORLD WAR II

ELITE FORCES OF WORLD WAR II

This Chevrolet truck of the Long Range Desert Group now resides in the Imperial War Museum. *(Creative Commons Jonathan Cardy via Wikipedia)*

Two Long Range Desert Group patrols rendezvous in the desert of North Africa. *(Public Domain United Kingdom Government via Wikimedia Commons)*

special equipment and techniques we had evolved for very long distance travel and for navigation would ever be put to serious use."

Actually, when Bagnold met with General Sir Arichibald Wavell, commander of British and Commonwealth forces in the Middle East, in Alexandria that summer of 1940, the reception was more positive than he had dreamed. Wavell had actually entered Jerusalem years earlier in company with T.E. Lawrence, the famed Lawrence of Arabia, and was quite enthusiastic.

"We ought to have some mobile ground scouting force, even a very small scouting force," Bagnold recalled telling Wavell, "to penetrate the desert to the west of Egypt to see what was going on. Because we had no information on what the Italians might be doing."

Wavell replied, "What if you find that the Italians are not doing anything in the interior at all?" Swiftly Bagnold offered, "How about some piracy on the high desert?"

Wavell's face broke into a broad grin, and he responded, "Can you be ready in six weeks?"

With that, the Long Range Desert Group (LRDG) was born. Wavell approved the allocation of equipment and manpower to the enterprise, and Bagnold began recruiting immediately. The nucleus of the LRDG came primarily from the 2nd New Zealand Division, as approximately 150 soldiers volunteered. These were hardy men, farmers and mechanics who could repair, if necessary, one of the burly American-made Chevrolet trucks that were chosen as operational vehicles. The trucks were modified with overflow radiator tanks to help cool the engines in the incredible heat of the desert, mounted with Lewis machine guns, and outfitted with plenty of storage for ammunition and foodstuffs.

The LRDG trained and became expert in deep penetration, explosives, and weaponry. It was understood that teams would spend weeks at a time in the field, behind enemy lines and beyond assistance if they encountered a difficult spot. Bagnold had his men ready in five weeks, and then for the next three years there was scarcely a day that went by without an LRDG patrol in harm's way. At times, the LRDG was audacious enough to pre-position ammunition and provisions deep in the desert in anticipation of future operations. In cooperation with the Special Air Service (SAS) formed later in 1941, the LRDG often provided ground transportation for its fellow elite force, including a September 1942 raid against the Libyan port city of Tobruk that covered 1,200 miles. An average LRDG mission included no more than 40 men travelling in 10 vehicles with a duration of up to three weeks and covering as many as 2,000 miles.

The LRDG men were hardened to the rigors of desert warfare, expected to perform on an intake of only 2.8 litres of water per day and often subsisting on substantially less than that. "You don't merely feel hot; you don't merely feel tired; you feel as if every bit of energy has left you, as if your brain was thrusting its way to the top of your head and you want to lie in a stupor until the accursed sun has gone down," commented one veteran who endured temperatures that sometimes soared beyond 120 degrees Fahrenheit.

The first LRDG mission took place as Bagnold led one of two groups that set out in September 1940 to harass Italian outposts and destroy supplies while gathering intelligence. The two groups covered 4,000 miles of desert and made a scheduled rendezvous as planned. The early success silenced some of those who had been sceptical of the concept from the beginning. In January 1941, the LRDG transported Free French troops more than 500 miles into the Libyan desert to capture the oasis at Koufrah.

During one particularly memorable mission in 1941, Captain A.M. Hay and LRDG Patrol G1 set out to disrupt the activities of the German Afrika Korps near the city of Benghazi, Libya. Travelling as rapidly as possible during the operation, the group was strafed and bombed twice by German and Italian aircraft but miraculously did not suffer any loss en route to their objective. After taking shelter in an old wadi and spending a rather uncomfortable night, Hay went looking for targets of opportunity. He came across a vehicle park that appeared to be a rest area for truck drivers shuttling men and supplies to Afrika Korps units fighting at Beda Fomm.

The LRDG moved forward and watched the coming and going of the German traffic for several hours prior to taking up positions near the rest area. When his men were in position, Hay gave the order to open fire. A fusillade of machine-gun and rifle bullets tore into the unsuspecting Germans, and hand grenades turned trucks into flaming wreckage. Although they searched quite a distance, the Germans never located their attackers, who melted away

An LRDG wireless operator sets up communications during a long patrol. *(Public Domain Imperial War Museum British/Commonwealth Military via Wikimedia Commons)*

www.keymilitary.com 11

into the desert. Patrol G1 played cat and mouse with German halftracks and infantrymen, hid from enemy aircraft during daylight hours, and retired to its base at Siwa Oasis without a scratch.

The reputation of the LRDG grew, and the elite force became a worrisome adversary for the Axis in the desert. Bagnold wrote, "To the Italians, the raiders seemed to appear from nowhere, as if from a fourth dimension, and to disappear rapidly."

Throughout its operations, the LRDG was governed by three "R's" that included reconnaissance, road watching, and raiding. Their ingenuity was beyond belief. A cracked engine block in one of their trucks was temporarily repaired with a mixture of sand and chewing gum. One man, Trooper R.J. Morse, became separated from his companions and walked more than 200 miles until he was located and rescued. The LRDG brought the use of camouflage and natural phenomena to new heights. Masters of concealment the men used netting and brush to hide their vehicles in plain sight. When trouble arose, they were known to drive straight into a swirling sandstorm to break off an engagement with the enemy or avoid detection.

While lustily pursuing Bagnold's envisioned "piracy" activities, roaring into enemy camps with machine guns chattering away, blasting parked aircraft and vehicles, and turning fuel dumps into flaming pyres, the LRDG also engaged in mine laying and gathering intelligence that proved invaluable as major operations got underway. General Bernard Montgomery, commander

Two men of the LRDG keep watch along a road in North Africa in May 1942. *(Public Domain Collections of the Imperial War Museums No 1 Army Film & Photographic Unit, Graham (Lt) via Wikimedia Commons)*

Men of the LRDG inspect new Chevrolet trucks that have just been delivered to them. *(Public Domain Collections of the Imperial War Museums Graham (Lt) No. 1 Army Film and Photo Section Army Film and Photographic Unit via Wikimedia Commons)*

Men of the Long Range Desert Group read mail during a period of relaxation at their base at Siwa Oasis. *(Public Domain Collections of the Imperial War Museums Cecil Beaton via Wikimedia Commons)*

Netting is deployed to camouflage a Chevrolet truck during a Long Range Desert Group mission in 1942. *(Public Domain Collections of the Imperial War Museum Graham (Lieut), No 1 Army Film & Photographic Unit via Wikimedia Commons)*

of the fabled Eighth Army, praised the LRDG reconnaissance that took place prior to an attack on the Mareth Line in Tunisia in 1943, and other officers recognized the value of the information on enemy movements that was provided during long hours of surveillance.

By the spring of 1943, Axis forces in North Africa had surrendered, and the LRDG was redeployed elsewhere. During the entirety of its desert campaign, the LRDG had lost but 16 men killed in action and 24 missing or taken prisoner. Subsequent operations were conducted against German occupation troops on islands in the Mediterranean Sea, in Italy, along the coast of the Adriatic Sea, and in the Balkans.

One raid into Nazi-occupied Albania left the Germans stunned as the LRDG killed 80 enemy soldiers. Another mission into Greece in the autumn of 1944 taxed the abilities even of these hardened veterans as a pair of LRDG teams parachuted into the country, mined a road that was frequently used by German convoys, and then fell upon a stalled string of vehicles when their lead truck struck one of the buried mines. The LRDG teams left 50 German soldiers dead in their wake. At the same time, the LRDG landed a single patrol on the Greek island of Naxos, and the raiders spent 17 days avoiding a pitched battle with the German garrison of 650 men while sending radio reconnaissance to the Royal Air Force, which was planning a heavy bombing raid against enemy shipping in the island's harbour.

Although their record is one of great triumph, the LRDG did pay a price for its daring forays into enemy territory. An ill-fated patrol inserted on the Greek island of Levitas in October 1943 lost 41 men killed, while Colonel Jake Easonsmith, who succeeded Bagnold in command of the LRDG, died in action during a mission on the island of Leros while more than 50 of his men were captured or wounded.

By the spring of 1945, World War II in Europe was winding down, and most LRDG personnel were eager to fight on, volunteering for redeployment to the Far East. However, the request for further service was denied. In August of that year, the LRDG was formally disbanded. Bagnold had retired from the army in June 1944 at the age of 48. He was later promoted honorary brigadier. He lived to see the results of his extensive research in the desert used by NASA (National Aeronautics and Space Administration), the US space agency, in its study of the terrain of the planet Mars.

Ralph Bagnold, a recipient of the Order of the British Empire and Fellow of the Royal Society, died on May 28, 1990, at age 94. His contribution to the Allied victory in the desert during World War II was immeasurable, and the elan of the Long Range Desert Group lives on in special operations forces today. ■

ELITE FORCES OF WORLD WAR II

SPECIAL AIR SERVICE

Second Lieutenant David Stirling, a veteran of Layforce and No. 8 (Guards) Commando, had time on his hands. Stirling had participated in an unauthorised parachute jump near Mersa Matruh, an Egyptian port city some distance west of Alexandria. The result was temporary paralysis from the waist down and a stay in the hospital. As he lay there, Stirling began to consider his recent experience in Commando operations.

Speed and firepower, shock and awe on a miniature scale, appealed to the brilliant young officer, and he came up with an idea that had far-reaching consequences. Asserting that small teams of specially-trained men might well be more effective in hit-and-run raids against enemy airfields, supply dumps, and communication centres than larger forces, Stirling envisioned these teams of elite Commandos, experts in small arms, navigation, communications, and explosives, riding into battle in fast Jeeps equipped with machine guns. When the damage was done, these teams would swifty melt away, leaving the enemy stricken and vexed.

The 25-year-old Stirling knew that approval of such a scheme would be a fight in itself, but he was willing to contend with the military bureaucracy. He wrote his proposal on a scrap of paper and then, once released from the hospital, made his way to Cairo and managed to slip into the building where General Sir Claude Auchinleck, commander of British forces in the Middle East, had established his headquarters. Although he did not meet Auchinleck face to face, Stirling did come across his chief of staff, General Neil Ritchie, who agreed to pursue the idea and present it to Auchinleck. Subsequently, after brief discussion, Auchinleck endorsed the proposition.

Detachment L, Special Air Service Brigade, was activated on July 1, 1941, and included a core cadre of 66 men, many of them fellow veterans of Layforce. The motto "Who Dares

This famous photo depicts SAS troopers in their element. This detachment has just returned from a three-month mission in North Africa. *(Public Domain Collections of the Imperial War Museum Keating (Capt) No 1 Army Film & Photographic Unit via Wikimedia Commons)*

Wins" was adopted, while the insertion of the word "Air" had been made to potentially confuse the enemy as to the unit's preferred method of transportation. Actually, SAS personnel were trained for deployment by land, sea, and air.

In September 1942, the unit's name was officially changed to the 1st Special Air Service Regiment. The SAS went into action just as General Auchinleck launched a major offensive, Operation Crusader, against the Axis enemy. On the night of November 16, 1941, five SAS teams were inserted by air transport to attack German airfields near Gazala.

Parachuting in, the SAS raiders were widely scattered amid high winds, and most of their equipment was lost in a sandstorm. Thirty-four of the 55 men involved failed to reach a rendezvous point where the Long Range Desert Group (LRDG) was to provide ground transport and became casualties. The disaster left Stirling convinced that the use of Jeeps was the best method of insertion, and soon afterward a second operation produced good results. The SAS roared into action at three airfields at Sirte, Aqedabia, and El Agheila. Guns blazing, they shot up 60 enemy aircraft on the ground. The LRDG had again provided the ground transportation, and an excellent tactical partnership developed between the two elite formations. At times the famed four-wheel drive trucks of the LRDG were utilized, but the SAS was known to ride into action even in Bentley touring cars! When the SAS did receive Jeeps of its own, the men mounted Vickers machine guns on them and adopted a tactic of approaching targets in a V formation at high speed with every available gun firing.

The element of surprise played a critical role in SAS operations, and one LRDG driver recalled a curious incident during a cooperative mission. "We drove through a huge German Army camp. The cooks were just getting up. Odd fellows walking about, going to the lavatories and having a wash. We just drove through them waving. They waved back. Why not? Five trucks driving through your camp, in the early morning, waving to you, why not wave back? Can't possibly be enemy, all that way behind German lines. Impossible."

Members of a SAS unit stand in formation during ceremonies in Italy. *(Public Domain Collections of the Imperial War Museum via Wikimedia Commons)*

SPECIAL AIR SERVICE

French SAS members visit with local tribesmen in North Africa in 1943. *(Public Domain Collections of the Imperial War Museums Currey (Sgt) No 2 Army Film & Photographic Unit via Wikimedia Commons)*

German patrols. Stirling and his companions hid in a depression, camouflage netting and scrub brush covering their remaining serviceable Jeeps. Luftwaffe aircraft flew over their heads during the day, so the various groups moved primarily after dark. After making rendezvous, the SAS men returned to base.

The results of the so-called "Jeep Raid" were outstanding. At least 25 German aircraft were destroyed, while an LRDG raid that occurred simultaneously destroyed another 15. Miraculously, only one SAS man died when he was struck by a mortar fragment.

In the wake of the Jeep Raid, German nerves were on edge. Security measures were stepped up, and General Erwin Rommel, commanding Afrika Korps forces, began to refer to Stirling as the "Phantom Major." Stirling continued to make the SAS a thorn in the Axis side until his luck ran out in January 1943. He was captured by Italian soldiers in Tunisia and spent the rest of the war as a prisoner.

The loss of Stirling was a blow to the SAS, but one of its original members with a fearsome reputation as a fighter stepped into his command shoes. Lieutenant Colonel

Stirling, promoted to major and later lieutenant colonel, relished a good fight and led from the front. And he experienced numerous close calls. One of these occurred on July 26, 1941, when the SAS men climbed aboard 18 Jeeps armed with a total of 60 machine guns and left their base at Bir Chalder to attack the German airfield at Sidi Haneish, 40 miles northwest.

Just as the SAS approached the airfield, a flood light snapped on, piercing the protective darkness. It appeared for a breathless moment as if the raiders had been discovered. But then the drone of aircraft engines was heard overhead and a German bomber was seen making its landing approach. Stirling watched the plane descend, and just as it touched down, he gave the order to attack with the ignition of a signal flare. The SAS cascaded upon the airfield and blasted row after row of Junkers Ju-52 transport planes, Heinkel He-111 bombers, and Junkers Ju-87 Stuka dive bombers.

The astonished Germans gathered themselves and quickly responded with small-arms and mortar fire. Four Jeeps, including Stirling's, were damaged beyond repair, and another was hit and broke down later. The SAS men retreated quickly, breaking up into small groups to evade

SAS troopers man a heavily armed Jeep near Geilenkirchen, Germany, in the autumn of 1944. *(Public Domain Collections of the Imperial War Museums No 5 Army Film & Photographic Unit, Hewitt (Sgt) via Wikimedia Commons)*

An SAS patrol returns to its base following a mission behind enemy lines in North Africa. *(Public Domain Collections of the Imperial War Museums via Wikimedia Commons)*

SAS troops pose for a group photo with a 75mm cannon in this 1945 image taken in Italy.
(Public Domain British Army via Wikimedia Commons)

Shown in the desert in 1942, Lieutenant Colonel Blair 'Paddy' Mayne commanded the SAS after David Stirling's capture.
(Public Domain Collections of the Imperial War Museums via Wikimedia Commons)

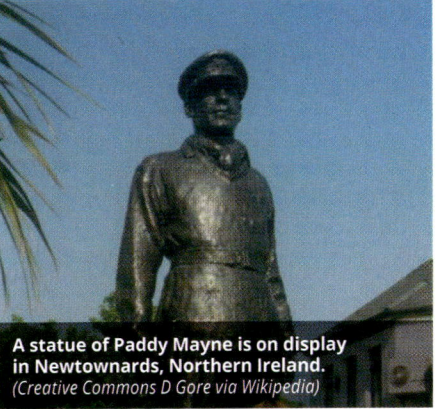

A statue of Paddy Mayne is on display in Newtownards, Northern Ireland.
(Creative Commons D Gore via Wikipedia)

Blair "Paddy" Mayne was well-known as a brawler who spent a considerable amount of time in the doghouse with army authorities. Nevertheless, he was an inspiring leader. Mayne was an imposing figure, standing 6 feet, 4 inches tall. He was a rugby player and a champion boxer in his native Northern Ireland. For the rest of the war, Mayne and Stirling's brother, Lieutenant Colonel William Stirling, who took command of the 2nd SAS Regiment formed in 1943, led the elite force in action.

Mayne became a legend as the SAS fought its way through Italy, France, Belgium, the Netherlands, Norway, and Germany in 1944-45. His exploits seemed at times to be superhuman. However, one episode stands out during his career, and in the eyes of many it should have garnered him the Victoria Cross. Some historians have speculated that the British Commonwealth's highest decoration for valour was denied because of his frequent run-ins with powerful authority figures.

The story speaks for itself. On April 9, 1945, Mayne and his SAS contingent were escorting an advance regiment of the Canadian 4th Armoured Division near the city of Oldenburg, Germany, en route to the port of Kiel. A group of German soldiers had taken up positions in a house along the roadside and unexpectedly opened fire on the advancing force. Mayne took charge – grabbing an automatic weapon, he dismounted and rushed into the house, where he killed every German he could find.

Mayne then ran back to his Jeep, ordered his men to fan out and be ready for action, and then gunned the engine. While another SAS man fired the vehicle-mounted machine gun, Mayne drove the Jeep a distance of 100 yards down the road, where German soldiers were still shooting at the Canadians. At various intervals, he slowed the Jeep to allow his gunner to spray the enemy with machine-gun bullets. Still under enemy fire, Mayne turned the Jeep around and drove back the way he had come, stopping to recover several wounded men and transport them to safety.

Those who witnessed that feat of derring do were astonished. The column advanced another 20 miles that day, well ahead of the main body of the Canadian 4th Armoured Division. The movement compelled German forces to fall back due to the emerging threat to their rear. Mayne, therefore, had ruptured an entire enemy defensive line and eased the way for an armoured division to quicken its pace.

Amid its recurring successes, the strength of the SAS increased steadily, reaching five regiments by 1944, including two British, two French, and one Belgian. Multiple SAS teams were regularly in the field, and during the Allied advance from the D-Day beaches in Normandy, SAS Operation Dunhill facilitated the breakout into the French countryside during the larger Operation Cobra. Fifty-nine SAS men in five teams freed 200 downed Allied airmen and linked up with advancing American forces after three weeks in the field. The SAS scouted drop zones and performed reconnaissance missions during Operation Market Garden in the Netherlands, but tragedy struck during Operation Loyton in the Vosges Mountains of France when 31 SAS men were captured and summarily shot by the Nazis. The ordeal of Operation Loyton lasted from August to October 1944, and another group of 24 SAS men and a captured American airman were also murdered.

The elite fighters of the SAS compiled a superlative record during World War II. Through 18 months of continual action, they destroyed 350 enemy aircraft, 89 wagons, 29 locomotives, seven trains, and more than 700 other vehicles. They killed more than 7,700 enemy soldiers and captured nearly 5,000. At its peak strength, the SAS numbered no more than 2,000 men, and 330 were killed in action.

The modern SAS continues the tradition of the elite fighting force, and today the insignia of the winged dagger is recognised the world over as a symbol of military excellence. ■

This museum display depicts an SAS detachment in the field during World War II. (Creative Commons Der Schimpf via Wikipedia)

LIEUTENANT COLONEL DAVID STIRLING

Lieutenant Colonel David Stirling founded the Special Air Service (SAS) in North Africa. *(Public Domain Collections of the Imperial War Museums Keating (Capt), No 1 Army Film & Photographic Unit via Wikimedia Commons)*

Always a bit of a maverick, Lieutenant Colonel David Stirling, father of the Special Air Service, was born into a military family on November 15, 1915, in Bridge of Allen, Scotland. The son of Brigadier Archibald Stirling and Margaret Fraser Stirling, daughter of Simon Fraser, 13th Lord Lovat, he was educated at Ampleforth College in Yorkshire and then entered Trinity College Cambridge. Soon enough, he was dismissed from the latter institution for gambling and drinking.

Young Stirling at first intended to become an artist, and ever the adventurer, he was training to climb Mount Everest when World War II broke out in 1939. He was athletic and stood tall at six feet, six inches. Commissioned in the Scots Guards in 1937, he volunteered for No. 8 (Guards) Commando. True to form, he was nearly killed in an unauthorised parachute drop that left him temporarily paralyzed and in hospital in Alexandria, Egypt. But during this period of physical inactivity his brain conceived to idea of the Special Air Service.

Stirling narrowly avoided capture or even worse during the daring Jeep Raid of January 1941, and continued to lead the SAS aggressively until he was captured in Tunisia. On January 10, 1943, Stirling was advancing with a column which came under attack by enemy troops. He managed to escape and took up with a group of apparently friendly Arabs – who sold him back to his captors for 11 pounds of tea. He was said to have awakened from a nap to find himself surrounded by 500 enemy soldiers.

Stirling attempted to escape from German prison camps on four separate occasions. Finally, he was shipped to the infamous Colditz Castle in the province of Saxony. Colditz was considered virtually escape proof, and he spent the rest of the war in confinement.

After the war, Stirling transferred to the reserves in 1947, officially retiring in 1965. From 1947 to 1959, he lived in Kenya and Rhodesia (territory roughly equivalent to the nation of Zimbabwe today). Meanwhile, he engaged in activities that led to some controversy. He founded the Capricorn Africa Society in 1949 with the intent to advocate racial equality; however, his views on limited voting rights quelled general support for the initiative. He resigned as chairman in 1959.

Stirling also engaged in the arms trade and facilitated the hiring of mercenary troops to various governments, primarily in the Middle East. With John Woodhouse, a former army lieutenant colonel, Stirling formed Watchguard International Ltd. in 1967 as a military and security consulting firm that dealt primarily with African countries, and the organisation came to be known as the "civilian branch of the SAS."

Stirling remained something of a controversial figure for the rest of his life, and news reports surfaced that he had even hatched a plan to restore and maintain order with private security forces while operating key industries in the event of a general strike or uncontrolled civil unrest in Britain. In the early 1970s, he was linked to an attempted coup d'etat in Libya intended to oust dictator Muammar al-Qaddafi. He also served as chairman of Television International Enterprises Ltd.

During World War II, Stirling had received the Distinguished Service Order, and in 1946 he was honoured with the Order of the British Empire. In 1990, he was appointed Knight Bachelor, and he died in London on November 4 at age 74. ■

After being captured, David Stirling was held at Colditz Castle in Saxony. This photo was taken in 1945. *(Public Domain US Military or Department of Defense via Wikimedia Commons)*

Lieutenant Colonel David Stirling poses with an SAS Jeep patrol on January 18, 1943. *(Public Domain Collections of the Imperial War Museums No 1 Army Film & Photographic Unit, Keating G (Capt) via Wikimedia Commons)*

ELITE FORCES OF WORLD WAR II

LAYFORCE

Shown in 1943, General Robert Laycock, founder of Layforce, rose to the post of Chief of Combined Operations. *(Public Domain Collections of the Imperial War Museums via Wikimedia Commons)*

The trailblazing Commando force of World War II arrived in the Mediterranean theatre in March 1941. Under the command of Colonel Robert "Lucky" Laycock, it bore his name, Layforce.

The honour was justified. Laycock had been instrumental in the formation of No. 8 (Guards) Commando, the 500-man nucleus around which Layforce was organized in Egypt. The son of Sir Joseph Frederick Laycock, a general of the Royal Artillery, Robert was educated at Eton College and the Royal Military College, Sandhurst, receiving a commission in the Royal Horse Guards in 1927.

Given charge of Commando operations the eastern Mediterranean, he was quickly promoted brigadier and assembled Layforce, initially about 2,000 in number, from his own No. 8 (Guards) Commando, No. 7 Commando, No. 3 Commando, and No. 11 (Scottish) Commando. Other units, including No. 50 and No. 52 Commando were added in March 1941. Layforce was composed of four battalions, each including headquarters, two Commando companies, and a signals section. One section was equipped with small collapsible watercraft called folbots.

When Laycock and company became operational in the Mediterranean, the concept of Commando warfare was still largely experimental. However, during its short tenure Layforce was to establish a basis for further such operations throughout World War II while spawning other specialised units as well. Among these were the Special Air Service (SAS), founded by Lieutenant Colonel David Stirling, and the Special Boat Service that evolved from the folbot section under the command of Major Roger "Jumbo" Courtney. Another notable officer who served with Layforce was Lieutenant Colonel Geoffrey Keyes, who later led men of No. 11 (Scottish) Commando in Operation Flipper, an attempt to kill or capture German General Erwin Rommel, and received a posthumous Victoria Cross.

Although Layforce operated only from February to August 1941, the unit was quite active. Intended to ride the crest of British victories against the Italians in North and East Africa, the outlook for raids and harassing operations of that nature evaporated with the arrival of the German Afrika Korps in Libya at about the same time as Layforce.

Still, there would be opportunities to conduct raids that were a bit less ambitious in nature than originally envisioned. Therefore, the Axis base at Bardia in eastern Libya was chosen for attack. On the night of April 19, 1941, No. 7 Commando and an attached group from the Royal Tank Regiment encountered problems from the outset, including difficulties debarking the assault force from the infantry landing ship HMS *Glengyle*. Several naval guns were disabled, a cache of truck tires was set alight, and a bridge was damaged, but further troubles were encountered during the withdrawal as more than 60 Commandos were marooned and later taken prisoner.

Nevertheless, the Bardia raid was a strategic success in that it prompted the Germans to defend against another such incursion, and the bulk of an Afrika Korps armoured brigade, much needed for frontline operations, was instead diverted from Sollum to protect the port facilities at Bardia.

Laycock and others saw promise in continuing raids against enemy supply and communications routes, but further efforts were hampered as the comprehensive situation in the eastern Mediterranean deteriorated. Luftwaffe aircraft increased patrols, limiting daylight movement by land or water, while the German invasion of Yugoslavia led to the redeployment of the majority of British and Commonwealth troops in the region to Greece. This substantial movement deprived Layforce of its waterborne

General Robert Laycock inspects Royal Marine Commandos prior to D-Day in 1944. *(Public Domain Collections of the Imperial War Museums War Office official photographer, Evans, J L (Capt))*

The infantry landing ship HMS *Glengyle* transported members of Layforce in the Mediterranean. *(Public Domain Collections of the Imperial War Museums via Wikimedia Commons)*

LAYFORCE

transportation, while the commitment to the Balkans stretched available manpower to the extent that the Commandos were the bulk of the available reserve troops in theatre.

The situation became even more critical in April 1941, as the Germans invaded Greece. Within three weeks, Allied troops were evacuated from the mainland and concentrated on the island of Crete. Elements of Layforce were sent to Crete with the hope of conducting raids that might slow down the German airborne operation that had begun on May 20. Circumstances prevented any real offensive effort, and by the end of the month the Commandos had been tasked with delaying the enemy and serving as a rear guard for the evacuation of British forces from the island. From May 26-31, Laycock led the Commandos, ill equipped for such an endeavour, in facilitating the evacuation of Crete around the port of Sphakia.

On the 28th, Laycock experienced a close call as his headquarters was ambushed. Luckily, three British tanks were in the vicinity. "By the most fortunate chance," he recalled, "the ambush was close to the tanks, and the Germans did not see them. The enemy were about 30 yards or less away from us when my Brigade-Major and I jumped into a tank and drove straight over the Germans."

Laycock and his intelligence officer, Captain and celebrated author Evelyn Waugh, were among the last of Layforce to leave Crete, and the losses were staggering. Of the 800 Commandos fighting on the island, 600 were killed, wounded or captured.

The remnants of Layforce regrouped and within days were organising a series of raids in the vicinity of the Libyan port of Tobruk, which was under siege by German and Italian forces at the time. The force designated for these operations numbered only five officers and 70 men of No. 8 Commando. However, there were notable successes.

On the night of July 18, the Commandos struck an Italian strongpoint nicknamed the Twin Pimples. After thoroughly reconnoitering the area, three officers and 40 men filtered through forward Italian positions, reaching a designated site to the rear of the objective. Indian troops to the front put on a diversion, and with perfect timing the raiders struck.

British Commandos crowd aboard a landing craft during training exercises. *(Public Domain Lt. Richard G. Arless Canada. Dept. of National Defence / Library and Archives Canada via Wikimedia Common)*

"The fight lasted about three or four minutes," a Commando remembered. "In order that we should not fight each other in the dark, we used a password 'Jock,' and I heard 'Jock' 'Jock' being shouted all over the place mixed with rifle shots and the explosion of grenades. The Italians rushed into their dugouts, and we bombed them out." One Commando died of his wounds, and three others were wounded but survived the stunning operation.

Meanwhile, No. 11 (Scottish) Commando had been detailed to Cyprus and then to Lebanon and Syria. During a fierce battle at the Litani River in June, the commander, Lieutenant Colonel R.R.H. Pedder, was killed. Keyes took command, crossing the river under fire, and leading the capture of the Vichy French gun emplacement that had hotly contested their advance. Roughly a quarter of the strength of No. 11 Commando, 123 officers and men, were lost in the fight.

By July 1941, it had become evident that strategic changes, casualty rates, and operational challenges had brought Layforce to its end. Although disbanded, it had nevertheless become a catalyst for other elite Commando units. Laycock, however, benefitted from a powerful ally. When Prime Minister Winston Churchill was apprised of the demise of Layforce, he ordered the formation of Middle East Commando and appointed Laycock as its commanding officer. Middle East Commando included the remaining elite forces in theatre, and among them were the handful of No. 11 (Scottish) Commando led by Keyes and L Force, the early designation of the SAS.

Laycock had some misgivings about Operation Flipper, particularly that Keyes was adamant about personally leading the raid on Rommel. He joined Keyes' command in the November 1941 mission as an observer and continued to lead Middle East Commando until August of 1942. For the next year, he commanded the five battalions of the Special Service Brigade. At war's end, Laycock held the rank of major general and the post of Chief of Combined Operations. ∎

Commonwealth forces bridge the Litani River during the campaign in Lebanon and Syria. *(Public Domain United Kingdom Government Chapter 10, Playfair, I.S.O. (1956). The Mediterranean and Middle East: "The Germans come to the Help of their Ally" (1941). HISTORY OF THE SECOND WORLD WAR. II. London: Her Majesty's Stationery Office via Wikimedia Commons)*

Commandos pause during operations surrounding the siege of Tobruk. Layforce conducted raids in support of the effort to raise the siege. *(Public Domain Collections of the Imperial War Museums via Wikimedia Commons)*

ELITE FORCES OF WORLD WAR II

LIEUTENANT COLONEL GEOFFREY KEYES

At age 24, Geoffrey Keyes was the youngest lieutenant colonel in the British Army, albeit the rank was temporary. World War II was underway, and the young officer, educated at Eton College and the Royal Military College, Sandhurst, had seen quite a bit of combat.

However, the military career that young Keyes had chosen had taken a detour sometime earlier – one that would lead him to command perhaps the most ambitious Commando raid of the conflict and earn him the Victoria Cross. The highest honour for valour in the armed services of the British Commonwealth was presented posthumously. Operation Flipper, the mission to capture or kill German General Erwin Rommel, would also cost him his life.

Geoffrey Keyes was the son of Admiral of the Fleet Sir Roger Keyes, a hero of the Boxer Rebellion and naval actions during World War I, and recently chosen by Prime Minister Winston Churchill as Chief of Commando Combined Operations. Geoffrey had hoped to emulate his father and pursue a commission in the Royal Navy; however, he failed the requisite eyesight test. Undaunted, he joined his uncle's cavalry regiment, the famed Royal Scots Greys, with the rank of 2nd lieutenant. He served in Palestine in the 1930s, and with the outbreak of war in 1939 he was back in England.

Yearning for a meaningful role in the war, he volunteered for service with the Commandos, and his father was delighted, writing, "I am so pleased you applied for the service – because

German General Erwin Rommel was the target of the abortive Operation Flipper in November 1941. *(Creative Commons Bundesarchiv Bild via Wikipedia)*

I was going to apply for you…" The younger Keyes was assigned to a mission in Norway, but that was cancelled when British forces withdrew from the country. He then returned to his former regiment and served as a liaison officer with the French Chasseurs Alpins and received the Croix de Guerre for bravery. When assignment to No. 11 (Scottish) Commando came through, Keyes endured the rugged

The grave of Lieutenant Colonel Geoffrey Keyes is located in Benghazi War Cemetery, Libya. *(Creative Commons Alloutlenses via Wikipedia)*

training regimen and deployed to the Middle East in early 1941. While fighting Vichy French forces in Lebanon during the invasion of Syria, he received the Military Cross for heroism.

By August, No. 11 Commando had moved to Cyprus for rest and then to Egypt to begin disbandment. However, with the help of his influential father, Keyes managed to hold onto 110 men, remain with Middle East Command, and seek further opportunities. He became the foremost proponent of Operation Flipper when intelligence reports seemed to confirm Rommel's presence at Beda Littoria in the Libyan desert.

Keyes was intent on leading the raid personally, although he was advised against such action. Nevertheless, he led 60 Commandos who boarded submarines in mid-November 1941, and came ashore on the Libyan coast amid rough seas. Torrential rain soaked the raiders as they broke into three groups to attack separate objectives.

When Keyes and his men reached Beda Littoria, the assault commenced with grenades, small-arms fire, and hand-to-hand combat. Rommel was actually in Rome at the time, and Keyes was mortally wounded in the chest. Carried outside one of the compound buildings, he died within minutes.

Operation Flipper ended in costly failure. Two Commandos – one of them a bright young officer – were dead and 28 were taken prisoner. When Prime Minister Churchill received word of the mission's outcome, he wrote to Admiral Roger Keyes, "I would far rather have Geoffrey alive than Rommel dead." ∎

Lieutenant Colonel Geoffrey Keyes was killed during Operation Flipper and received a posthumous Victoria Cross. *(Public Domain Collections of the Imperial War Museums via Wikimedia Commons)*

THE CHINDITS

A Chindit column crosses a river in Burma during a deep penetration foray. (Public Domain Collections of the Imperial War Museums No. 9 Army Film and Photographic Unit via Wikimedia Commons)

Weary, some ill and wounded, they trudged out of the jungle in clusters of a few here and there. These were the fighting men whom Brigadier Orde Wingate, their charismatic leader, had named the Chindits, after the word "chinthe" that described the mythical lions prominent in art and architecture of the Burmese people.

The Chindits had been born of Wingate's will and the support of powerful individuals, including General Archibald Wavell, commanding British forces in India, and the towering figure of Prime Minister Winston Churchill. Their raison d'etre was to execute deep penetrations behind Japanese lines in the China-Burma-India theatre, exacting as many enemy casualties as possible and wreaking destruction on their resources.

The Chindits were formally organised in late 1942 after Wavell authorised Wingate to raise a force of 3,000 men to endure rigorous training and then undertake some of the most hazardous missions of World War II. Constituted as the 77th Indian Infantry Brigade, the Chindits embarked on their first offensive penetration on February 13, 1943. Intent on cutting the rail line and destroying bridges along a principal Japanese supply route to frontline positions, they crossed the River Chindwin near the town of Imphal and spent the next two months behind enemy lines.

Wingate had devised an operational plan that obliged his command to complete long marches in stifling heat through thick jungle rife with malaria-bearing mosquitoes. Some men fell out with heat prostration, while others were taken seriously ill. However, the Chindits were a fighting force that engaged the Japanese wherever possible. In fact, the enemy was noticeably alarmed when the Chindits were discovered operating 125 miles behind their front. After their lightning conquest of much of Southeast Asia, the Japanese had earned a reputation as superb jungle fighters. Even so, as sharp clashes occurred and the hunt for the elite force intensified, they acknowledged a grudging respect for their Chindit opponents.

The Japanese were compelled to transfer substantial forces toward their rear areas to confront the Chindit threat, and Wingate divided his force into five separate columns for the long march across the broad plain of the River Irrawaddy. As they advanced, the Chindits found the surrounding terrain unsuitable for sustained resupply and extended operations. Japanese strength grew by the day, and Wingate responded to the deteriorating situation by breaking up his columns into small groups that could more easily avoid enemy patrols and filter back into the relative safety of India.

Subsequently, the Chindits conducted a fighting retreat. Although their ranks were thinned by death and disease, those who were able to shoulder a weapon fought the Japanese tenaciously. When the first foray was concluded, Wingate and his senior officers were appalled at the heavy losses suffered. Three thousand men had started the long-range penetration, and more than 800 casualties had been sustained – killed, wounded, captured, or incapacitated by disease. Although approximately 600 of these recovered and rejoined the Chindit ranks, the entire affair was held up to close scrutiny.

Brigadier Orde Wingate conceived of the deep penetration tactic in jungle warfare and created the Chindits to carry out such operations. (Public Domain Collections of the Imperial War Museums No. 9 Army Film and Photographic Unit via Wikimedia Commons)

ELITE FORCES OF WORLD WAR II

Chindits board a transport aircraft during the opening phase of Operation Thursday. (Public Domain United Kingdom Government via Wikimedia Commons)

The No. 77 Brigade patch features the mythical Burmese lion, namesake of the Chindits. (Creative Commons Coldstreamer20 via Wikipedia)

The Chindits had probably given at least as good as they had received during their long march, but the leader was taken to task by some senior officers who had never endorsed the concept of deep penetration and raiding. They felt it was a rather frivolous waste of men's lives and war materiel that could be put to better use elsewhere. The most vocal opponents of the Chindit concept harped on these aspects in the mission debriefings.

Nevertheless, Prime Minister Churchill was impressed with the result, noting that the Chindits had carried the fight to the Japanese in their own back yard and in the type of warfare which they had been known to excel. At the very least, the effort had put the enemy on notice that more such operations could be in the offing, and it required them to divert resources to guard against future incursions. Churchill relished the notion of attacking the enemy in any sort of special operation and pointed to the tangible worth of having a well-trained force that destroyed supplies and communications centres while killing Japanese soldiers. After the Japanese had won a string of victories in the CBI early in the war, the Chindits had accomplished something significant as he saw it.

Further, at this stage in World War II, the British people were in need of heroes. The press could provide a valuable tool in presenting the Chindits and their colourful commander as such. Wingate was a reporter's delight, and he cut an adventuresome figure. Therefore, leveraging the positive aspects of the first Chindit expedition, he was promoted major general and given increased logistical and fire support. The Chindits grew to 20,000 personnel, and American transport aircraft, gliders, fighters, and bombers were put at Wingate's disposal under the capable command of US Colonel Phil Cochrane, later the inspiration for the comic strips Terry and the Pirates and Steve Canyon, penned by cartoonist Milton Caniff.

Churchill even briefly considered elevating Wingate to command of all British and Commonwealth troops then operating in Burma. But the headwinds against such a move might well have been more than even a man of the prime minister's immense political stature could achieve. While Wingate had his advocates in the higher echelons of command, his opponents were powerful as well. Never afraid to speak his mind or ruffle feathers, the eccentric brigadier had made quite a few enemies during a career that was sometimes stormy.

Wingate's opponents were well aware of his eccentricities. He was known to hold meetings with his staff officers while not wearing a stitch of clothes. He had been seen boiling tea while using his socks as strainers. He harboured a robust Zionist perspective, and his willingness to breach protocol was well-known. Still, he was a brilliant tactician, a visionary, and an articulate individual. Supremely intelligent, he carried copies of the Greek classics by Homer and Plato for reading while on the jungle trail.

While his command was revived and grew in strength, Wingate was determined to undertake another long-range penetration mission against the Japanese. By early 1944, he and his staff envisioned a new foray in cooperation with an elite American force dubbed Merrill's Marauders and troops of the Chinese Army then under the command of US General Joseph "Vinegar Joe" Stilwell.

During the Quebec Conference of August 1943, Wingate presented his plan for a second Chindit mission that would involve the Americans to British senior commanders and the Joint Planning Staff. Despite the objections of some, including Field Marshal Claude Auchinleck, who declared, "In my opinion the proposal is unsound and uneconomical as it would break up divisions which will certainly be required for prosecution of the main campaign of 1944/45," the Chindit commander prevailed. Churchill retorted and later wrote that Auchinleck's "high command in India had been dragging its feet far too long... Wingate won the contest hands down..."

The mission was code named Operation Thursday. Supplies and ammunition were to be prepositioned at six sites deep behind enemy lines. Resupply would be conducted by air, and Stilwell would coordinate a complementary offensive with Chinese troops that would hopefully push the Japanese completely out of northern Burma, seize the tactically critical town of Myitkyina and its adjacent airfield, and facilitate an overland supply route for Allied forces between India and China. Once the Chindits were on the ground, they would attack targets of opportunity and sow chaos.

The offensive got underway in early March 1944 as the Chindits were inserted by glider and organised several bases, including White City, Piccadilly, Broadway, Aberdeen, and others. Although several Dakota transport aircraft crashed when their engines gave out with the burden of towing two gliders and late reconnaissance photos indicated that Piccadilly was strewn with logs and tree stumps making

American transport planes tow gliders to landing zones during Operation Thursday. (Public Domain Collections of the Imperial War Museums via Wikimedia Commons)

www.keymilitary.com **21**

THE CHINDITS

Chindits of the Hong Kong Volunteer Company pause for a photo in Burma. *(Public Domain via Wikimedia Commons)*

Orde Wingate confers with British generals in East Africa. *(Public Domain Collections of the Imperial War Museums No 1 Army Film & Photographic Unit, Palmer F E (Mr) via Wikimedia Commons)*

General Masakazu Kawabe led Japanese troops opposing Chindit operations in Burma. *(Public Domain Japanese Press Showa Era Japan (1930s-1940s) via Wikimedia Commons)*

it unsuitable for landings, Operation Thursday proceeded. Gliders previously designated for Piccadilly were diverted to Broadway, but just 35 of 61 landed without damage or casualties.

The opening phase of Operation Thursday was disappointing. It became impossible to maintain a timeline as evidenced by the fact that Brigadier Bernard Ferguson's 16 Brigade took 23 days to hack its way to the banks of the Chindwin, the halfway point in its route of march. At the same time, the Japanese responded swiftly to the renewed threat.

Lieutenant General Masakuzu Kawabe ordered 10 battalions of veteran Japanese troops into the thick jungle intent on overrunning the Chindit lodgements. Chindit 77 Brigade, under heroic Brigadier Mike Calvert, fought doggedly against an immense force of 6,600 Japanese soldiers at White City, while two Japanese battalions struck Broadway like a sledgehammer. Both sites were soon abandoned, but Calvert remained belligerent. Although his command had been reduced to just 2,000 effectives, he seized the town of Mogaung but lost half his force killed or wounded. Meanwhile Chindit 111 Brigade maintained a grim hold on a hastily built strongpoint named Blackpool.

These initiatives were enough to provide a bit of breathing room – but just barely. The Japanese pressure was relentless, and by the end of August it was time for the Chindits to retire. Operation Thursday ended six months after it began. As the Chindits pulled out of the jungle, they brought as many of their 5,000 dead and wounded back as possible.

By this time, Wingate was dead. His specially fitted Consolidated B-24 Liberator bomber had crashed into a mountainside southwest of Imphal as he returned from an assessment of the situation on the ground at Aberdeen.

With the death of Wingate, some British officers evidently saw no great loss. They said as much in post-war memoirs and interviews. Wavell was among those who criticised his former protégé in writing in the mid-1950s. However, on the day of Wingate's funeral, he stood by the grave and remarked, "The number of men of our race in this war who are really irreplaceable can be counted on the fingers of one hand. Wingate is one of them. The force he built is his own; no one else could have produced it. He designed it; he raised it; he led it, inspired it and finally placed it where he meant to place it – in the enemy vitals."

Debate as to the cost versus benefit of Chindit operations continues to this day; however, their willingness to persevere and sacrifice against long odds remains readily apparent. ∎

After graduating from Chindit training, the Hong Kong Volunteer Company is pictured in late 1944. *(Public Domain via Wikimedia Commons)*

22 ELITE FORCES OF WORLD WAR II

ELITE FORCES OF WORLD WAR II

BRIGADIER ORDE WINGATE

Some considered him mad, others a genius of war. Regardless, there is no doubt that Brigadier Orde Wingate was aggressive and quite willing to carry the fight to the Japanese where they might be most vulnerable in the China-Burma-India (CBI) theatre of World War II – behind their lines where skilled, elite troops could attack vulnerable supply dumps, troop concentrations, and communications centres, gather intelligence, inflict casualties, and then withdraw.

Wingate was an enigma. While he exhibited flashes of brilliance in tactical planning and was an inspirational leader of men, his eccentric behaviour was a concern for some superiors who often expressed concerns as to his fitness for senior command. Nevertheless, Wingate had advocates in high places and organised his famous Chindits for long-range penetration operations deep into the jungles of the CBI. The exploits of the Chindits and their noble sacrifice against a determined foe in perhaps the most inhospitable climate on earth are well remembered.

Born to devoutly Christian and Puritan parents in India on February 26, 1903, Wingate grew up in England, gaining admission to the Royal Military Academy, Woolwich. He showed promise but was known to challenge authority and question orders. Between the world wars, Wingate served in the Sudan and the Middle East, nurturing an innate Zionist perspective that fuelled a desire to strike back at Arab terrorists during counterinsurgency efforts in Palestine.

Brigadier Orde Wingate led the Chindits behind Japanese lines in Burma. *(Public Domain US Military Photo via Wikimedia Commons)*

During this period, Wingate became the protégé of General Sir Archibald Wavell and persuaded his commander in 1937 to authorise the formation of the "Special Night Squads," composed of British soldiers and Jewish militiamen. Their covert anti-terrorist effort was successful, forcing the Arabs on the defensive as Wingate's men took the offensive against Arab gunmen and destroyed oil pipelines and production facilities to choke off their funding.

Orde Wingate points to a location on a map while conferring with Haile Selassie in Ethiopia. *(Public Domain Collections of the Imperial War Museums No 1 Army Film & Photographic Unit, Palmer F E (Lieut) via Wikimedia Commons)*

With the outbreak of World War II, Wingate commanded Gideon Force in East Africa, harassing the Italian enemy in Ethiopia throughout 1940 and burnishing his reputation as an outstanding tactician. Wingate likely hatched the concept of the Chindit force at that time as his command executed extended patrols against the Italians while proving itself highly trained and motivated. By late 1942, Wavell, then commanding British and Commonwealth forces in India, saw potential for similar operations against the stubborn Japanese in the CBI, accepting Wingate's proposal to form the special operations unit that would become legend.

Wingate went on to lead the Chindits in memorable but costly operations. Although he had gained the favour of Wavell, other officers, and even Prime Minister Winston Churchill, who praised his dogged determination and zeal to fight, Wingate had his formidable enemies, who continually decried the losses incurred when weighed against the Chindit achievements. Still, the Chindits did create headaches for the Japanese, proving that they could take on the enemy – superb jungle fighters that they were – and exact an appreciable toll.

Wingate was promoted major general and commanded the two largest Chindit incursions behind Japanese lines, the first in early 1943 and the second, Operation Thursday, in the spring of 1944. His controversial career, however, ended abruptly when he died in a plane crash on March 24 at the age of 41. ∎

Wingate stands with Chindit leaders during operations in Burma, 1944. *(Public Domain Collections of the Imperial War Museums via Wikimedia Commons)*

BRITISH ARMY AND MARINE COMMANDOS

In the difficult days of 1940 when Great Britain stood alone against Nazi Germany, Prime Minister Winston Churchill understood the importance of maintaining some offensive posture against the enemy. He knew well that an invasion of western Europe would require some time and rebuilding of forces, and perhaps the active participation of the United States as an Allied co-belligerent as well.

In the meantime, the prime minister sought methods of making the Nazis at least uneasy in their occupied territories, of causing them to be wary and take measures to defend against aggressive British forces that would raid, destroy, and then disappear. Churchill told Parliament on June 4, 1940, "…We shall not flag or fail. We shall go on to the end, we shall fight in France, we shall fight on the seas and oceans, we shall fight with growing confidence and growing strength in the air, we shall defend our island, whatever the cost may be, we shall fight on the beaches, we shall fight on the landing grounds, we shall fight in the fields and in the streets, we shall fight in the hills; we shall never surrender…"

As evidence of this willingness to continue alone in the struggle against the Nazis, Churchill advocated military formations of skill combat troops that would conduct hit-and-run

Men of No. 4 Commando are shown after returning from a raid near Boulogne in 1942. *(Public Domain Collections of the Imperial War Museums Malindine E G (Lt) War Office official photographer via Wikimedia Commons)*

attacks against the Nazis, striking hard blows and sowing confusion wherever possible. And so, two days after his stirring speech to Parliament, Churchill tasked the Army Chiefs of Staff with developing such an elite body of fighting men. Utilising his long-time friend and staff officer General Sir Hastings Ismay as his messenger, Churchill conveyed his idea.

"Enterprises must be prepared, with specially trained troops of the hunter class, who can develop a reign of terror down these coasts, first of all on the 'butcher and bolt' policy; we could surprise Calais or Boulogne, kill or capture the Hun garrison…and then away…they can crawl ashore, do a deep raid inland, cutting a

Troops of No. 3 Commando are shown after the ill-fated Dieppe Raid in August 1942. *(Public Domain United Kingdom Government Lt J H Spender J H (War Office official photographer) via Wikimedia Commons)*

Field Marshal Sir John Dill, Chief of the Imperial General Staff, gave the Commando initiative his full support. *(Public Domain Collections of the Imperial War Museums Jarche, J (Mr) via Wikimedia Commons)*

ELITE FORCES OF WORLD WAR II

German soldiers escort Commando prisoners following Operation Chariot. *(Creative Common Bundesarchiv Bild via Wikipedia)*

vital communication, and then back, leaving a trail of German corpses behind them…"

The famed Commandos of the British military in World War II, then, came about with a shaking fist of bravado and a desperate yearning to strike back. The first Commando formations were developed from volunteers who heeded the call to participate in "independent mobile operations." Lieutenant Colonel Dudley Clarke, a veteran of the Boer Wars in South Africa, remembered the hard-hitting Boer irregulars who were then known as Commandos and had studied their methods as they traversed the Transvaal. He suggested the Commando name for these new fighting units, and it stuck.

Clarke had already been an early advocate of the Commando concept and had suggested raising such units in a letter to Sir John Dill, Chief of the Imperial General Staff. Dill had heard Churchill's words loud and clear and pledged to Clarke, "I will get you what you want."

Astonishingly, just three weeks later, the first so-called Commando Raid of World War II was executed as 115 men, their faces blackened and laden with substantial kit to perform sabotage, slipped across the English Channel. It was hardly a noteworthy operation in itself, but the quick strike was a harbinger of things to come. Two German sentries became the first casualties of Commando warfare, but there was little intelligence gleaned in this pin prick on the French coast at Boulogne. All had not gone completely as planned – one small boat full of Commandos had become disoriented and paddled around in the darkness before returning to its mother transport.

By mid-July, the second Commando raid was launched against the island of Guernsey, one of the Nazi-occupied Channel Islands. There was plenty of confusion, and the result confirmed that there was still much to learn. One group of Commandos landed on the wrong island, while electrical wiring caused compasses to spin wildly, disorienting the attackers. One boatload of fighting men exited into water above their heads. When the Commandos finally organised on shore, they burst into a building that supposedly served as a German barracks and found only an empty warehouse. Meanwhile, heavy swells had forced the launch that delivered the Commandos to pull away from the shore, compelling many men to shed equipment and swim some distance to the boat.

Although there were hard lessons, it was clear by the autumn of 1940 that the Commandos might provide valuable service in the future. More than 2,000 soldiers had volunteered for the hazardous duty, and the Commandos were officially designated the Special Service Brigade with General Joseph Haydon as commanding officer. An original authorised strength of 10 Commando units was increased to 12, each of them 450 strong, commanded by a lieutenant colonel, and containing a headquarters group, heavy weapons and assault formations. Each unit was further divided into troops of 75 men and sections of 15. Training was intense, and tactics were refined as a wider variety of weapons was made available as well.

By mid-1942, the Royal Marines had been authorized to develop their own Commando units, and the appeal was wildly successful as 6,000 men volunteered. A healthy rivalry soon developed between the Commando units of the Army and Royal Marines.

Admiral Sir Roger Keyes was named the first Chief of Combined Operations. He resigned in October 1942, giving way to Lord Louis Mountbatten. During this period, other Commando type formations were being developed, including the Special Air Service (SAS) and Special Boat Service (SBS).

Less than a year after the Commandos were officially constituted, they validated the concept of hard-hitting raids against high value targets with tremendous elan. In 1941, operations were staged against plants in Norway that converted fish oil to glycol for use in the German armaments industry.

At the time, plans for Operation Chariot, one of the most ambitious and dangerous raids of World War II, were underway. The 42,900-ton Kriegsmarine battleship Tirpitz was a continuing menace to Allied merchant shipping, and the only drydock on the Atlantic coast of France capable of handling the behemoth was located

On the morning after the St. Nazaire Raid, HMS *Campbeltown* **is wedged into the drydock gate.** *(Creative Commons Bundesarchiv Bild via Wikipedia)*

Motor Gun Boat 314 is shown underway prior to the raid on St. Nazaire. *(Public Domain United Kingdom Government Imperial War Museum via Wikimedia Commons)*

www.keymilitary.com 25

BRITISH ARMY AND MARINE COMMANDOS

at the port of St. Nazaire. Built between the wars to accommodate the French luxury liner Normandie, the drydock, as well as U-boat pens and installations at St. Nazaire had been targeted by Royal Air Force bombers, but high altitude bombing was relatively inaccurate, and the results were disappointing.

The components of a Commando raid against St. Nazaire came together quickly. The old American destroyer USS Buchanan had been given to the Royal Navy during the historic Destroyers for Bases Deal of 1940 and renamed HMS *Campbeltown*. For Operation Chariot, Campbeltown would be modified to mimic the silhouette of a German Mowe-class torpedo boat, and the nose of the old warship would be packed with 400 pounds of high explosives. The destroyer crew would ram the bow of the *Campbeltown* into the drydock, and when the destructive payload detonated, the facility would be rendered useless to the Nazis. Commandos would meanwhile rush ashore and destroy vital port facilities to cripple the functioning of the base.

While the modifications were made to HMS *Campbeltown*, Royal Navy Captain Robert "Red" Ryder and Lieutenant Colonel Charles Newman of No. 2 Commando trained their men hard for the upcoming assault. The Commandos would come ashore in three groups, 75 of them

German soldiers inspect the wrecked HMS *Campbeltown* moments before the explosives aboard detonated. *(Creative Commons Bundesarchiv Bild via Wikipedia)*

debarking from the deck of Campbeltown while the remainder came rushed in from motor launches. The moon and tides indicated the most favourable conditions would occur on March 27, 1942, and in the days leading up to the event the force assembled at Falmouth.

The Commandos began arriving on March 13, and 12 days later the *Campbeltown*, with Lieutenant Commander Sam Beattie in charge, steamed into the harbour. Altogether the force included *Campbeltown*, the motor gunboat *MGB-314*, two escorting destroyers, and 16 motor launches carrying a complement of 611 men, 257 Commandos, 345 Royal Navy officers and ratings, and three liaison officers.

Navigating through the mouth of the River Loire, the task force approached St. Nazaire in darkness. German suspicions were aroused at 1:15 a.m. with a lookout's report, and no German ships were expected at the time. *Campbeltown* was flying a German naval ensign, and *MGB-314* transmitted, "Proceeding up harbour in accordance with orders. Two damaged ships in company. Request permission to proceed in without delay."

Within minutes, a German antiaircraft vessel opened fire. The Commandos remained cool and flashed a warning of "friendly fire." For a moment it appeared that the ruse was continuing to work. But then heavy fire erupted from across the harbour. Enemy guns pounded *Campbeltown*, but the old destroyer ran full speed ahead, slamming into the drydock gate at 20 knots and crumpling her bow an incredible 36 feet. Impact had occurred only four minutes behind schedule.

Meanwhile, the Commando teams came ashore under heavy fire, assaulting various objectives including the winding houses that opened the drydock gates, the pump house that filled the drydock with water, power stations that supplied electricity, and underground fuel tanks. The motor launches took the brunt of the German response, their wooden hulls shredded by enemy shells. One erupted in a sheet of flame, killing eight of 11 Commandos aboard before they set foot on land. Another just aft of *Campbeltown* took a direct hit, and 15 of 17 Commandos aboard were killed.

Nevertheless, the Commandos that made it ashore set to work. Two of the five men detailed to blow up the large pump house were wounded immediately. The commander, Lieutenant Stuart Chant, was hobbled with a knee injury, but the team blasted open a steel door, lugged 189 pounds of explosives 40 feet down stairs, and set the charges at 90 seconds. Chant and a Sergeant named Dockerell remained behind to make sure all was prepared and ordered the others out. Chant then miraculously hopped on one leg up the stairs and outside. Seconds later, the pump house blew sky high.

All Commando objectives were achieved, but there were heavy casualties. Of the 611 Commandos and Royal Navy personnel participating, 169 were killed and 232 taken prisoner. Beattie and Ryder were pulled from the water and taken for interrogation the next morning. While they refused to divulge any information, a massive explosion rocked the port of St. Nazaire at about 10:30 a.m. Late, but with shattering results, the explosives aboard *Campbeltown* had detonated. The drydock was a shambles, and more than 400 Germans were killed or wounded in the blast.

Operation Chariot symbolised the dedication and unbridled determination of the Commandos. Five of their number received the Victoria Cross for heroism at St. Nazaire, and 74 other medals were presented for valour.

Throughout the remainder of World War II, the Commandos etched a glorious chapter in the history of the British armed forces. ∎

Commando leader Lieutenant Colonel Charles Newman received the Victoria Cross for heroism during Operation Chariot. *(Public Domain Collections of the Imperial War Museums via Wikimedia Commons)*

Commandos watch fish oil tanks burn during a raid on the Lofoten Islands in Norway. *(Public Domain Collections of the Imperial War Museums Tennyson d'Eyncourt (Capt), War Office official photographer via Wikimedia Commons)*

ELITE FORCES OF WORLD WAR II

BRITISH AIRBORNE
DIVISIONS

General Roy Urquhart had never jumped from an airplane or ridden a glider into a landing zone, but General George Hopkinson, commander of the Red Devils, the 1st Airborne Division of the British Army, had been killed in action in Sicily.

Reports had filtered back to I Airborne Corps headquarters that Urquhart had acquitted himself well in command of the 231st Infantry Brigade, and so he became the choice to lead the 1st Airborne Division. General Frederick "Boy" Browning made the decision, and even Urquhart was shocked. After all, he was prone to airsickness.

Urquhart did take command of the 1st Airborne Division and led it through the terrible fighting of Operation Market Garden in the autumn of 1944. The British Army fielded only two full airborne divisions during World War II, and the other was the 6th Airborne, which covered itself in glory on D-Day, June 6, 1944. By the very nature of their operations, insertions by parachute and glider to execute missions behind enemy lines, these divisions were elite.

The 1st Airborne Division was formed in late 1941 and originally commanded by Browning. Its early components were the 1st, 2nd, 3rd, and 4th Parachute Brigades and supporting formations such as medical, communications, airborne artillery, and headquarters.

Paras of the 1st Airborne Division crouch by a roadside and await orders during Operation Market Garden. *(Public Domain Collections of the Imperial War Museums Smith D M (Sgt), No 5 Army Film & Photographic Unit via Wikimedia Commons)*

Early combat experience was gained in Operation Biting, the famed Bruneval Raid when elements of 2 Para under Major John Frost seized components of the Wurzburg radar system in a raid on the coast of France. In Operation Freshman, glider-borne troops made the first such Allied effort of the war in an attempt to disrupt German production of heavy water in Norway. That raid ended in tragedy.

General Roy Urquhart stands outside his headquarters at Arnhem on September 22, 1944. *(Public Domain Collections of the Imperial War Museums Smith, D M (Sgt), Army Film and Photographic Unit via Wikimedia Commons)*

British airborne soldiers advance in the Netherlands during the ill-fated Operation Market Garden. *(Public Domain)*

www.keymilitary.com 27

BRITISH AIRBORNE DIVISIONS

Major John Frost was a decorated hero of the 1st Airborne 'Red Devils' during World War II. *(Public Domain United Kingdom Government via Wikimedia Commons)*

Further 1st Airborne operations were conducted in North Africa, Sicily, and Italy by both parachute and glider.

By the autumn of 1944, General Bernard Montgomery, commander of the Allied 21st Army Group, had devised an ambitious plan dubbed Operation Market Garden. A combined airborne and ground thrust into the German-occupied Netherlands would open a direct route into the Ruhr, the industrial heart of Germany. The capture of the Ruhr might well end the war by Christmas 1944. However, the entire scheme was fraught with peril. Three airborne divisions, the British 1st and US 82nd and 101st, would seize and hold key bridges until relieved by the spearhead of the XXX Corps advancing up a single road from one bridge to the next. The toughest assignment fell to Urquhart and the Red Devils. They were to capture the bridge that spanned the Neder Rhine at the town of Arnhem, the most distant of the airborne objectives.

In the event, the Allies suffered tremendous losses as the airborne forces came to earth in the vicinity of two German panzer divisions, the 9th and 10th SS, which had been sent to the area to rest and refit after being roughly handled in Normandy. The lightly armed paras in the vicinity of Arnhem fought with distinction, enduring hardships beyond the capabilities of ordinary combat troops.

Urquhart led 10,000 men into battle during Market Garden, and the division pulled out with less than 2,000. Just about everything that could go wrong did. Even the radios that were vital to communications had been sent with the wrong crystals.

The fighting around Arnhem lasted nine agonising days, and only a single battalion of Frost's 2 Para reached the town and fought for control of the bridge. When surrender became inevitable, Frost's command had been shattered. Urquhart actually became isolated from his own headquarters for an extended period.

At Arnhem, there was no shortage of heroism; however, the 1st Airborne Division never fully recovered from its devastating losses. At war's end, the division was moved to Norway to handle the repatriation of German prisoners, and Urquhart remained in command until the division was disbanded in August 1945. He retired in 1955 and served as an advisor to the feature film A Bridge Too Far, chronicling the story of Market Garden. His character was portrayed by famed actor Sean Connery. Urquhart died in December 1988 at age 87.

The 6th Airborne Division was formed in England in the spring of 1943 and initially consisted of the 3rd and 5th Parachute Brigades and the 6th Airlanding Brigade. Its commander, General Richard N. Gale, is rightly considered the father the airborne in the British Army. Gale had spent a remarkably long period – 15 years – between the wars without advancing beyond the rank of lieutenant. However, by 1940 he was in command of an infantry battalion. A year later he was ordered to form the first parachute brigade in the army.

Gale was subsequently elevated to Director of Airborne Forces and then the 6th Airborne Division. Preparations were swiftly undertaken for the airborne phase of Operation Overlord, the Normandy invasion of June 1944, and Gale went into France with glider troops under his command.

Although the weather was far from ideal, the order was given to proceed with Overlord, and the first Allied troops into France were the glider-borne soldiers of the 6th Airborne Division. The division was given the task of anchoring

The insignia of the 6th Airborne Division features the mythical winged horse Pegasus. *(Creative Commons Joeyeti via Wikipedia)*

the eastern flank of the Normandy invasion beaches. Its objectives were the capture of the bridges over the Caen Canal and River Orne along with the destruction of five key bridges across the River Dives to impede any German counterattack against the landings, and the silencing of a battery of heavy guns at Merville that might, if intact, wreak havoc on the Allied soldiers coming ashore at Sword Beach.

At 12:15 a.m., six Airspeed Horsa gliders, towed behind Douglas C-47 Dakota transports whisked their way toward the Caen Canal bridge. Aboard were five platoons of the 2nd Battalion, Oxfordshire and Buckinghamshire Light Infantry along with a company of Royal Engineers under the command of Major John Howard.

In one of the most spectacular aerial feats of World War II, one of the glider pilots put his wood and canvas aircraft down in a clearing just 22 yards from the far end of the bridge. Seconds later, two other pilots brought their gliders in a scant 25 yards from the first. German Private Helmut Romer, walking sentry duty, was shocked and retreated with other guards. The Germans were taken completely by surprise.

Howard's men rushed the bridge and captured it in 10 minutes. Casualties were light, but a burst of German machine-gun fire cut down Lieutenant Den Brotheridge, who is believed to have been the first Allied casualty of Operation Overlord.

Air Chief Marshal Trafford Leigh Mallory called the landing at the Caen Canal the most

The debris of battle is strewn around the bridge across the Neder Rhine at Arnhem after the battle during Operation Market Garden. *(Public Domain Collections of the Imperial War Museums via Wikimedia Commons)*

ELITE FORCES OF WORLD WAR II

General Richard Gale was the first commander of the 6th Airborne Division. *(Public Domain Collections of the Imperial War Museums Christie (Sgt), No 5 Army Film & Photographic Unit via Wikimedia Commons)*

Paras of the 6th Airborne Division board a glider for transport into France on the night of June 5, 1944. *(Public Domain Collections of the Imperial War Museums Malindine E G (Capt), War Office official photographer via Wikimedia Commons)*

After capturing Pegasus Bridge, men of the Ox and Bucks pause on D-Day, June 6, 1944. *(Public Domain Collections of the Imperial War Museums Loughlin (Sgt) No 2 Army Film & Photographic Unit via Wikimedia Commons)*

outstanding feat of airmanship in all of World War II, and from June 6, 1944, on, the span has been known as Pegasus Bridge, in reference to the depiction of the mythical winged horse on the insignia of the 6th Airborne Division.

Although two more gliders carrying the Ox and Bucks were tardy and a third failed to reach its assigned landing area, the Orne River bridge was also captured quickly. The code words "Ham and Jam" were broadcast to convey the success of the operations. Howard and his command held against counterattacks until relieved at 1:30 p.m. by Commandos under Lord Lovat.

Meanwhile, Lieutenant Colonel Terence Otway and the 9th Parachute Battalion, 650 men, were tasked with silencing the Merville Battery. Otway and his men, however, faced serious difficulties from the start. Gliders filled with vital radio equipment and anti-tank weapons had broken their tow lines and spiralled into the English Channel. Heavy antiaircraft fire scattered the transports, and the paras came down widely dispersed.

Otway actually fell atop a German command post and had to stealthily slip away as enemy soldiers poured out the front entrance. Some men came down in the marshy environs of the River Dives and drowned under the weight of their heavy kit. Otway rounded up only a single machine gun and 155 men. Nevertheless, they set out on their mission. As they approached the battery, the paras saw two gliders full of reinforcements that should have landed nearby soar into the distance, too far to lend a hand to the deadly business.

Small-arms fire broke out as the paras blasted gaps in the barbed wire. They tangled with enemy soldier in the trenches surrounding the battery, and hand-to-hand fighting erupted. While the outer defences were breached, several men ran toward the battery's steel doors. The paras forced their way inside and shot the surprised artillerymen, disabling the guns with explosives. When the situation calmed temporarily, Otway had lost 65 men dead or wounded, and more than 100 Germans lay strewn across the vicinity.

A recognition flare was sent skyward to signal that the Merville Battery had been neutralize just moments before a naval bombardment was set to commence with the assumption that the parachute effort had failed.

Two brigades of 3rd Para dropped near Troarn after running into high winds, mismarked drop zones, and heavy antiaircraft fire. Although these men were scattered as well, four of the five bridges over the Dives were blown up quickly. The fifth was something of a different matter, but a group of nine enterprising paras found a Jeep that had been intended for medical use and pressed the vehicle into service. Speeding into Troarn, they cut their way out of a barbed wire entanglement and roared through the town's main street, rifles and automatic weapons chattering. Once they reached the bridge, the paras sprinted forward, planted their explosives, and blasted the span sky high.

The rapid movement of the 6th Airborne Division and the ingenuity of its junior ranks locked up the eastern flank of the invasion beaches on D-Day and significantly delayed a counterattack organised by the 21st Panzer Division. For the next two months, the 6th Airborne Division was engaged as the Allied beachhead expanded east of the River Orne. In September, the division was withdrawn for reorganisation in England after suffering 4,000 casualties.

Later in the war, the 6th Airborne Division, commanded by General Eric Bols, fought in the Battle of the Bulge in late December 1944 and January 1945. By the spring, the division was across the Rhine after jumping in Operation Varsity. In April, the 6th Airborne met Soviet troops at the port of Wismar, Germany, on the Baltic Sea. General Gale went on to serve post-war as NATO Deputy Supreme Commander and Commander-in-Chief of the British Army of the Rhine. ■

COCKLESHELL HEROES

COCKLESHELL HEROES

At first, Royal Marine Major Herbert G. "Blondie" Hasler's discourse on the use of two-man canoes to slip into enemy harbours, attach limpet mines to moored ships, and then silently paddle their way to safety was brushed off.

However, after his initial attempt to gain support foundered in early 1942, it was revived again in August and given the go-ahead. Why the change? Lord Louis Mountbatten, then Chief of Combined Operations, and his staff were looking for some sort of response to recent Italian successes in similar covert operations in the Mediterranean theatre.

Hasler was soon stationed at the Combined Operations Development Centre at Southsea, Hampshire, and allowed to recruit volunteers for a unit of only 24 men, first called the Royal Marine Beach Patrol Detachment and later the Royal Marine Boom Patrol Detachment, a name that had nothing to do with its real, clandestine purpose. Each of the recruits was required to be familiar with small boats, capable of conducting light repairs, and willing to participate in high-risk operations.

While they "guarded" the Boom, the channel between the Isle of Wight and southern England, Hasler's elite command trained in small boats, practicing the laying of limpet mines, navigation, and techniques of escape and evasion. Both motorboats and folding canvas craft called folbots were found unsuitable for the anticipated operations, and it was decided that the men would paddle the Mark 2 semi-rigid two- or three-man canoe into action.

As they trained, the target for the first mission of Hasler's "Cocklemen" was being determined. By the autumn of 1942, it was decided that German merchant ships, sometimes successful in slipping past the Royal Navy blockade of French ports, would be worthy of attention. The docks at Bessens-Bordeaux, roughly 75 miles up the estuary of the River Gironde

Commandos train in two-man canoes prior to Operation Frankton. (Public Domain United Kingdom Government via Wikimedia Commons)

in southern France looked promising since high-value traffic involving exchanges of resources between Axis partners Germany and Japan was known to frequent there.

The plan, code named Operation Frankton, was set for November-December 1942, when the moon and tides were expected to be most favourable. Six two-man canoes would be launched from a submarine, and the Cocklemen would paddle upriver, moving at night and laying up during the day. Once they reached the Bessens-Bordeaux docks, they would find appropriate targets, attach their limpet mines, paddle away into the night, and then escape via the land network established by MI-9 of British intelligence and the French Resistance to repatriate downed Allied airmen. Exercises took place in the Thames estuary and in Scotland.

Twelve Cocklemen manning six Mark 2 canoes were to be inserted near the mouth of the Gironde from the submarine HMS *Tuna* on December 7. They would then cover 91 miles under their own power to complete the mission.

The elite raiders included Major Hasler and Marine William Sparks in the canoe nicknamed *Catfish*; Corporal A.F. Laver and Marine W.H. Mills in *Crayfish*; Sergeant Samuel Wallace and Marine Robert Ewart in *Coalfish*; Lieutenant Jack MacKinnon and Marine James Conway in *Cuttlefish*; Marines W.A. Ellery and Eric Fisher in *Cachalot*; and Corporal C.G. Sheard and Marine David Moffatt in *Conger*. History would remember these dozen intrepid Royal Marine Commandos as the "Cockleshell Heroes."

Operation Frankton ran into difficulties from the beginning. As *Cachalot* was brought up for launch, its canvas hull was snagged and torn on *Tuna's* torpedo hatch. Ellery and Fisher were sidelined to their great dismay. The remaining five teams were in the water by 5:30 p.m., avoiding detection by two German trawlers that happened past. After paddling for three hours, the Cocklemen were confronted with an unforeseen hazard, a tide race with white water breaking in steep waves in the shallows of the Gironde estuary.

Operation Frankton was undertaken in the estuary of the River Gironde. (Creative Commons Franck-fnba via Wikimedia Commons)

ELITE FORCES OF WORLD WAR II

The submarine HMS *Tuna* transported the Cockleshell Heroes during Operation Frankton. *(Public Domain Collections of the Imperial War Museums Zimmerman, E A (Lt) Royal Navy official photographer via Wikimedia Commons)*

Jose Ferrer directed and starred in the 1955 film The Cockleshell Heroes. *(Public Domain eBay no copyright registered via Wikimedia Commons)*

This original Cockleshell canoe is now a museum piece. *(Creative Commons Deben_Dave via Wikipedia)*

At 800 yards distant, Laver and Mills attached their limpet mines to two cargo vessels.

Their task complete, the Cocklemen paddled as swiftly as they dared out of the harbour. Abandoning their boats before daybreak, the teams travelled separate escape routes. Although they had been gratified to hear the sounds of distant explosions, the damage to the targeted ships had been fairly light. Some of the limpet mines had fallen off their hulls or failed to detonate.

After hiding and evading for more than six weeks, Hasler and Sparks crossed the Pyrenees into Spain and presented themselves at the British consulate in Barcelona for repatriation. Laver and Mills were at large for two days before they were arrested by French collaborationist Gendarmes and joined MacKinnon and Conway as prisoners. The Germans showed no mercy. All four were transported to Paris and executed in March 1943.

Prime Minister Winston Churchill was briefed on the outcome of Operation Frankton and fantastically concluded that the raid had shortened the war by six months. Mountbatten crowed that Frankton was "the most courageous and imaginative of all the raids ever carried out by the men of Combined Operations commands."

In the aftermath of Operation Frankton, the Germans did take extraordinary measures to guard against other such incursions.

Major Hasler received the Distinguished Service Order for his gallantry after a recommendation for the Victoria Cross was denied oddly because his deeds were not done "in the face of the enemy." Sparks was presented the Distinguished Service Medal. Laver and Mills were Mentioned in Despatches. Hasler remained a small boat enthusiast and competitor for the rest of his life. In the 1980s, he returned to Bordeaux to pay tribute to his fellow Cocklemen who had been executed by the Nazis. He died in 1987 at age 73.

A 1955 British film, extensively fictionalised, celebrated the clandestine raid and was appropriately titled The Cockleshell Heroes. Two books, Cockleshell Heroes and The Last of the Cockleshell Heroes, by C.E. Lucas-Phillips and William Sparks and Michael Munn respectively, were published. ■

Coalfish disappeared. Although Wallace and Ewart had paddled through the tide race, their boat capsized. They were taken prisoner by the crew of a German flak gun on the morning of December 8. The two were interrogated but refused to divulge the nature of their mission. Hitler had just released his infamous Commando Order in October, and the prisoners were taken to Bordeaux and shot on December 11.

Conger capsized on its second attempt to negotiate the tide race. Sheard and Moffatt were towed to within a mile of shore by *Catfish* and *Crayfish*. At Pointe de Grave, where a lighthouse marked the entrance to the Gironde, they set off to swim to shore, just as the giant light snapped on. However, no alarm was raised. Both swimmers drowned. Sheard's body was never found, while Moffatt's washed ashore some hours afterward. The situation deteriorated further when an underwater obstacle sank *Cuttlefish*. MacKinnon and Conway attempted to reach neutral Spain but were arrested by French gendarmes and handed over to the Nazis.

Catfish and *Crayfish* carried on, their crews approaching exhaustion as freezing temperatures numbed extremities and made conditions miserable. On the night of December 8, Hasler, Sparks, Laver and Mills covered 22 miles in six hours. Continuing to paddle by night and hide in daylight hours, the Cocklemen battled an ebb tide on the night of the 10th, and Hasler chose to postpone the actual attack for 24 hours. That meant another 20 miles of paddling.

In the darkness of December 11, the two canoes parted company, *Catfish* heading west and *Crayfish* east. Hasler and Sparks attached three limpet mines to a 7,000-ton cargo ship and two more to a minelaying destroyer, two to a small cargo vessel, and their last to a tanker. As they drifted, a German sentry swung a light in their direction and they were certain they had been discovered. However, he turned away.

A monument to the participants of Operation Frankton sits near the mouth of the River Gironde. *(Creative Commons VVVF via Wikipedia)*

www.keymilitary.com **31**

POPSKI'S PRIVATE ARMY

When the two Long Range Desert Group (LRDG) patrols swept into the German airfield at Barce in Libya in September 1942, their machine guns blazed and hand grenades exploded. The surprised guards were shot dead or bewildered, unable to offer coordinated resistance. As the LRDG faded into the blackness of the North African night, 24 German planes were destroyed and 12 damaged along with 10 transport vehicles.

One participant in the successful raid was Vladimir Peniakoff. Officially an observer, the Belgian adventurer born to parents of Russian lineage had a finger smashed by a German bullet. It was amputated the next day, and shell fragments were picked out of his wounded leg as well.

Despite the injuries, Peniakoff had experienced a natural high. He was determined to constitute his own elite independent fighting unit, emulating the LRDG and the British Special Air Service in sowing destruction and confusion among the Axis enemy during World War II in the desert. Peniakoff had worked as an engineer in the region before the war and drifted from job to job in Egypt. When war came, he had attempted to enlist in the LRDG, but the British recruiters looked at him with a bit of disdain and brushed his application aside.

Peniakoff was persistent, however, and he was subsequently given a major's commission to command an obscure outfit known as the Libyan Arab Force Commando. In a rather undefined role, he was then free to organise his own elite but irregular hit-and-run outfit. Dependent on the largesse of the LRDG for supplies and equipment, Peniakoff organised this group of fewer than 30 men into a highly mobile fighting force.

In the spring of 1942, Peniakoff's band of desert buccaneers destroyed an enemy fuel dump, and thousands of gallons of precious Axis gasoline went up in flames. However, the LRDG and Peniakoff's command were pulled back, and to his consternation his little but mighty force was summarily disbanded. Then came the Barce raid and a re-energizing of Peniakoff's penchant

Major Valdimir Peniakoff led Popski's Private Army in irregular operations in the desert and Italy during World War II. *(Public Domain United Kingdom Government via Wikimedia Commons)*

En route to the Barce Raid, Major Vladimir Peniakoff leans against a heavily armed LRDG vehicle. *(Public Domain United Kingdom Government via Wikimedia Commons)*

Soldiers of Popski's Private Army are shown in Venice in 1945. *(Creative Commons Cocai via Wikipedia)*

for combat. As he recovered, the eager officer visited Colonel Shan Hackett, then controller of irregular forces in the Middle East. With a sympathetic ear, Hackett listened to Peniakoff's plea for another independent command.

Soon enough, Peniakoff was given charge of the No. 1 Demolition Squadron, comprised of five officers and 18 men and charged to seek and destroy fuel dumps, aircraft and installations behind enemy lines. There was little enthusiasm for the drab and bland name of the unit, and Hackett proposed Popski's Private Army (PPA), referencing a nickname given to the commander by LRDG intelligence officer Bill Kennedy when his radio operations were having trouble pronouncing his name.

Never numbering more than 120 men, the PPA was equipped with four jeeps armed with twin .303-calibre Vickers machine guns and a pair of three-ton trucks carrying 11 days' worth of supplies, fuel for a trek of 1,500 miles, and more than a ton of explosive charges. In early 1943, the PPA set out from Cairo, but the journey to Jebel Akhdar did not provide any targets of opportunity since the British Eighth Army had already pushed the Axis forces back into Tunisia at the Mareth Line. Training continued with the LRDG, which PPA personnel accompanied on several missions. However, one of them nearly ended in disaster as a German fighter plane shot up their encampment, destroying three Jeeps and wounding two LRDG men while most of the others were away from the site.

Popski sent the remaining three Jeeps back the safety of Tozeur, 200 miles away, while the rest of the men walked a great distance until they were

ELITE FORCES OF WORLD WAR II

Royal Navy warships and other craft mill about offshore during Operation Slapstick in September 1943. *(Public Domain Collections of the Imperial War Museums Priest L C (Lt), Royal Navy official photographer via Wikimedia Commons)*

Popski's Private Army hunted Nazi Reichsführer SS Heinrich Himmler as he fled Allied justice. *(Creative Commons Bundesarchiv Bild via Wikipedia)*

picked up by an American patrol and taken to US II Corps headquarters where they were given food and new clothing. Popski took advantage of his group's notoriety and newly found reputation for toughness after its long desert trek and wrangled a transfer for his PPA from the Eighth Army to temporary American command.

Within days, the PPA had Jeeps armed with Browning .50-calibre and .30-calibre machine guns. The replenished force took to the desert wasteland again and hit Axis sites in several locations. In short order, they destroyed 34 enemy planes, 112 vehicles, six tanks and armoured cars, and a fuel depot. During other operations at this time, Popski's men covered as many as 4,000 miles and even impersonated a German patrol to bluff their way through a checkpoint. On March 19, 1943, three of Popski's men took the surrender of 600 Italian soldiers who were trapped in a dry wadi. The PPA suffered only one man taken prisoner and two wounded during the entire foray – remarkably no one had been killed.

When the Axis forces surrendered in North Africa in May 1943, the PPA was assigned to the British 1st Airborne Division, landing by sea at the port of Taranto with Popski and a contingent of five Jeeps in the vanguard of Operation Slapstick on September 9. The PPA took part in the fight to expand and break out of the Anzio beachhead south of Rome and conducted amphibious raids along the coast of the Adriatic Sea. During one raid on the German garrison at the medieval fortress of Caserma dei Fiumi Uniti, just 45 of Popski's men surprised the enemy infantry, bluffing them into surrendering. After the bastion was taken without firing a shot, the PPA bagged a patrol of German soldiers that arrived late. For good measure, a third group of Germans was cornered and forced to surrender. When the action ended, the PPA had capture 152 German soldiers and killed 40 against a loss of only three dead and five wounded.

Popski lost his left hand during a heated firefight with German troops outside Ravenna in December 1944. He was evacuated to recover in Britain and received the Distinguished Service Order. However, he refused to remain out of the waning fight.

In the spring of 1945, the PPA reached the Italian coastal town of Chioggia and again executed a bluff. A full 700 enemy troops marched into captivity, and a detachment of heavy artillery was captured. The German commander was chagrined when he learned that his entire force had been surrendered to a mere handful of intrepid PPA fighters. In separate actions during a 10-day period, the PPA captured 1,335 prisoners and 16 pieces of artillery. This was the unit's last combat, and Popski rejoined his command at Chioggia, brandishing a hook where his lost hand had been.

During the last weeks of World War II in Europe, the PPA engaged in hunting down fugitive Nazi officials, including Reichsführer SS Heinrich Himmler, Hitler's notorious head of the SS and supposedly loyal "Bloodhound." The PPA engaged in tense negotiations with communist Yugoslav partisans, persuading them to refrain from encroaching on the territory of Austria, and then disarmed bands of Italian Partisans who had fought the Nazis from the hills and wilderness of their country.

Popski's Private Army disbanded in Austria on September 14, 1945, having spent 20 months of its 29-month existence deployed on operations. Popski remained in Austria and served as a liaison officer between the British and Soviet armies. Discharged in 1946, he died of a brain tumour in London in May 1952 at the age of 55. Popski's Private Army, successful beyond its commander's dreams and its naysayers' expectations, had etched a heroic chapter in the history of the desert war. ■

British troops approach the landing area at Taranto, Italy, in September 1943. *(Public Domain Collections of the Imperial War Museums Priest L C (Lt), Royal Navy official photographer via Wikimedia Commons)*

NO. 617 SQUADRON RAF

Air Vice Marshal Ralph Cochrane, Air Officer commanding No. 5 Group, was stunned when he departed the meeting at RAF High Wycombe, headquarters of Royal Air Force Bomber Command.

It was wartime, and Cochrane was well aware that extraordinary commitment was required of every man and woman serving in the RAF. As a matter of fact, No. 5 Group had already contributed mightily to the war effort. But now Cochrane was handed a monumental task, and he wondered just how he might manage to pull it off.

Cochrane had been ordered to assemble a new bomber squadron, coordinate its training, and then see that it completed one of the most famous missions in the history of the Royal Air Force, and no doubt its most celebrated bombing raid of World War II. At the same time, Operation Chastise, as the effort was called, had to be conceived and executed under a veil of secrecy… and, oh yes, Cochrane was to continue to run the daily affairs of No. 5 Group as well.

On the face of it, Operation Chastise was a daunting challenge. The pilots and airmen of the newly-formed squadron were to board Avro Lancaster heavy bombers, fly over

The badge of No. 617 Squadron RAF was chosen by King George VI. *(Public Domain Royal Air Force via Wikimedia Commons)*

This scale model of the Möhne Dam was used during No. 617 Squadron training. *(Public Domain Collections of the Imperial War Museums via Wikimedia Commons)*

Scientist and engineer Barnes Wallis and other officials watch the Upkeep bomb during trials. *(Public Domain Collections of the Imperial War Museums via Wikimedia Commons)*

Nazi-occupied territory and across the frontier of the Fatherland, and deliver specially designed bombs that would explode and breach the dams that blocked the Rivers Möhne, Eder, and Sorpe. Hydroelectric power generated from these dams supplied energy to much of the Ruhr, the industrial heart of Germany, and the Nazi war machine depended greatly on the output from the factories in the region.

Earlier efforts to bomb the dams had been unsuccessful. They were generally well defended by antiaircraft guns, and high-altitude bombing was woefully inaccurate, particularly using the conventional ordnance then available. However, a new weapon conceived just for the purpose at hand might indeed get the job done. The crux of Cochrane's task was to find the right airman to lead the squadron and ensure that the men were thoroughly trained in the deployment of the new weapon, code named Upkeep.

Coincidentally, Upkeep had been designed by an old friend of Cochrane's, engineer Sir Barnes Neville Wallis. After analysing the shortcomings of conventional bombs, Wallis and his colleagues concluded that the best way to breach a dam was to fashion a bomb, or perhaps more accurately a depth charge. The scientists discovered that an explosive device such as Upkeep, when released at the proper speed and altitude, would rotate and then skip across the surface of the water like a stone, slam into the

ELITE FORCES OF WORLD WAR II

An Upkeep bomb is shown mounted beneath the Avro Lancaster heavy bomber of Wing Commander Guy Gibson. *(Public Domain United Kingdom Government National Archives Imperial War Museum via Wikimedia Commons)*

for good measure. Training began immediately, and cricket screens were hoisted at Wainfleet on the coast of Lincolnshire to represent the towers at each end of the targeted dams. Mock low-level bombing runs were practiced until they could be completed with methodical precision. Local farmers and townspeople looked up in amazement as the big bombers flew dangerously close to the ground and crossed the still waters of nearby reservoirs time after time.

The date of May 16, 1943, was chosen for Operation Chastise. Primary and secondary targets were identified and studied meticulously. The bombers were organised into three waves, and as the day approached the participants wondered whether they would survive such a daring endeavour. Thirty minutes past the appointed hour, at about 10 p.m., on the fateful night, the first of the Lancasters rose into the dark sky from RAF Scampton. Cochrane had stopped by to wish the crews well and then proceeded to RAF Grantham, where he would wait along with a cluster of other senior officers, including Harris, for word of success or failure. The news would be delivered by telephone.

The second wave actually departed ahead of the first and met heavy German flak over dam, sink to the appropriate depth, and then detonate. Since Upkeep weighed a staggering 9,250 pounds while measuring five feet long and almost as wide, the bomb bays of the big Lancasters were to be modified to accept them.

Even as the design team worked diligently, there were those among the highest echelons of RAF command that believed the entire scheme was preposterous. Foremost among the naysayers was Cochrane's friend Air Chief Marshal Sir Arthur "Bomber" Harris, commander-in-chief of RAF Bomber Command, who declared, "This is tripe of the wildest description… The war will be over before it works, and it never will." For some, the Lancaster bombers themselves were assets that the RAF could ill afford to lose in some frivolous effort, not to mention the lives of numerous trained aviators that would no doubt be forfeited.

Nevertheless, as Cochrane had received orders to form "Squadron X" demonstrations of Upkeep looked promising and Wallis campaigned for the project with vigour. In his zeal, though he developed support in some quarters, Wallis's solicitations rankled several influential officers. When informed of the situation, the scientist offered to tender his resignation. Then, amazingly, despite the objections, approval was received two days after the project seemed virtually dead. In short order, Avro was given the go-ahead to modify the workhorse Lancasters and Vickers was contracted to produce the weapons of decision.

There was little doubt in Cochrane's mind as to the best choice to lead Squadron X. Wing Commander Guy Gibson was a young and daring bomber pilot who had already demonstrated the requisite qualities to execute such an ambitious undertaking. With a bit of convincing, Gibson was aboard. He was handed the details of the mission, and his new command was christened No. 617 Squadron.

It was Gibson's prerogative to pick the pilots and aircrew who would fly with him, and he chose them from across the Commonwealth. The men represented Britain, Canada, Australia, and New Zealand. There was even an American thrown in

The crew of Lancaster AJ-T poses at RAF Scampton prior to the Dambuster Raid. *(Public Domain Collections of the Imperial War Museums via Wikimedia Commons)*

Water spills from the breached Eder Dam on May 17, 1943, following the Dambuster Raid. *(Creative Commons Bundesarchiv Bild via Wikipedia)*

NO. 617 SQUADRON RAF

King George VI, centre right, listens to Air Vice Marshal Ralph Cochrane and Wing Commander Guy Gibson, along with Group Captain John Whitworth on May 27, 1943. *(Public Domain Collections of the Imperial War Museums Hensser (F/O), Royal Air Force official photographer via Wikimedia Commons)*

This aerial photograph depicts the breached Möhne Dam on May 17, 1943. *(Public Domain United Kingdom Government Flying Officer Jerry Fray RAF via Wikimedia Commons)*

the coast of the Netherlands. Within minutes two Lancasters were shot down, a third had its Upkeep torn from the suspension apparatus in its belly, and a fourth evidently hit power lines and crashed, killing its entire crew on impact.

Gibson led the first wave against the Möhne Dam, dropping his weapon short of the target and watching in disappointment as it exploded without doing appreciable damage. The leader remained in the vicinity to observe the other bombers' results and to draw antiaircraft fire away from them during their bomb runs. The second Lancaster was hit by flak just as its Upkeep exploded. The bomber crashed, and only two men survived. The third and fourth Lancasters nailed the target, and after an anxious moment or two, the wall of the Möhne Dam ruptured spectacularly. A torrent of water cascaded into the river valley below.

Leading the remaining bombers of the first wave to the Eder Dam, where no antiaircraft fire greeted them, Gibson watched as a single Upkeep breached the target. Meanwhile, the third wave, accompanied by the lone surviving Lancaster of the ill-fated second wave, attacked the Sorpe Dam but failed to cause any damage.

At 3:30 a.m. on March 17, 1943, Operation Chastise, now known popularly as the Dambuster Raid, was over.

At RAF Grantham, the big brass of the Royal Air Force sweated out the minutes. When the telephone rang the initial report was negative, and an air of gloom settled over the smoke-filled room. Minutes later, however, there was jubilation as the telephone rang again and news was received of the successes at the Möhne and Eder Dams.

Even Harris was ecstatic. He shook Wallis's hand vigorously, avowing that his early scepticism had given way to celebration and that in the future he would be willing to purchase a pink elephant from the scientist. Cochrane, apparently with the weight of the world finally off his shoulders, congratulated Wallis as well. Then the two men fairly ran to their car and sped off to RAF Scampton to attend the immediate debriefing of the returning aircrews.

Cochrane managed to dash off a congratulatory message to Gibson: "All ranks in 5 Group join me in congratulating you and all in 617 Squadron on a brilliantly conducted operation. The disaster which you have inflicted on the German war machine was a result of hard work, discipline, and courage..."

Although the actual consequences of Operation Chastise remain the subject of debate among historians to this day, it has been confirmed that German war production was adversely affected for a brief period. There is no question, however, as to the bravery of the RAF airmen who executed the hazardous mission. Fifty-three airmen died in the effort, and eight of the 19 precious Lancasters committed to the raid had been lost.

Numerous medals were presented to the participants, and Wing Commander Gibson received the Victoria Cross. Tragically, he was later killed in action.

Ten days after the Dambuster Raid, King George VI and the Queen visited No. 617 Squadron at RAF Scampton. After the royal couple were briefed on the details of the mission, the King was asked to choose between two renderings of an appropriate badge for the heroic squadron. His choice has become famous – lightning bolts are shown striking a ruptured dam, and beneath the image the French inscription reads, "Apres moi le deluge," or "After me the flood." ∎

King George VI visits No. 617 Squadron at RAF Scampton, May 27, 1943. *(Public Domain Collections of the Imperial War Museums via Wikimedia Commons)*

ELITE FORCES OF WORLD WAR II

WING COMMANDER GUY GIBSON

When Wing Commander Guy Gibson was summoned to the office of Air Vice Marshal Ralph Cochrane, Air Officer commanding No. 5 Group RAF, the two exchanged pleasantries and then got down to serious business. Gibson, who had already proven himself a dynamic and fearless combat leader, would be offered another exceptional challenge.

After the meeting in mid-March 1943, Gibson remembered, "In one breath he congratulated me on my bar to the DSO, in the next he suddenly said, 'How would you like to do one more trip?' I gulped. More flak, more fighters, but said aloud, 'What kind of trip, sir?'

'A pretty important one, perhaps one of the most devastating of all time. I can't tell you more now. Do you want it?' I said I thought I did, trying to remember where I left my flying kit."

Gibson had applied to the RAF for pilot training in the mid-1930s. Just a teenager at the time, he was rejected because his legs were too short. He was persistent, and finally in 1936 he was accepted with the notation in his personnel file: "satisfactory leg length test carried out."

When war broke out, Gibson was among the few RAF bomber pilots who flew in the earliest attempted raid against Nazi Germany, when bombers tried to attack elements of the German Navy near the port of Wilhelmshaven. Bad weather forced the raid to be recalled, but from April to September 1940, Gibson took part in 34 air missions and gained a reputation for bravery in the air. He received the Distinguished Flying Cross for valour during a raid on July 9, 1940, and was credited with a probable kill when he engaged a Luftwaffe Dornier Do-215 light bomber on his return flight from a mission against the port of Lorient, in Nazi-occupied France on August 27. Gibson later flew the Bristol Beaufighter and was credited with several aerial victories.

With his third operational tour, Gibson was promoted wing commander at age 23 and flew various minelaying and bombing missions with No. 106 Squadron. In November 1942, he received the Distinguished Service Order (DSO) for heroism. On March 12, 1943, he flew his final mission with the squadron, a raid on the city of Stuttgart, Germany. After his Lancaster was hit by German flak, he completed the mission on three working engines. Recommended for a second DSO, Gibson's recognition was initially downgraded to a bar to his Distinguished Flying Cross at headquarters No. 5 Group. However, when Air Chief Marshal Sir Arthur "Bomber" Harris, head of RAF Bomber Command, reviewed the mission's record he immediately reinstated the recommendation for a bar to the DSO.

Harris was emphatic in his admiration of Gibson's air combat record and commented, "... Any Captain who completes 172 sorties in outstanding manner is worth two DSOs if not a VC. Bar to DSO approved."

When Operation Chastise was getting underway, Air Vice Marshal Cochrane was confident that Gibson was the man to lead No. 617 Squadron. Indeed, the young pilot did not disappoint, and the Dambuster Raid lives on in the annals of aerial warfare. Gibson did receive the Victoria Cross for the mission against the Ruhr dams.

On September 19, 1944, Gibson was piloting a de Havilland Mosquito twin-engine light bomber over the Netherlands when his plane plunged earthward. Gibson and his navigation officer were killed. The hero of the Dambuster Raid was dead at age 26. ■

Wing Commander Gibson and his crew board their Avro Lancaster bomber for Operation Chastise. *(Public Domain Collections of the Imperial War Museums Bellamy W (F/O), Royal Air Force official photographer via Wikimedia Commons)*

Wing Commander Guy Gibson led No. 617 Squadron in the Dambuster Raid. *(Public Domain Collections of the Imperial War Museums Royal Air Force official photographer Stannus (F/O) via Wikimedia Commons)*

Wing Commander Guy Gibson talks with Squadron Leader David Maltby at RAF Scampton in July 1943. *(Public Domain Collections of the Imperial War Museums via Wikimedia Commons)*

1ST SPECIAL SERVICE BRIGADE

The components of the 1st Special Service Brigade and their leader, Brigadier Simon Fraser, 15th Lord Lovat, were experienced Commando warriors when the formation was brought together in 1943 to train as a unit for the D-Day landings in Normandy on June 6, 1944.

At its inception, the brigade consisted of No. 3, No. 4, and No. 6 Commando, No. 45 Royal Marine Commando, and No. 10 Inter-Allied Commando. These units had operated separately in several raids on Nazi-occupied Europe, and Lord Lovat had previously risen to command of No. 4 Commando. In early March 1941, No. 3 and No. 4 Commando assaulted the Lofoten Islands of Norway in Operation Claymore. Their objective was the destruction of large factories that produced fish oil and glycerine that was a component of munitions then being used for the Nazi war effort.

During Operation Claymore, the initial objective was partially achieved with the sinking of several enemy ships and damage to the factories; however, the recovery of a rotor wheels used in the German Enigma cipher machine and accompanying code books became a boon to British intelligence which enabled cryptanalysts to decode significant enemy radio traffic.

In December 1941, Operation Archery was undertaken by elements of Nos. 2, 3, 4, and 6 Commando, its objective the destruction of German installations at Vaagso, Norway. Four groups of Commandos landed at different points in the area and made a shambles of the German communications, warehouses, and equipment at Vaagso. They also destroyed fish oil processing facilities and took 98 German soldiers prisoner. The German garrison was stronger than intelligence reports had indicated, and the raiders called in a floating reserve as house-to-house fighting erupted in the town.

Commandos march toward their embarkation point in Britain just prior to D-Day. *(Public Domain Collections of the Imperial War Museums No 5 Army Film & Photographic Unit via Wikimedia Commons)*

The Commandos withdrew after inflicting 150 casualties on the enemy, while 19 British soldiers were killed and 57 wounded. In the wake of Operation Archery, the Nazis exacted reprisals against Norwegian civilians they deemed sympathetic to the Allies.

By August 1942, a major Commando raid had been planned against the Germans at the French coastal resort town of Dieppe. Operation Jubilee was a primarily Canadian operation, and both No. 3 and No. 4 Commando were tasked with silencing heavy enemy artillery batteries. No. 3 was to blow up the guns at Berneval east of Dieppe, while No. 4 was to take out the artillery at Varengeville to the west. In the event, a large number of landing craft carrying No. 3 Commando were scattered, and many of its personnel rounded up a captured.

No. 4 Commando followed a strafing run by Royal Air Force Hawker Hurricane fighters. With fixed bayonets the men charged the gun emplacements and destroyed them. However, 45 men were lost in the effort. The success at Varengeville was the high point of Operation Jubilee. Overall the raid on Dieppe was a terrible failure with more than 4,000 Allied casualties suffered. Still, valuable lessons were learned that would assist planners with the D-Day landings in Normandy nearly two years later.

The leader of No. 4 Commando at Dieppe, Acting Lieutenant Colonel Lord Lovat received the Distinguished Service Order for his heroism. He had been instrumental in Commando training as early as 1941, and had commanded a detachment of 100 men from the unit along with 50 Canadian troops in the April 1942 raid on the French village of Hardelot. Dubbed Operation Abercrombie, the effort had been intended to conduct reconnaissance of the surrounding beaches, take prisoners for interrogation, and destroy equipment and weapons, including a searchlight battery.

After a postponement, Lovat's Commandos embarked on April 21. The Canadian contingent became separated and failed to disembark on the French coast. The Commandos came ashore in the wrong place and attempted to carry out assigned tasks, but the allotted time was short and the men were recalled soon after landing. Although the results of the raid were somewhat disappointing, equipment and tactics were tested, proving to be of value for future operations.

Lord Lovat was promoted brigadier and ordered to prepare his new command, the 1st Special Service Brigade, for D-Day operations. The plan

Landing craft deliver men of No. 4 Commando to the beach during Operation Jubilee. *(Public Domain Collections of the Imperial War Museums Mr A D C Smith via Wikimedia Commons)*

ELITE FORCES OF WORLD WAR II

Men of No. 4 Commando gather after returning from Operation Abercrombie in April 1942. *(Public Domain Collections of the Imperial War Museums Malindine E G (Lt), War Office official photographer via Wikimedia Commons)*

Simon Fraser, 15th Lord Lovat, led the 1st Special Service Brigade on D-Day. *(Public Domain via Wikimedia Commons)*

Commandos stare from aboard their landing craft during the approach to Sword Beach on D-Day. *(Public Domain Collections of the Imperial War Museums No 5 Army Film & Photographic Unit, Wilkes (Sgt) via Wikimedia Commons)*

Just as Lovat prepared to leap into the frigid water off Sword Beach, the man standing behind him was struck in the face by a German bullet and fell. Undeterred, Lovat pushed forward, shouting encouragement to his men. Millin followed and soon found himself floundering at a depth that was up to his armpits. Above the din, he heard his commanding officer order, "Give us Highland Laddie, man!"

Once they had reached the shore, the soaked and shivering piper saw Lovat standing with his brigade major and gesturing. Again, an order came to pipe a popular tune, The Road to the Isles, to bring the rest of the Commandos ashore. "That sounded rather ridiculous to me to play the bagpipes and entertain people just like on Brighton sands in peacetime," Millin remembered later. "Anyway, I started the pipes up, and marched up and down."

Just after 1 p.m., the leading elements of the 1st Special Service Brigade reached the now famous Pegasus Bridge to the great relief of the glider men. Lovat apologized for being about an hour behind schedule. His Commandos took up defensive positions east of the River Orne near Ranville and held until the vanguard of the 3rd Division came up from Sword Beach in the afternoon. Just six days later, Lovat was seriously wounded when a British shell fell short during a bombardment around Breville. He was succeeded in command by Brigadier Derek Mills-Roberts.

The brigade returned to Britain in September 1944 for rest and replenishment. Rather to soon though, No. 4 Commando was sent back to France to replace the depleted No. 46 Royal Marine Commando. In late 1944, the special service brigades of the British Army were renamed as Commando brigades, and the 1st Commando Brigade was back in action on the continent in January 1945.

Subsequent operations included clearing German forces from the Roer Triangle and the crossing of the River Rhine during Operation Plunder. The 1st Commando Brigade was disbanded in 1946, and future such units were to be under the auspices of the Royal Marines. ■

involved landing of the brigade in the Queen Red sector of Sword Beach, the most eastward of the five landing beaches. After coming ashore, the brigade was to press inland and relieve the Ox and Bucks glider infantrymen of the 6th Airborne Division who had seized the bridge over the Caen Canal in the predawn hours of June 6. Embarking from the docks of Warsash at the mouth of the River Hamble in Hampshire, the brigade was 2,500 strong as it boarded 22 landing craft for the English Channel crossing.

The landings at Sword Beach followed aerial and naval bombardment and commenced around 7:30 a.m. with infantry and tanks of the 3rd Division coming ashore. The 1st Special Service Brigade hit the beach near the village of Colleville in the second wave with No. 4 Commando and French Commandos leading the way.

The entry of the brigade was quite a D-Day spectacle. Lord Lovat instructed his personal piper, Bill Millin, to pipe the Commandos ashore. Millin hesitated and expressed his concern for army regulations. Lovat retorted, "Ah, but that's the English War Office. You and I are both Scottish, and that doesn't apply."

Piper Bill Millin is shown in the foreground of this D-Day photo, while Lord Lovat is just to his left shoulder and in the water approaching Sword Beach. *(Public Domain Collections of the Imperial War Museums Evans, J L (Capt), No 5 Army Film & Photographic Unit via Wikimedia Commons)*

X-CRAFT SUBMARINERS

The German battleship *Tirpitz* was the target of X-Craft midget submarines during Operation Source. *(Public Domain via Wikimedia Commons)*

From the onset of World War II, the British Isles were dependent on trans-Atlantic convoys delivering vital supplies, including foodstuffs, fuel, and war materiel. During the Lend-Lease era, the Soviet Union was also sustained in part by the cargo vessels that made perilous voyages to Arctic ports.

And throughout the conflict, Nazi Germany did its utmost to attempt to sever these seaborne lifelines. During the Great War of 1914-1918, the Germans had nearly succeeded in bringing Britain to its knees with relentless U-boat attacks and the continuing menace of surface raiders, both stalking and sinking ships at an alarming pace. A generation later, the Kriegsmarine had embarked on an ambitious naval construction program that would perhaps even challenge the British Royal Navy's 300 years of domination of the world's oceans.

During the 1930s, the Germans constructed powerful pocket battleships with formidable 11-inch main batteries, battlecruisers *Scharnhorst* and *Gneisenau* also with 11-inch guns, an array of heavy and light cruisers, and scores of U-boats. Most impressive were the sister battleships *Bismarck* and *Tirpitz*, mounting 15-inch main guns, stout secondary armament, and displacing more than 42,000 tons. Achieving some degree of parity with the strength of the Royal Navy was one pillar on which the Kriegsmarine had undertaken its building program. The other was sanguine indeed. A single surface warship, or raider, might wreak havoc with a convoy rendered defenceless and send millions of tons of precious cargo to the bottom of the sea.

In response to the threat and ever-present urgency to win the Battle of the Atlantic, the Royal Navy aggressively pursued German surface warships. In 1939, the pocket ship Admiral Graf Spee had been cornered at the mouth of the River Plate in the South Atlantic and scuttled after a running battle with a trio of Allied cruisers. In the spring of 1941, the *Bismarck* had been hunted down and sunk after an epic chase that covered thousands of miles of open sea – but not before the behemoth and her consort, the heavy cruiser *Prinz Eugen*, had sunk the battlecruiser HMS *Hood*, pride of the Royal Navy, in the Battle of the Denmark Strait.

Tirpitz, however, remained a constant threat, obliging the Royal Navy to maintain a powerful presence at its Scapa Flow anchorage in the Orkney Islands of Scotland. In 1943, the great battleship was safely ensconced at Kaafjord on the coast of Norway, and she was capable of putting to sea within hours of receiving such orders. Neutralizing *Tirpitz* became a priority for the Admiralty and the Royal Air Force. High altitude bombing, however, was inaccurate and achieved little result as the battleship was sheltered amid the sheer cliffs of the fjord and ringed with antiaircraft guns. An attack by submarine offered different challenges that proved equally problematic. The approaches to the *Tirpitz* anchorage were narrow and hazardous, while the battleship was swathed in anti-torpedo netting.

There was a third option to get at *Tirpitz*, but it was fraught with risk and would require men with nerves of steel, determination, and a literal willingness to die in the attempt.

The Admiralty actually did identify both the weapon and the stout-hearted men who would risk their lives to deliver the blow.

Since late 1941, the Royal Navy had been experimenting with midget submarines, and the design work had produced the X-Craft, 51 feet long, weighing nearly 34 tons, and with interior space to accommodate up to four crewmen in cramped quarters. By March 1942, a pair of prototypes, dubbed *X-3* and *X-4*, had been completed, and within weeks six more operational boats, *X-5* through *X-10*, were produced and deemed ready for assignment. Designated the 12th Submarine Flotilla, the X-Craft were to be manned by volunteers.

Recruiting commenced, and the response was satisfactory. However, some men dropped out during the course of the rigorous training program. Obviously, the men realised that they were being prepared for a mission against a high value target, and along with that the associated risk had to be tremendous. In the spring of

The German battleship *Tirpitz* is partially obscured by a smokescreen in Kaafjord in this aerial photograph. *(Public Domain Collections of the Imperial War Museums via Wikimedia Commons)*

ELITE FORCES OF WORLD WAR II

Royal Navy Lieutenant Henty Henty-Creer and the crew of *X-5* were lost during Operation Source, the attack on the German battleship *Tirpitz*. *(Public Domain Collections of the Imperial War Museums via Wikimedia Commons)*

X-24, the only preserved X-Craft midget submarine is on display in a museum. *(Creative Commons Geni via Wikipedia)*

The interior of *X-24* reveals the cramped conditions for the crew of four. *(Creative Commons Geni via Wikipedia)*

1943, the elite men who had graduated their regimen began specific training for a mission called Operation Source, and they deduced that their target was *Tirpitz*. Training for Operation Source was cloaked in secrecy and took place at Port HHZ in Loch Cairnbawn on the remote coast of northern Scotland, far from prying eyes. The X-Craft crewmen learned to steer their small submarines, navigate in confined spaces, and to deploy their "side cargoes," a pair of two-ton explosive amatol charges.

By September, everything appeared to be in readiness. On the night of the 11th, the six X-Craft left Scotland bound for Norwegian waters and under tow from conventional submarines. The distance to the target was a gruelling 1,100 miles, and the X-Craft were manned by transit crews that would turn the midget submarines over to the combat crews at a rendezvous point at Soroy Sound, 100 miles from the entrance to Kaafjord. The long voyage was hazardous in itself, and bad weather – howling winds and heaving seas – set in on the 15th. Three tow lines snapped amid the lashing waves. *X-8* foundered and had to be scuttled, but worse, the waterlogged tow line of *X-9* grew so heavy that it dragged the small craft and its transit crew to the bottom of the sea.

The original plan for Operation Source included attacks on *Tirpitz* as well as *Scharnhorst* and the pocket battleship *Lutzow*, believed to also be anchored in Kaafjord. However, the loss of *X-8* and *X-9* altered the scheme. The remaining X-Craft were all to attack *Tirpitz*, slipping beneath its massive hull to drop the side cargoes to the shallow fjord bottom with timed fuses set to detonate in one hour. As it turned out, neither *Scharnhorst* nor *Lutzow* was in Kaafjord.

As the date of the attack approached, *X-10* developed electrical problems and had to be withdrawn from Kaafjord waters. However, the remaining X-Craft combat crewmen boarded their boats on the afternoon of September 22, 1943, and penetrated the outer defences of the fjord at about 7 p.m. Royal Navy Lieutenant Henty Henty-Creer commanded *X-5*, while

X-25 makes its way through waters while participating in training operations. *(Public Domain Collections of the Imperial War Museums Beadell, S J (Lt), Royal Navy official photographer via Wikimedia Commons)*

X-CRAFT SUBMARINERS

Lieutenant Duncan Cameron was aboard *X-6*, and Lieutenant Godfrey Place skippered *X-7*.

Cameron spotted a German patrol boat and followed it through an opening in the cordon of anti-torpedo netting. As he oriented himself, Cameron peered through his small periscope and spotted *Tirpitz* 200 yards distant. He ordered *X-6* to dive, and the midget submarine crashed into an underwater rock formation, recoiling and bobbing to the surface just 75 yards from the giant battleship. Lookouts shouted, and the secondary armament of *Tirpitz* opened fire. Cameron had just enough time to jettison his explosives beneath the forward 15-inch gun turrets. He then surrendered to Germans who were approaching aboard a motor launch. Minutes later the prisoners were aboard *Tirpitz* and warned their captors, who were sending divers over the side, that explosives might erupt at any time.

Simultaneously, Place and *X-7* became tangled in the anti-torpedo netting, slipped free, and popped to the surface just 25 yards from *Tirpitz*. The crew released one of its charges forward and the other amidships. *X-7* scraped the battleship's hull and then became tangled in the anti-torpedo netting again, struggling for some time until a massive explosion shook the entire anchorage at 8:12 p.m. The detonation of one explosive had set them all off. The blast threw *X-7* free of the netting but with serious damage. Guns aboard *Tirpitz* fired at the little craft, killing two crewmen. Place and another crewman were taken prisoner.

The fate of *X-5* remains something of a mystery. At least one German destroyer attacked Henty-Creer's craft and dropped depth charges. Smaller boats were also seen in the vicinity where *X-5* was thought to have gone done, but there

Lieutenant Godfrey Place and the crew of *X-7* participated in Operation Source. *(Public Domain Collections of the Imperial War Museums via Wikimedia Commons)*

A crewman tends the engine aboard an X-Craft submarine. *(Public Domain Collections of the Imperial War Museums via Wikimedia Commons)*

were no survivors. In 2003, Norwegian marine archaeologists located wreckage believed to be *X-5*, and its explosives were missing. Therefore, Henty-Creer may have been able to place them before the midget submarine sank.

The multiple explosions rocked *Tirpitz*, blasting a gaping hole in her hull and wrecking steering gear while the big 15-inch guns were dislodged from their mounts. *Tirpitz* was put out of action for at least six months, never actually returning to service. On November 12, 1944, the battleship was sunk in Tromso Fjord by RAF bombers delivering massive 13,000-pound Tallboy bombs.

Ten X-Craft crewmen were killed during Operation Source. Cameron and Place, prisoners of the Germans for the rest of the war, received the Victoria Cross. Three other survivors received the Distinguished Service Order, and the fourth the Conspicuous Gallantry Medal. Commander Elliott Smart of *X-8* was appointed Member of the Order of the British Empire. Although Henty-Creer was only Mentioned in Despatches, there have been efforts to award him a posthumous Victoria Cross.

In the spring of 1944, *X-24* attacked the Laksevag floating drydock at Bergen, Norway, laying mines beneath the merchant ship Barenfels, which did sink although the drydock sustained little damage. X-Craft crews also performed reconnaissance missions on the coast of Normandy prior to the D-Day landings of June 6, 1944.

In August 1945, *XE-1* and *XE-3* raided Japanese ships in the harbour of Singapore. *XE-3* attached limpet mines to the hull of the cruiser *Takao* and dropped external explosive charges nearby. *XE-1* joined that attack on *Takao*, sinking the cruiser when its crew failed to locate its primary target, the cruiser *Myoko*. During Operations Sabre and Foil, *XE-4* and *XE-5* cut communications cables between the cities of Singapore, Saigon, Hong Kong, and Tokyo.

This wreckage of the midget submarine *X-7* was recovered from Kaafjord sometime after Operation Source. *(Creative Commons Enter via Wikipedia)*

ELITE FORCES OF WORLD WAR II

SPECIAL INTERROGATION GROUP

They spoke the German language fluently. They wore the uniform of the Deutsches Afrika Korps. They conversed easily and even possessed a grasp of the latest Wehrmacht slang. But these soldiers were hardly in the service of the Nazis.

In fact, most of them were German-speaking Jews who had fled Hitler's relentless persecution and found their way to Palestine. Some of them already had combat experience and came from other organisations, including the French Foreign Legion. Together, they formed the Special Interrogation Group (SIG), and their purpose was to infiltrate German lines while passing themselves off as soldiers of the Fatherland.

As long as their ruse held, the men of the SIG were to support the operations of other clandestine British forces, such as the Special Air Service (SAS) and the Long Range Desert Group (LRDG), conduct sabotage, gather intelligence, and create confusion in rear areas. Although the exact strength of the SIG is the subject of debate, it generally numbered only a few dozen men willing to risk probable torture and summary execution if captured.

Its existence was short-lived, but the SIG brought a new dimension to covert operations. The brainchild of Captain Herbert Cecil Buck, the unit came into being after his own experience. Captured in North Africa in January 1942, he managed to escape and return to active duty after donning various German uniforms and bluffing his way along with his mastery of the German language. He had succeeded so easily, he believed, that a force such as the SIG might well perform outstanding service in the desert war.

Buck recruited his prospects and then presented them with an odd circumstance.

Wrecked Axis planes are shown on the airfield at Derna, target of an SAS raid. *(Public Domain Australian Armed Forces via Wikimedia Commons)*

Italian gunboats fire at British craft in the harbour at Tobruk during Operation Agreement. *(Public Domain an Unnamed Member of the Regia Aeronautica Peter E. Smith (2008) Massacre at Tobruk. Stackpole books, p. 83 via Wikimedia Commons)*

Soldiers of the Royal Pioneer Corps congregate. When the SIG disbanded a number of its former members joined this corps. *(Public Domain Collections of the Imperial War Museums Ministry of Information Photo Division Photographer via Wikimedia Commons)*

They were to be trained at a base near Suez, and their instructors were two German prisoners who had sworn that their true sentiments were anti-Nazi. Although some of the men were sceptical, Buck was not concerned about the prospect of a betrayal. And so, former POWs Herbert Brueckner and Walter Essner put the SIG recruits through a harsh regimen that mimicked the day-to-day life of a German soldier, complete with love letters from fake girlfriends back home, false identities with papers to match, and knowledge of the lyrics to popular German songs of the day.

Within weeks, the SIG was in business, driving captured enemy vehicles through checkpoints, gleaning valuable intelligence in conversations with German soldiers, and blowing up targets of opportunity. At one point, SIG operatives even joined the line at a German field kitchen and ate their meals undisturbed.

In June 1942, the SIG was ordered to support an SAS raid against airfields at Derna and Martuba, west of the Libyan port of Tobruk. The SIG detachment operated in two groups, one headed to each airfield. The Derna group was betrayed by Brueckner, who feigned engine trouble with a truck and slipped away. Brueckner returned with a group of German soldiers, and only one SIG operative managed to evade death or capture. When the Martuba group returned to base, Essner was taken into custody by military police. He was later killed during an escape attempt.

In September, SIG personnel participated in Operation Agreement, a large-scale raid on German and Italian fortifications around the harbour of Tobruk. The raid ended in disaster as nearly 800 Royal Marines and soldiers were killed and 576 captured. In addition, a cruiser, two destroyers, and numerous smaller craft were sunk.

Following Operation Agreement, SIG was disbanded and its remaining members assigned to other units. Aged 28, Captain Buck was killed in a plane crash near Chard, Somerset, on November 22, 1945. ■

NO. 62 COMMANDO

Dangerous things may come in small packages, and in the case of No. 62 Commando, also known as the Small Scale Raiding Force (SSRF), such was definitely the case.

While the number, size and type of Commando forces within the British military proliferated, the Special Operations Executive (SOE) retained control of a unit that mustered only 55 men on its roster. Highly trained in Commando tactics, this intrepid handful of daredevils was in business to keep the Germans off balance. Never intended for more than a pinprick of a destroy-and-dash mission, No. 62 Commando conducted numerous raids against the Axis enemy from its beginning in 1941 until it was disbanded two years later.

The precursor to the Small Scale Raiding Force, the Maid Honour Force, had been named after a trawler requisitioned by the leader of the group, Major Gustavus Henry March-Phillipps. This group initiated the actions that would be credited to SSRF with Operation Postmaster. In August 1941, March-Phillipps led 30 men to West Africa in an attempt to seize a German tanker then in harbour at the island of Fernando Po, which was actually territory of neutral Spain. That, however, was just a minor detail.

The Maid Honour Force executed its mission brilliantly, not only snatching the tanker but taking an Italian freighter for good measure. To reach their objectives, they had employed motor torpedo boat *MTB 344*, nicknamed the Little Pisser because of its lightning speed. The captured prizes were towed from Fernando Po to the port of Lagos, Nigeria.

The success of Operation Postmaster brought further opportunities for March-Phillipps and his band of marauders. March-Phillipps received the Distinguished Service Order for his heroism. Soon enough, more missions were under consideration. A couple of minor successes spurred the command to undertake Operation Aquatint.

MTB 344 relied on speed, but the little craft was also armed with a pair of Vickers machine guns on either side of the bridge and Lewis guns aft. Her skipper was a rugged seaman named Freddie Bourne, who was unafraid to venture with his crew of seven men wherever orders might take his small motorboat. Aquatint was to be the greatest challenge yet for the SSRF. Landing on the beach at Baie de la Seine near the great French port of Cherbourg, the Commandos were to gather information on shore defences and grab a German prisoner for interrogation before quickly departing. Only 11 men, including March-Phillipps, were to take part.

Aquatint was to be executed on the night of September 11, 1942, but fog and foul weather forced its postponement to the following night, when *MTB 344* departed Portsmouth with its small contingent of Commandos aboard. The group departed *MTB 344* in a Goatley boat but came ashore in the wrong place, mistaking it for the preselected landing area. Realising that a cluster of nearby houses was too close to leave the Goatley boat in plain sight, the Commandos decided to drag their boat into some brush 200 yards away.

On their return toward the beach, a German patrol was alerted to their presence when its dog began to bark. A brisk firefight broke out, and one man left to watch the boat was wounded. He was believed dead and left behind as the others paddled toward the waiting *MTB 344*. Suddenly, machine-gun fire from three German positions erupted, and then a heavier calibre gun opened. The combined fire from four locations riddled the Goatley boat, which began to sink. *MTB 344* was taking fire, but Bourne waited to pick up the men swimming toward him. Bourne pulled those he saw aboard, moved out of range of the German guns, and a few moments later went back in again to search for more survivors. Engine damage forced *MTB 344* to retire, at only half power, and the wounded MTB limped into Portsmouth later that night.

Three Commandos were killed, including Major March-Phillipps, four were captured, and four others managed to escape. The raid had taken place just a month after Operation Jubilee, the costly defeat during the raid on the

Major Gustavus March-Phillipps led the SSRF. He was killed in action during Operation Aquatint. *(Public Domain United Kingdom Government British Army via Wikimedia Commons)*

MTB 344 was a similar craft to this speedy boat shown underway. *(Public Domain Collections of the Imperial War Museums via Wikimedia Commons)*

The Italian freighter *Duchess D'Aosta* was captured by SSRF men during Operation Postmaster. *(Public Domain Item is held by John Oxley Library, State Library of Queensland via Wikimedia Commons)*

British Commandos march past a Goatley boat such as the one used in Operation Aquatint. *(Public Domain United Kingdom Government via Wikimedia Commons)*

French port of Dieppe undertaken by primarily Canadian forces and Nos. 3 and 4 Commando. No doubt, in the wake of Dieppe the Germans had been on high alert across occupied France.

One Commando, Captain Graham Hayes, managed to avoid capture and make contact with the French Resistance. Eventually making his way to Spain, he was given up by a French double agent and taken into custody by the Germans. He spent nine months in prison at Fresnes, France, and was executed on July 13, 1943.

Major Geoffrey Appleyard took command of the SSRF after the loss of March-Phillipps, and the command was in action again in October 1942. This time in company with a few selected men of No. 12 Commando, the target was Sark, a spit of land in the occupied Channel Islands. Code named Operation Basalt, this mission was again an effort to perform reconnaissance and bring back German prisoners. *MTB 344* was repaired and sortied on the night of September 18. However, bad weather forced cancellation and delayed Basalt until October 3.

That night, the 12 Commandos involved slipped past German sentries after climbing cliffs at the water's edge. They reached a house, where the cooperative female resident alerted them to the presence of 20 Germans nearby and politely declined an offer to take her back to England when the mission was completed.

Danish Commando Anders Lassen killed one German sentry with his knife, and five German soldiers were roused from a sound sleep. Their hands were bound – among other standard measures that would make their escape difficult as other prisoners were sought. As the Commandos moved out, one of the German captives ran and began shouting, prompting the others to attempt escape. In the melee that followed, two prisoners were shot and another stabbed. Altogether, including Lassen's victim, three Germans were killed. A single prisoner was taken aboard *MTB 344* and brought to England.

In the aftermath of Operation Basalt, the two dead Germans were apparently discovered with some manner of binding still intact. Hitler was enraged and ordered harsher measure for Allied soldiers and Commandos who had been captured at Dieppe. It is further believed that the circumstances contributed to the Führer's issuing of the infamous Commando Order, which led to the execution of many Allied soldiers and to charges of war crimes against numerous Nazi perpetrators after World War II ended.

The SSRF was disbanded in April 1943, and a number of its members were transferred to Algeria, where they joined No. 2 Special Air Service (SAS). This unit, just forming, was commanded by Colonel William Stirling, brother of Colonel David Stirling, founder of the SAS. Major Appleyard was appointed deputy commander.

On the night of July 12, 1943, Appleyard was in charge of an airborne operation to insert SAS personnel in support of the Allied landings on the island of Sicily. The drop was concluded without incident, but during the return flight the Armstrong Whitworth Albemarle transport plane which he was aboard was lost. The circumstances are unknown, and his body was never found. However, it is widely believed that the aircraft was shot down by friendly fire. ■

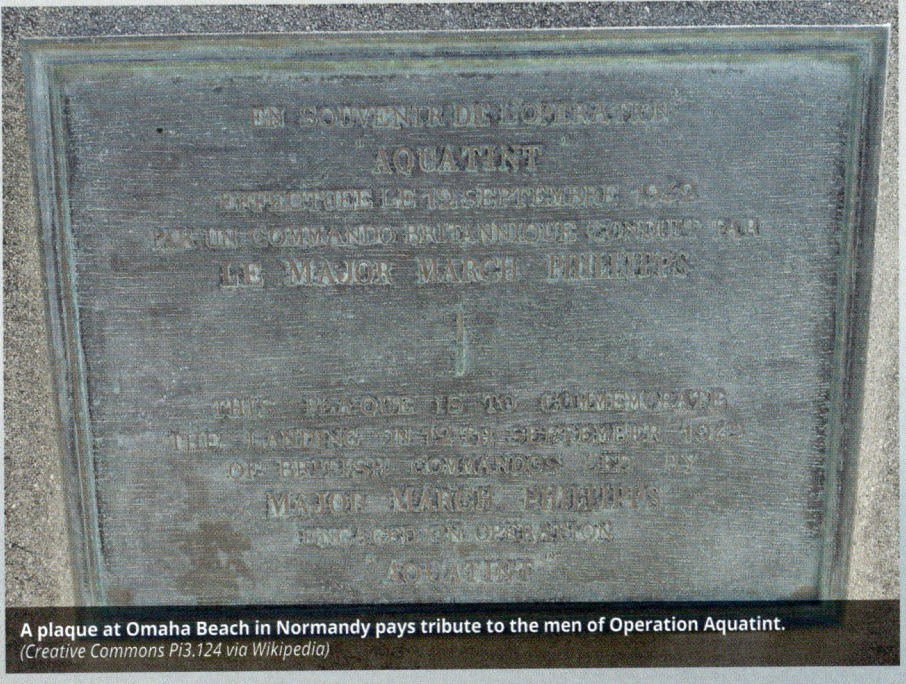

A plaque at Omaha Beach in Normandy pays tribute to the men of Operation Aquatint. *(Creative Commons Pi3.124 via Wikipedia)*

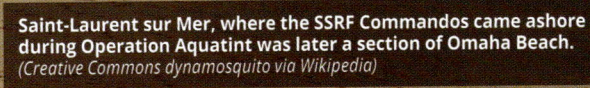

Saint-Laurent sur Mer, where the SSRF Commandos came ashore during Operation Aquatint was later a section of Omaha Beach. *(Creative Commons dynamosquito via Wikipedia)*

Men of No. 6 Polish Troop, No. 10 Inter-Allied Commando operate a Bren gun during exercises in Scotland. *(Public Domain Andrzej Perepeczko "Komandosi w akcji". (Commandos in action) Gdańsk 1978. via wikimedia Commons)*

Commandos train at Eastbourne in the summer of 1943 prior to a hazardous mission. *(Creative Commons Onbekend via Wikipedia)*

NO. 10 INTER-ALLIED COMMANDO

As the German juggernaut rolled across Europe in the early days of World War II, many refugees were displaced. Some of these made their way to Britain and were determined to resist the Nazis. Even so, the early attempts in the summer of 1940 to organise a special operations group of expatriate men who were from non-English speaking countries failed to gain a sufficient response.

Therefore, the idea was shelved for a time but not forgotten. The concept was revived in early 1942, and No. 10 Inter-Allied Commando was born. By July the multinational force included recruits from France, The Netherlands, Belgium, Denmark, Norway, Yugoslavia, and Poland. These recruits were organised into troops, as was a contingent of Jewish fighters. These sub-units were designated as follows: Headquarters; Nos.1 and 8 French; No. 2 Dutch; No. 3 (Refugee, Jewish, or X); No. 4 Belgian; No. 5 Norwegian; No. 6 Polish; and No. 7 Yugoslavian. Two more Belgian troops were organised just prior to the end of the war.

No. 3 Refugee did not function as a unit but supplied individual Commandos to units in need of specialised personnel, particularly those requiring German interpreters. Troop X was primarily composed of Jewish troops, and these men hailed from Germany, Austria, Czechoslovakia, and Hungary, as well as other European nations.

Activated on July 2, 1942, under the command of Lieutenant Colonel Dudley Lister, No. 10 Inter-Allied Commando was comprised of foreign personnel with the exception of its British headquarters apparatus, communications, medical, and supply functions. A six-week training course at Achnacarry in Scotland included the art of clandestine operations, demolitions, small unit tactics, amphibious landings, and hand-to-hand combat. In the spring of 1943, No. 10 Inter-Allied Command relocated to Eastbourne, Sussex, and parachute training was added to the curriculum.

In the meantime, Lieutenant Colonel Peter Laycock, already a hero of covert operations in the North African desert war, became commanding officer. Under Laycock, the individual troops engaged in some operations independently. No. 2 Dutch Troop, for example, deployed with more than 80 officers and other ranks to the China-Burma-India theatre and conducted operations against the Japanese in concert with No. 5 Commando and No. 44 Royal Marine Commando, moving from India into Burma.

The Dieppe Raid of August 19, 1942, brought elements of No. 10 Inter-Allied Commando into action with No. 3 and No. 4 Commando, as all three formations were to be components of the 1st Special Service Brigade under Brigadier Lord Lovat. Some of the Commandos were captured, and at least one was executed under the infamous Commando Order recently issued by Adolf Hitler.

Commandos gather to listen to an instructor during intense training in the Scottish Highlands. *(Creative Commons Onbekend via Wikipedia)*

ELITE FORCES OF WORLD WAR II

Frequent raids along the coast of Norway kept the Germans off balance and contributed to Hitler's concern over the covert operations. The subsequent issuing of the Commando Order resulted in numerous atrocities against captured raiders and prompted war crimes charges against several German officers and soldiers after World War II concluded.

No. 5 Norwegian Troop was involved in coastal operations launched from its base in the Shetland Islands, while X Troop was inserted into Sicily in 1943. Multiple operations were conducted along the French coastline in the summer, and these efforts were intended to assess the strength of German beach fortifications, gather intelligence, and perform acts of sabotage as they were identified. In November, No. 4 Belgian and No. 6 Polish Troops were assigned to the 2nd Special Service Brigade on the Italian front.

No. 7 Yugoslavian Troop reached the Adriatic coast in an attempt to support partisan activities in the Balkans, but the small unit was continually burdened with internal political strife and eventually disbanded. At the same time, No. 4 Belgian Troop engaged in raids on enemy shipping off the Italian coast. Operational control of No. 6 Polish Troop was handed over the II Polish Corps of the British Eighth Army in Italy in the spring of 1944.

The most notable operation of World War II involving No. 10 Inter-Allied Commando was the landing on Sword Beach in Normandy on D-Day. The French Commandos, 185 strong, assaulted the prominent Riva Bella Casino near the town of Ouistreham, calling on armoured support to subdue the stubborn German defenders when their own light arms were inadequate to dislodge the enemy. By evening, No. 10 Inter-Allied Commando had crossed the River Orne and penetrated inland with other units of the 1st Special Service Brigade to relieve British glider troops at the Caen Canal bridge, also known today as Pegasus Bridge. The French Commandos sustained heavy casualties, their numbers dwindling to only 40 effective men by the time the Allies reached the River Seine in late summer.

X Troop fought in Normandy, losing 27 men killed in action, wounded or captured. Although they were regularly detached to fight with other units rather than conducting operations as a cohesive formation, they demonstrated

Commandos fight house to house near Riva Bella Casino and Ouistreham on D-Day off Sword Beach. *(Public Domain Collections of the Imperial War Museums Laws, G (Sgt), Army Film and Photographic Unit via Wikimedia Commons)*

Men of No. 2 Dutch Troop smile during Operation Market Garden in September 1944. *(Public Domain Dutch Ministry of Defence Italiaander, T. (Tom) - Collectie Nederlands Instituut voor Militaire Historie via Wikimedia Commons)*

Shown standing with Belgian Prime Minister in Exile Hubert Pierlot, General Robert G. Sturges praised the work of X Troop Commandos. *(Public Domain Collections of the Imperial War Museums via Wikimedia Commons)*

their bravery on numerous occasions. Many of its men were given false nommes de guerre, fake personal histories, and fictitious family information because of their Jewish heritage. Captured Jewish Commandos would probably have otherwise faced immediate execution due to their ethnicity and the terms of the harsh Commando Order.

By February 1945, X Troop had compiled an outstanding, if little known, combat record. Major General Robert G. Sturges, commander of the Special Service Group, wrote that the unit had been "trained for and employed on work of a highly combatant nature and are good volunteers… their behaviour and work has always been most satisfactory… this is a good sub group, well able to look after itself, and has done excellent work."

After the war, X Troop disbanded, but many of its veterans continued to serve in clandestine roles, tracking German war criminals and translating captured documents, fully utilising their command of the German language.

During Operation Market Garden in September 1944, No. 2 Dutch Troop supplied men to each of the three Allied airborne divisions involved, 12 to the British 6th Airborne, five to the US 101st, and 11 to the US 82nd. Others were allocated to General Frederick "Boy" Browning's 1st Airborne Corps headquarters. No. 4 Belgian Troop was attached to the 4th Commando Brigade for landings on the island of Walcheren during the clearing of the Scheldt estuary.

By 1945, separate raids around the Belgian port of Antwerp were conducted, while No. 5 Norwegian Troop was dispatched to participate in the liberation of its homeland in cooperation with the Free Norwegian Brigade. During the Allied crossing of the great River Rhine, X Troop provided German-speaking personnel to the 1st Commando Brigade.

No. 10 Inter-Allied Commando officially disbanded on September 4, 1945. However, its veterans did provide experience in the formation of numerous special forces organisations in their home countries. ■

German aircraft being serviced at Maleme on the island of Crete were targets of the SBS in Operation Albumen. *(Creative Commons Bundesarchiv Bild via Wikipedia)*

SPECIAL BOAT SERVICE

Major Roger Courtney was persistent. He failed to convince Admiral Roger Keyes, Chief of Combined Operations, that his concept of Commando raids conducted with small canvas folding boats, called folbots, was viable.

So Courtney went a step further. He executed a one-man operation to prove his point. Stealthily climbing aboard the infantry landing ship HMS *Glengyle*, anchored in the River Clyde, he snatched the cover of a deck gun and scratched his initials into the door of the captain's cabin. He then appeared before a group of senior Royal Navy officers at the Inverary Hotel and presented his trophies. In short order, Courtney was authorised to raise a dozen volunteers and form the Folbot Troop of No. 8 Commando.

Courtney's vision became reality as the Folbot Troop trained incessantly and then deployed to North Africa with Layforce in the winter of 1940-1941. Training continued at the Great Bitter Lake in Egypt, and the unit was renamed the No. 1 Special Boat Section as it completed beach reconnaissance missions and participated in the withdrawal of British and Commonwealth forces from the island of Crete the following spring.

In December 1941, Courtney was ordered to England and formed a second unit, No. 2 Special Boat Section. Meanwhile, functioning as the Folbot Section, No. 1 SBS was attached to the Special Air Service and participated in various raids, including a series of operations against airfields on Crete to interrupt Luftwaffe support for Axis operations in North Africa. Collectively known as Operation Albumen, these hit-and-run

George Jellicoe, 2nd Earl Jellicoe led elements of the Special Boat Service in the Mediterranean. *(Creative Commons Rodolph at English Wikipedia via Wikimedia Commons)*

An SBS corporal sharpens a blade prior to the raid on the island of Symi in 1944. *(Public Domain Collections of the Imperial War Museums No 1 Army Film & Photographic Unit, Turner (Sgt) via Wikimedia Commons)*

attacks destroyed 25 enemy planes and damaged scores more at Maleme, Kastelli, Tympaki, and Heraklion. Operation Albumen was conducted in early June 1942 with follow-up in July.

Further SBS operations included a September 1942 raid against a pair of enemy airfields on the island of Rhodes. During Operation Anglo, eight men of the SBS and four Greek partisans landed on Rhodes from the submarine HMS *Traveller* and the Greek submarine *Papanikolis*. Splitting into two groups, the Commandos infiltrated the airfields and planted

48 ELITE FORCES OF WORLD WAR II

ELITE FORCES OF WORLD WAR II

Tough German paratroopers prepare for action on the island of Leros in the Mediterranean. *(Creative Commons Bundesarchiv Bild via Wikipedia)*

SBS personnel assisted General Mark Clark when he came ashore to negotiate with the Vichy French in North Africa in 1942. *(Public Domain Collection Brazilian National Archives via Wikimedia Commons)*

the Greek Sacred Band, a battalion and later regimental sized formation of special forces that cooperated with the British and Commonwealth forces in the Mediterranean theatre.

In mid-1944, the SBS joined the Greek formation to execute Operation Tenement, a raid on the island of Symi in the Aegean. The raiders included 100 SBS men under the command of Major Ian "Jock" Lapraik and 224 Greek fighters. They reached the island aboard 10 motor launches after departing from small support vessels. At dawn on July 14, they surprised the German garrison with small-arms and mortar fire, and when a pair of German coastal barges that had been shadowing the British boats ventured into the harbour they were riddled with bullets and sank in the shallow water.

The raiders advanced toward high ground, and when they reached the crest of a hill they were counterattacked by a German unit that had been in retreat moments earlier. Just as the British Commandos came under enemy fire, a platoon of Greek fighters rolled up behind the Germans and compelled them to surrender. A large castle dominated much of the island, and its capture was a focus of the raid. Mortar and machine-gun fire were concentrated on the objective, but the Italian Carabinieri that garrisoned the old fortification responded and pinned down the SBS men for some time. Eventually, a captured German officer was brought up to negotiate with the Italians. Together with a Royal Navy liaison officer of the SBS, he convinced the Italians to march out peacefully following a three-hour battle and the ensuing uneasy standoff.

With the situation temporarily in hand, the SBS men planted explosives to destroy several supply caches, gun emplacements, and even more than a dozen small watercraft in the harbour. About 150 tons of materiel were destroyed, and while the demolitions were being concluded German aircraft flew over, some of them dropping bombs and strafing. However, the air attack had little effect on the progress of the demolitions.

When the raiders determined to withdraw, they took prisoners and wounded along toward the coastline. Two German motor launches were set ablaze as they tried to reach the shore, and a heavily armed E-boat made a run against the withdrawing force. The E-boat was riddled with bullets and set on fire as the raiders departed.

The raid on Symi was a spectacular success. Two SBS men died by drowning, and explosives, which detonated and damaged or destroyed at least 30 enemy aircraft.

Only two of the raiders were able to return to *Traveller*, which had waited offshore. After they boarded, the submarine was spotted by an Italian patrol boat. Executing an immediate crash dive, *Traveller* survived a depth charge attack and made good its escape. The remaining raiders were captured, and a Greek partisan was later executed. The story of the raid was recounted in the 1954 film *They Who Dare*. Captain David "Dinky" Sutherland was one of the SBS men who evaded capture. Seriously ill, he was hospitalised after the raid but fully recovered to later assume command of all SBS units operating in Italy, Greece, and the Aegean Sea.

After being absorbed into the SAS in November 1942, No. 1 SBS was redesignated the Special Boat Squadron and led by Major the Earl Jellicoe. Numbering about 250 men, this unit transferred to the port of Haifa in Palestine and trained with eight others were wounded. Twenty-one German and Italian troops were killed.

Subsequent operations were conducted around the coast of the Aegean for the remainder of the war. Jellicoe received the Military Cross for actions in 1944. The SBS participated in the fighting on the islands of Leros and Kos in the Dodecanese through the autumn of 1943.

Meanwhile, No. 2 SBS, which retained the designation of Special Boat Section throughout World War II, provided escort for Major General Mark Clark during his clandestine mission in North Africa to carry on negotiations with Vichy French officials prior to the Allied landings of Operation Torch on November 8, 1942. When Allied troops were poised for landings on the Italian mainland at Salerno, a group of personnel named Z SBS performed reconnaissance missions on the designated beaches.

While operating from the island of Ceylon, the SBS cooperated with Special Operations Executive groups in the Pacific. At any given time, multiple small boat organisations were at work in various theatres. ■

The submarine HMS *Traveller* transported SBS men on Operation Tenement. *(Public Domain Collections of the Imperial War Museums via Wikimedia Commons)*

MAJOR ANDERS LASSEN

There was never any shortage of bravery among the men of the Special Boat Service and the various iterations of elite forces that went to war in small watercraft.

Major George Jellicoe, the 2nd Earl Jellicoe, was only in his mid-20s during World War II. The son of Admiral John Jellicoe, famed commander of the Royal Navy Home Fleet during the epic World War I Battle of Jutland, was a stalwart, wounded in the desert and rising to command the SBS.

Jellicoe realised that he was in the presence of an extraordinary man the day he met an expatriate Dane who had volunteered for the service. "In England, I met a marvellous Dane named Andy Lassen," he recalled. Major Anders Lassen was one of the most decorated soldiers of World War II. He was awarded the Victoria Cross and three Military Crosses for valour and was said to have killed more Germans than any other Allied soldier in the conflict.

Lassen was well known to Axis troops, and they nicknamed this Mediterranean menace the "Terrible Viking." Of course, Lassen was prone to chart his own course, and throughout his time with the SBS he was headstrong. Once at a bar in Palestine, an incident between Lassen and Jellicoe might have jeopardised the Dane's future. "I must have said something that offended and ignited his quick fuse," Jellicoe laughed sometime afterward. "Two or three minutes later I found myself getting up from the floor."

Instead of having Lassen arrested, Jellicoe handed him an opportunity to properly vent whatever anger he held inside. One SBS comrade remembered that Lassen "... was brave with such a calm, deadly, almost horrifying courage born of a berserk hatred of the Germans who had overrun his country. He was a killer, too, cold and ruthless – silently with a knife or point-blank with a pistol. On such occasions, there was a froth of bubbles round his lips, and his eyes were dead as stones."

Lassen was front and centre during numerous SBS raids. In Yugoslavia, he led a party of 11 in blowing up a bridge, and at Salonika in Greece he charged a German barracks accompanied by only a sergeant. Rushing like an angel of death from room to room, Lassen shot enemy soldiers and blew them away with hand grenades. He killed 41 of them, wounded 27, and captured 19. The accompanying sergeant commented years later, "That was the only time I was in action side-by-side with Lassen, and it's one of the reasons I'm trying to forget the war. It's no fun throwing grenades and shooting sleeping men. That garrison could have been captured."

But war is war. On the island of Santorini, Lassen found a local bank building full of Germans and Italians. Along with 11 other SBS

Shortly before his death, Major Anders Lassen (right) discusses operations at Lake Comacchio. *(Creative Commons unknown author via Wikipedia)*

The grave of Major Anders Lassen is located at Argenta Gap War Cemetery in Italy. *(Creative Commons Olsok29 via Wikipedia)*

men, he attacked. Fifty-eight enemy soldiers were killed, and only 10 got away, some of whom leaped from upper floor windows to escape the wrath of the Terrible Viking.

Lassen lost his life on April 9, 1945, during Operation Roast. After putting several German bunkers and machine-gun nests out of action in the vicinity of Lake Comacchio in northern Italy, he stepped forward to accept the surrender of a group of Germans holed up in a strongpoint. As Lassen emerged from cover, an enemy soldier shot him dead. Some reports state that no prisoners were taken when the position was subdued.

"Major Lassen refused to be evacuated as he said it would impede the withdrawal and endanger further lives, and as ammunition was nearly exhausted, the force had to withdraw," read his Victoria Cross citation. Anders Lassen was 24 years old when he died. ∎

Amphibious Buffalo vehicles transport German prisoners past Lake Comacchio, Italy, where Anders Lassen was killed during Commando Operation Roast. *(Public Domain Collections of the Imperial War Museum No 2 Army Film & Photographic Unit, Wooldridge (Sgt) via Wikimedia Commons)*

ELITE FORCES OF WORLD WAR II

THE DEVIL'S BRIGADE

One of the toughest outfits to engage in combat during World War II was the brainchild of a British scientist. Geoffrey Pyke was an eccentric, to say the least, and most of his ideas were considered wild schemes that would never amount to much of anything.

However, one of Pyke's imaginative proposals did draw some favourable attention and actually came into being. Pyke believed that a joint elite force of American and Canadian troops should be organised, trained in Commando type operations, and then unleashed on the Axis enemy wherever an opportunity – Europe or the Pacific theatre – presented itself.

The First Special Service Force, as the experimental unit was designated, came into being on June 1, 1942, and its volunteers congregated for training at Fort William Henry Harrison, a remote location in the wilderness of Montana not far from the state capital at Helena. Roughly 2,200 American and Canadian men formed the nucleus of the force, and about one-third of them had been drawn from the Royal Winnipeg Rifles and the Queen's Own Cameron Highlanders of the Canadian Army. The remainder were American soldiers who were hoping to avoid lengthy terms in prison through volunteering for the new unit, lumberjacks, drifters, and adventurers seeking an extraordinary experience in wartime.

They were not disappointed. From rigorous training through the end of its existence late in the war, the First Special Service Force deployed to the Aleutians during the recapture of the island of Kiska from the Japanese, fought with reckless abandon during the Italian Campaign, and then took part in Operation Anvil-Dragoon, the Allied landings in Southern France. From

Devil's Brigade officers confer at headquarters in Venafro, Italy. *(Public Domain Library and Archives Canada via Wikimedia Commons)*

Robert T. Frederick, shown here with the rank of brigadier general, led the Devil's Brigade. *(Public Domain US Government via Wikimedia Commons)*

the outset, the unit exemplified the rough-and-tumble background from which its men had been drawn, and in combat it became known by a well-earned nickname, the Devil's Brigade.

The training regimen was more than the common soldier would have bargained for, as the men learned to snow ski, climb mountains, and fight hand-to-hand. They became experts with a variety of weapons and explosives, and they were survivalists, acclimated to the harshest of climates. Their leader was Colonel Robert T. Frederick, and a better choice could hardly have been made. Frederick was a 35-year-old graduate of the US Military Academy at West Point, class of 1928. He was rugged and earned the respect of his men, even as they tested one another in barroom brawls and fistfights among themselves or at times when they encountered civilians in the towns around Fort William Henry Harrison.

With Frederick, who later would command the US 45th Infantry Division, leading them, the force found unit cohesion. The men took great pride in their distinctive insignia, a roughly hewn Native American spearhead emblazoned with the legend, "USA Canada." Anticipation grew as rumours of deployment were rife in the autumn of 1942, but the first opportunity for action was a false start. Operation Plough, a raid on Nazi hydroelectric facilities in Norway, was abruptly cancelled, and there was no assignment for the First Special Service Force until the summer of 1943.

First Special Service Force soldiers undergo airborne training at Fort William Henry Harrison. *(Public Domain Signal Corps Archive via Wikimedia Commons)*

www.keymilitary.com

THE DEVIL'S BRIGADE

Men of the First Special Service Force prepare to go on patrol in Italy, 1944. (Public Domain Library and Archives Canada via Wikimedia Commons)

In June 1942, Japanese forces had seized the islands of Attu and Kiska in the Aleutians during their Midway operations. The following year, US forces mounted an effort to take the islands back. Attu was reclaimed after a pitched battle in May 1943, and a similarly tough fight was expected when the force boarded transports on July 10, bound for landings on Kiska.

The First Special Service Force was a component of the 34,000 Allied soldiers who stormed ashore at Kiska on August 15, 1943, only to find that the Japanese had executed a brilliant evacuation. The heavy naval bombardment that preceded the landings was later deemed a "live fire exercise." The men were greeted by several dogs, one of them named Explosion, who had been with 10 Americans manning a weather station at Kiska when the Japanese struck months earlier. The dogs had been cared for by the Japanese and then "liberated."

Although their disappointment at finding no enemy to fight was tremendous, the men of the First Special Service Force would soon encounter plenty of German soldiers. Weeks after returning to the US, the unit shipped out for Casablanca, Morocco, arriving in November. From North Africa, the force finally deployed along the Allied front in Italy beside the 36th Infantry Division confronting the stout German Winter Line defences.

By December, the force had experienced combat and received accolades from Lord Louis Mountbatten, Allied chief of Combined Operations. However, its greatest tests lay ahead. In the midst of bitter winter weather, Frederick and his command were given the tough assignment to dislodge German defenders from the summit of Monte la Difensa, which towered 3,120 feet above sea level. An assault could only be made by scaling the jagged face of the mountain and taking on the enemy in close combat at the top.

Frederick led a battalion, roughly 600 men, toward the objective in predawn darkness. Climbing stealthily, the attackers pitched into the enemy, and a brisk battle ensued. One soldier recalled, "When we first got to the top we were pinned down. I ran a little way and lay down beside a soldier and talked to him for a long time before I found out that he was dead. I recall borrowing Captain Border's rifle when I came across him in a kneeling position observing the enemy through binoculars on the opposite ridge. When I returned with his rifle some 30 minutes later, he was dead with a sniper's bullet in the head."

Outnumbered, the force prevailed in a spectacular feat of arms at Monte la Difensa. When an officer stepped forward and tried to accept the surrender of a group of German soldiers, one of them raised a rifle and shot him in the face. The Canadian and American men responded quickly, killing every German in sight. From that time forward, they were reluctant to take prisoners, and word of their ferocity swept the Italian battlefields. Monte la Difensa had been taken in two hours, and over the next two days several German counterattacks were beaten back. Victorious, the First Special Service Force suffered 511 killed or wounded.

After Monte la Difense, the Devil's Brigade gained accolades from senior officers and attention from the press. Clark Lee of the International News Service wrote, "This feat captured the imagination of the entire Fifth Army, and overnight Frederick and his soldiers became almost legendary figures in a battle area where heroism was commonplace."

The Force earned other nicknames, including simply the "North Americans," or the "Thugs," or "Freddie's Freighters," and their reputation struck fear into the hearts of the enemy. Their hard-driving commander also earned promotion to brigadier general.

Devil's Brigade soldiers attend a briefing prior to a mission during the Italian campaign at Anzio. (Public Domain Library and Archives Canada via Wikimedia Commons)

Japanese soldiers occupy the island of Kiska in the Aleutians in June 1942. (Public Domain under Uruguay Round Agreements Act via Wikimedia Commons)

ELITE FORCES OF WORLD WAR II

American soldiers march towards landing craft during preparations to land on Kiska in 1943. *(Public Domain US Government Lt. Horace Bristol, USNR, Steichen photographic unit via Wikimedia Commons)*

The distinctive patch of the First Special Service Force incorporates a Native American spear point. *(Creative Commons Bassoonstuff via Wikipedia)*

"The Black Devils are all around us, every time we come into the line," wrote one German lieutenant. The haunting statement was scrawled in his diary, recovered next to his lifeless body after he was strangled with piano wire and left in the wake of the advancing Devil's Brigade.

More action followed as the Devil's Brigade claimed additional high ground in the rugged mountains of Italy. Monte la Remetanea was taken in December, followed by Monte Sammucro on Christmas Day 1943, and Monte Vischiataro in January 1944. Casualties were high in the winter months, and some units experienced rates of more than 70 percent due to enemy action or illness.

On February 1, 1944, the Devil's Brigade was relocated to the Anzio beachhead, roughly 35 miles south of Rome, where an Allied lodgement had failed to provide the quick strike envisioned to outflank the formidable German defences at the Gustav Line and seize the Italian capital city. The Devil's Brigade was called in to reinforce the defensive perimeter at Anzio, as enemy artillery hammered the beleaguered enclave on a daily basis.

The Devil's Brigade spent 99 straight days at Anzio, and though its mission was ostensibly defensive in nature, Frederick and his men were intent on taking the fight to the enemy. Small groups of force men were regularly infiltrating and harassing the Germans, leaving dead sentries or unwary enemy soldiers with their throats slit. The raiders crossed the opposing lines at night with blackened faces and armed with their trusty V-42 combat knives. When their work was done, they often left a calling card that read ominously, "The Worst is Yet to Come."

Elements of the Devil's Brigade slogged into Rome on June 4, 1944, following the success of Operation Diadem and the breakout from the Anzio beachhead. From there, Operation Anvil-Dragoon, the Allied invasion of southern France, brought the force back into action against the Germans in the mountainous terrain along the Italian frontier. As the campaign wore on, the brigade suffered 60 percent casualties, and its stamina was sorely tested. By the end of the year, the need for replacements among Allied infantry divisions had contributed to the decision to disband the First Special Service Force in December.

While many of the former Devil's Brigade men were absorbed into divisions of Third Army under General George S. Patton, Jr., others went to airborne units, where their skills were put to good use.

Meanwhile, Frederick's performance had earned significant praise. British Prime Minister Winston Churchill crowed, "If we had a dozen men like him, we would have smashed Hitler in 1942. He is the greatest fighting general of all time!"

Frederick was promoted major general and later commanded the 1st Airborne Task Force and the 4th and 6th Infantry Divisions as well as the 45th Division. Always willing to lead from the front, he had been wounded eight times, more than any other general officer in the US Army during World War II, and received the Purple Heart medal for each. He was also a recipient of the Distinguished Service Cross, the second-highest award for valour in the American military, the Silver Star, Bronze Star, two Distinguished Service Medals, two Legion of Merit awards, and the British Distinguished Service Order.

The Devil's Brigade engaged in combat deployment for 18 months, and during that time it is believed to have inflicted 12,000 casualties on the enemy and captured more than 7,000 prisoners. Its record during World War II served as an inspiration for the modern US Special Forces, as well as the Canadian Joint Task Force 2.

Major General Robert T. Frederick was wounded eight times during World War II. *(Public Domain US War Department via Wikimedia Commons)*

RAF LYSANDER SQUADRONS

The Westland Lysander did not cut the figure of a hero's aircraft. Rather stubby with high-mounted wings and oversized fixed landing gear, the plane looked rather ungainly. Its early role was limited reconnaissance and artillery spotting, and on those few occasions when German fighters were about, the lightly armed and slow-flying Lysander had to beat a hasty retreat.

There was, however, an opportunity to excel. The Lysander possessed an attribute that few other aircraft could claim. It needed only a sliver of land, a pasture, a forest clearing or a stretch of old road, to take off and land. A modified version of the Lysander was fitted with a 682-litre external long-range fuel tank, and its rear area with a ladder for quick ingress and egress from cramped seating. In the hands of a skilled and mostly fearless pilot, the Westland Lysander would make a perfect vehicle for the insertion and extraction of covert agents and operational flights into Nazi-occupied Europe and Japanese-held areas in the Pacific theatre, as well as the delivery of critical supplies.

And so, these modified "Black Lysanders," flying from bases in Tempsford and Newmarket, completed more than 400 such missions during World War II under the direction of the Special Operations Executive (SOE). Squadron Nos. 138, 148, and 161 RAF flew missions in Europe, and No. 357 conducted missions in the Pacific. During the run-up to the D-Day landings in Normandy on June 6, 1944, Lysanders flew more than 60 missions into hostile territory. They inserted 101 agents and brought 128 out safely while losing only two planes.

Flight Lieutenant Murray Anderson flew with three photographic reconnaissance units, snapping shots of the German heavy cruiser *Prinz Eugen* in harbour at Kiel, and continued

Pilots of No. 161 Squadron pose with their dogs in front of a Westland Lysander at RAF Tangmere in 1943. (Creative Commonw G.Garitan via Wikimedia Common)

flying the Lysander with No. 161 Squadron, having trained in the aircraft in 1940. Anderson flew a pair of Lysanders on six hazardous and became famous for his navigational skills. On one occasion he helped the leader of a three-plane flight correct his orientation merely by providing a description of the terrain below.

Flight Lieutenant Peter Arkell transferred to No. 161 Squadron after flying Supermarine Spitfire and North American P-51 Mustang fighters. During one harrowing mission, he witnessed another Lysander crash with the loss its pilot and two agents aboard. He flew with No. 357 Squadron in Burma and nearly lost his life as he attempted to land during a monsoon. Another Lysander pilot came to his rescue, landing and pulling Arkell and his injured passenger from the wreckage and whisking them to safety.

Lysander pilots pore over a map of their landing area in enemy territory prior to a hazardous mission. (Public Domain Collections of the Imperial War Museums via Wikimedia Commons)

Pilot Lewis Hodges had flown Handley Page Halifax and Lockheed Hudson bombers on secret missions before transferring to the China-Burma-India theatre to lead No. 357 Squadron and rising to the rank of air chief marshal during a 49-year career in the RAF.

Flight Lieutenant R.G. Large flew a stint with the Lysander between assignments to RAF fighter squadrons. During his epic forays, Large piloted solo, double and triple missions, conducting aerial surveillance, delivering supplies, and safely transporting covert operatives with No. 161 Squadron. He later was among the earliest pilots to fly the Gloster Meteor jet fighter.

A total of 1,786 Westland Lysander aircraft were built from the mid-1930s until the type was retired from active service in 1946. ∎

A flight of stubby-winged Westland Lysanders is airborne over England during World War II. (Public Domain United Kingdom Government via Wikimedia Commons)

ELITE FORCES OF WORLD WAR II

RAF EAGLE SQUADRONS

A wealthy American businessman living in London, Charles Sweeney knew that his country was officially neutral as World War II engulfed Europe in 1939-1940. Still, he wanted to do all he could to assist in the fight against Nazi Germany.

Remembering the band of patriotic American pilots of the LaFayette Escadrille that had come to the aid of France during the Great War a generation earlier, Sweeney began recruiting American fliers to join the French Air Force even as the situation on the continent steadily deteriorated. With the fall of France in the summer of 1940, he was still determined and continued his effort – this time on behalf of the British Royal Air Force (RAF).

Sweeney, who had also worked with Billy Bishop, a Canadian ace of World War I, to entice American pilots to join the Royal Canadian Air Force (RCAF), persuaded 12 American pilots to enlist with the RAF. He further paid the cost of their travel to Britain and their training in RAF fighters, about $100,000 per pilot, and offered to do so for any others who followed.

Sweeney's resolve and seed money spurred the formation of the legendary RAF Eagle Squadrons composed of expatriate Americans who ventured to Britain, some via Canada, to volunteer their services even though such action was in violation of the US Neutrality Acts. These were not the only American pilots who willingly went abroad as war clouds gathered. Others had ventured to Finland to fly against the Soviet Air Force during the brief Winter War of 1939-1940 but never saw action, and still others joined the RCAF. Prior to the formation of the Eagle Squadrons, at least eight American pilots had flown missions against the Luftwaffe during the Battle of Britain, several of them with No. 609 Squadron.

The first Eagle Squadron, No. 71, was organised in September 1940 and based initially at Church Fenton, about 200 miles north of London. Eugene "Red" Tobin, Vernon "Shorty" Keough, and Andrew Mamedoff, the first three pilots on the squadron roster, were all veterans of No. 609 Squadron. Two months later, No. 71 Squadron received nine Hawker Hurricane fighters, and in early February 1941, the unit became operational from its new base at Martlesham Heath, 65 miles northeast of London.

In the spring of 1941, No. 121 Squadron was formed, and by August, No. 133 Squadron, the last of the three Eagle Squadrons, was activated. The former was based at Kirton-on-Lindsey, and the latter at Duxford. Each of the squadrons began operations flying the Hurricane, but within days these slower fighters were replaced by the sleek Supermarine Spitfire. During the first Eagle Squadron encounter with the Germans on July 2, 1941, the RAF pilots of No. 71 Squadron shot down three German Me-109s.

At peak strength, 244 American pilots served as members of the Eagle Squadrons, and 16 British air officers commanded either squadrons or flights at any given time. During their brief tenure, 82 of these gallant pilots were killed in action. Seventy-seven of them were American. The three Eagle Squadrons flew together into hostile skies only once. In August 1942, the pilots provided air cover for Operation Jubilee, the tragic raid on the French port city of Dieppe.

The first Eagle Squadron pilot to shoot down an enemy aircraft was Pilot Officer William R. Dunn of No. 71 Squadron, a native of Minneapolis, Minnesota, who had enlisted in the Canadian Army within a week of the outbreak of war in September 1939 and then moved on to the RAF 15 months later. He was also the first Eagle Squadron ace, claiming his fourth and fifth aerial victories on August 27, 1940, but nearly losing his life in the process.

On that fateful day, Dunn shot down a pair of Luftwaffe Messerschmitt Me-109 fighters and went after a third. Suddenly, he was jumped by four enemy fighters and seriously wounded. Drifting in and out of consciousness, he managed to maintain control of his Spitfire, which had been seriously damaged, and land at Hawkinge, Kent, just inland from the English Channel. Dunn

Eagle Squadron pilots stand on the wing of a Hurricane fighter. *(Public Domain Collections of the Imperial War Museums)*

Eagle Squadron pilots Mamedoff, Keough, and Tobin admire their new shoulder patch. *(Public Domain Collections of the Imperial War Museums Royal Air Force official photographer, Daventry B J (Mr) via Wikimedia Commons)*

American pilots of N0. 71 Squadron RAF rush to their Hawker Hurricanes on March 17, 1941. *(Public Domain Collections of The Imperial War Museums via Wikimedia Commons)*

spent three months in hospital in England and then another three months recovering in the United States. He was then ordered to Canada as a pilot instructor and transferred to the US Army Air Forces (USAAF) in June 1943, retiring 30 years later with the rank of lieutenant colonel.

Squadron Leader Gregory Augustus "Gus" Daymond shot down seven German planes with No. 71 Squadron. Three of these kills, a pair of Me-109s and a Dornier Do-17 bomber, were recorded flying the Hurricane in July and August 1941. A month later, he shot down another Me-109, and in October a fifth victory brought ace status.

Daymond was born in Great Falls, Montana, and grew up in California, where he worked in the film industry and took flying lessons, qualifying as a pilot at age 16. When war broke out, he went directly to Britain and joined the RAF. In August 1942, he was promoted commander of No. 71 Squadron, and later he received a commission in the USAAF with the rank of major and led the 334th Fighter Squadron, 4th Fighter Group. Daymond received the British Distinguished Flying Cross. He retired from the US Air Force Reserve with the rank of lieutenant colonel.

Pilots of No. 121 Squadron RAF run to their Spitfire fighters in August 1942. *(Public Domain Collections of the Imperial War Museums via Wikimedia Commons)*

American pilots of Eagle Squadron No. 121 await the call to action in August 1942. *(Public Domain Collections of the Imperial War Museums via Wikimedia Commons)*

Eagle Squadron Spitfire fighters make landing approaches at RAF Rochford, Essex. *(Public Domain Collections of the Imperial War Museums via Wikimedia Commons)*

The top-scoring Eagle Squadron ace was pilot officer Carroll W. McColpin, who was credited with 12 aerial victories, five probable kills, and a dozen enemy aircraft damaged while flying with No. 71 Squadron and as commander of No. 133 Squadron. McColpin later shot down eight more enemy planes while flying with the US Ninth Air Force. On two occasions he shot down a pair of Me-109s, and during air combat he demonstrated such skill that he caused three enemy pilots to lose control of their planes and crash into the ground without ever opening fire on them.

A native of Buffalo, New York, McColpin accepted a major's commission in the USAAF in September 1942. He remained in the Air Force following the war and retired in 1968 with the rank of major general after holding numerous high command posts.

After the US entry into World War II, the Eagle Squadrons remained with the RAF for some time due to logistical issues and the discussions between American and British officers surrounding the transition to the USAAF. In September 1942, the three squadrons were officially incorporated as the 334th, 335th, and 336th Fighter Squadrons, 4th Fighter Group, US Eighth Air Force. Most of the pilots received rank and privileges equivalent to those they had earned in the RAF. During less than two years of active service, Eagle Squadron pilots claimed 73½ German planes destroyed, 41 by No. 71 Squadron, 18 by No. 121 Squadron, and 14½ by No. 133 Squadron.

Several former Eagle Squadron pilots went on to compile impressive records with the 4th Fighter Group, including Colonel Don Blakeslee, commander of the group from January to October 1944. He ended the war with 15½ victories, and three of these were confirmed while flying 120 missions with No. 121 and No. 133 Squadrons. Major Don Gentile finished the war officially credited with 21.84 kills, two of which occurred while he flew with No. 133 Squadron.

ELITE FORCES OF WORLD WAR II

UNDERWATER DEMOLITION TEAMS

The modern elite SEALS (Sea, Air, and Land) of the United States Navy trace their lineage to the Underwater Demolition Teams (UDT) of the World War II era. In numerous instances, the conflict was one of amphibious operations, Allied forces storming ashore on enemy-held beaches or coastline.

Therefore, the need for solid reconnaissance and the demolition of obstacles and other hazards that might impede the progress of those coming ashore were essential functions. Whether a stretch of beach or shoreline was contested or uncontested, the work of the UDTs was among the most hazardous of assignments.

In the autumn of 1942, the Navy had established its Bomb Disposal School at Washington, DC, under the direction of Lieutenant Commander Draper Kauffman. By mid-1943, Kauffman had also helped to establish a similar school for the US Army at Aberdeen Proving Ground in Maryland. The UDT school was a logical step in the progression, and the naval officer took charge of its establishment in Fort Pierce, Florida.

More than 500 men answered the call for UDT volunteers, many of them already members of the famed Seabees, the Navy's rugged construction battalions. US Army Rangers and British Commandos were also seconded to attend sessions at Fort Pierce. Originally, the UDT men were intended to concentrate on preparations for the expected invasion of Normandy in June 1944, but their areas of operation steadily increased to involvement in Operation Anvil-Dragoon, the invasion of southern France in August 1944, and extensive island missions against Japanese strongholds in the Pacific.

In Europe, operations were typically conducted under cover of darkness, while in the Pacific the hazardous undertakings were often executed in daylight. Regularly, naval gunfire support personnel accompanied the UDT teams, assisting in removing obstacles and performing reconnaissance. Practical experience during early amphibious operations in Europe and the Pacific demonstrated the need for such skilled men as the UDTs. At Dieppe in 1942, it was determined too late that the sandy beach was not practical for the heavy Churchill tanks intended to support the Canadian soldiers and Commandos that landed during Operation Jubilee. At Tarawa in the Gilbert Islands of the Pacific, a coral reef presented a nearly insurmountable barrier for landing craft loaded with combat Marines.

A total of 31 UDT teams were constituted during World War II, and their first deployment occurred at the island of Kwajalein in the Marshalls archipelago in February 1944. The UTD men used drone boats steered by remote control and reported that the invasion beaches were clear of appreciable impediments. During the mid-June invasion of the Marianas Islands, Kauffmann earned the Navy Cross leading one of two UDT teams, each comprised of 96 men, in a daylight reconnaissance. As the UDT teams set about their business, measuring distances and sounding the depths offshore, Japanese fire killed four men despite the cover of a naval gunfire barrage.

At Omaha and Utah beaches on D-Day, UDT teams used two-pound explosive charges

Rear Admiral Draper Kauffman founded the Underwater Demolition Teams (UDT) of the US Navy. *(Public Domain US Navy via Wikimedia Commons)*

to clear a variety of obstacles, including teller mines, Belgian gates, and concrete and steel tetrahedra. One entire team was wiped out as it approached Omaha, a direct hit destroying its landing craft. UDT men earned seven Navy Crosses on June 6, 1944.

Kauffmann served through the remainder of the Pacific War, rose to the rank of rear admiral, and became superintendent of the US Naval Academy at Annapolis, Maryland, in 1965. ∎

Explosive charges set by a UDT team blast a channel off the island of Morotai in the Pacific. *(Public Domain National Archives via Wikimedia Commons)*

The US Navy Combat Demolition insignia featured a cartoon octopus. *(Public Domain US Navy via Wikimedia Commons)*

THE JEDBURGHS

From the earliest days of their formal alliance against the Axis in Europe, Britain and the United States cooperated in a variety of endeavours as they worked toward final victory in World War II. A primary goal of the Western Allies was the return of their armed forces to the European continent, and even as landings were accomplished on the mainland of Italy in September 1943, plans proceeded apace for Operation Overlord, the invasion of Normandy, which ultimately took place on June 6, 1944.

Not only was the invasion a prerequisite for victory over Nazi Germany, but it also was a critical element in support of the Soviet Union, whose armies had borne the brunt of Hitler's military juggernaut for three years by the time the Normandy landings occurred. Soviet Premier Josef Stalin had clamoured for the opening of a second front against the common enemy in northwest Europe for many months. In response, the foundation for that operation was laid, day after day, as American men and materiel flooded into Britain.

At the same time, the D-Day invasion took shape with 150,000 combat infantrymen and airborne troops assaulting the coast of French Normandy, the former splashing ashore at five landing beaches designated Gold, Juno, Sword, Utah, and Omaha, while the latter parachuted into the Norman countryside to seize key objectives and link up with the troops advancing from the beachhead.

Another aspect that was vital to the success of the Allied invasion was the coordination of the French Resistance to provide intelligence and execute missions of sabotage and ambush, destroy supply, communications, and transportation infrastructure, and generally disrupt the Nazi response to the landings while spreading chaos and confusion in the occupied areas. To maximize the effectiveness of the Resistance effort, leaders of the US and British intelligence communities gathered in the spring of 1943 to discuss tactical operations.

The British Special Operations Executive (SOE) and the American Office of Strategic Services (OSS) organised a partnership that would assist in the effectiveness of the French Resistance effort. Code named Operation Jedburgh, referencing a training facility located in the Scottish borders, the effort was designed to assist the Free French Forces of the Interior (FFI), who specialised in sabotage and hit-and-run tactics, along with the Maquisards, or Maquis, bands of guerrillas who operated primarily in the French countryside.

Operation Jedburgh would consist of elite, highly-trained three-man teams of French, Belgian, British, and American volunteers inserted into France and the Low Countries to recruit, train, equip, and coordinate activities to assist with the coming Allied offensive. From June to September 1944, a full 93 Jedburgh teams, a total of 276 men, parachuted into Nazi-occupied France, Belgium, and the Netherlands. The Jedburgh volunteers completed training in Scotland and at Milton Hall, a sprawling estate in the English countryside about 100 miles from London, and then as the war progressed and their numbers grew teams were activated in Southeast Asia as well.

The first Jedburgh team to parachute into France was code named Hugh and came to earth near the town of Chateauroux, contacting the Maquisards and setting up communication

Jedburgh operatives receive instructions prior to setting out on a dangerous mission in 1944. *(Public Domain US National Archives and Records Administration via Wikimedia Commons)*

Jedburghs are shown wearing parachutes prior to departing from an RAF airfield outside London. *(Public Domain US National Archives and Records Administration via Wikimedia Commons)*

Jedburgh recruits undergo intense training at Milford Hall outside London, 1944. *(Public Domain US National Archives and Records Administration via Wikimedia Commons)*

links between the guerrillas and the Allied troops then coming ashore in Normandy. As the Allied armies advanced, breaking out of their beachhead and moving across France, Jedburgh activities increased. Between September 1944 and April 1945, eight Jedburgh teams were inserted into the Netherlands, and these cooperated with the Dutch Underground during the airborne/ground offensive of Operation Market Garden in the autumn of 1944.

The Jedburghs regularly fought the Germans in uniform, but in October 1942, Hitler had issued his infamous Commando Order, which decreed that operatives captured while participating in clandestine missions were subject to summary execution. Nevertheless, there was no shortage of Jedburgh volunteers willing to risk their lives to defeat the Nazis.

One of the most notable examples of Jedburgh success occurred during the mission code named Bugatti undertaken on June 28, 1944. The Bugatti mission was led by US Marine Lieutenant Colonel Horace Fuller, a Harvard University graduate and veteran of the French Army who had fought during the dark days of the Battle of France and managed to return to the United States. Fuller joined the Marines and participated in the landings at Guadalcanal in the Pacific in August 1942. While recovering from wounds, Fuller was approached by OSS chief General William "Wild Bill" Donovan. He joined the OSS and became a Jedburgh the next year.

As Bugatti got underway, Fuller and two French officers parachuted into the Pyrenees Mountains of southern France and linked up with a group of Maquis. After narrowly averting capture, the Jedburghs were vexed by faulty radio equipment, finally swiping a working set in a quick raid on the town of Lannemezan while avoiding a direct engagement with the 1,200 Germans stationed there. A desperately needed supply drop was received in mid-July, and on the 17th the Jedburghs and Maquis fought a pitched battle against 800 German soldiers intent on eradicating

French Maquisards such as these pictured in the autumn of 1944 cooperated with Jedburghs from 1944 until the end of the war. *(Public Domain Library and Archives Canada Donald I. Grant, Department of National Defence via Wikimedia Commons)*

Resistance efforts in the region. After hours of combat, the Germans withdrew, losing 16 of their number dead and 20 wounded. There were no casualties among the Jedburghs or Maquis.

In the coming weeks, the Bugatti team received orders to engage the Germans in full-scale guerrilla warfare in support of the Allied landings in southern France during Operation Anvil-Dragoon, which began on August 15, 1944. Fuller organised a major attack on the enemy near the village of Luchon as the US Seventh Army advanced from the south. He set a trap, which was sprung with deadly precision. After making initial contact with the enemy, a group of Maquis led its pursuers into the teeth of an ambush. The Jedburghs and Maquis routed the Germans, inflicting heavy casualties, and the local population showed its gratitude by presenting Fuller with 48 bottles of vintage champagne.

The most famous of the Jedburghs was US Marine Colonel Peter Ortiz, a veteran of the French Foreign Legion who had served in North Africa between the world wars. Ortiz was of Spanish and French heritage and was living with his family in California when the war broke out. After recovering from wounds sustained while fighting with the Free French Brigade in North Africa, he enlisted in the Marines and was recruited by the OSS.

Along with British covert operative H.H.A. Thackwaite and a French radio operator named Monnier, Ortiz parachuted into the Haute-Savoie region of occupied France on D-Day. He quickly organised a raid on a German installation, stealing 10 vehicles and a Gestapo identification pass. Soon afterward, he was enjoying a drink in a local bar when a group of German soldiers at a nearby table began to talk of the "tall American Marine" who was wreaking havoc.

Ortiz left the bar, returned to his safe house, and put on his Marine uniform. He re-entered the bar with a .45-calibre pistol under his raincoat, tossed the coat aside, and revealed his identity. He ordered the Germans to their feet and compelled them to drink a toast to President Franklin D. Roosevelt. Ortiz was withdrawn for a short time but returned to France during Jedburgh Operation Union II. He was captured, escaped twice, and was liberated from a German POW camp in April 1945.

After the war, Ortiz pursued a successful career in the motion picture industry. He had earned the French Croix de Guerre with two Palms and gold and silver stars, the US Navy Cross with gold star, and the Order of the British Empire among other honours. ■

US Marine Colonel Peter Ortiz exhibited great bravado as a Jedburgh in Nazi-occupied France. *(Public Domain US Marine Corps via Wikimedia Commons)*

Jedburghs train at Milton Hall for a coming deployment in support of the Allied advance across northwest Europe. *(Public Domain US National Archives and Records Administration via Wikimedia Commons)*

DOOLITTLE RAIDERS

The Japanese high command was stunned. Bombs had fallen on the capital city of Tokyo. The American planes had seemed to come from nowhere. Days later when he met with reporters, President Franklin D. Roosevelt publicly acknowledged the raid. Beaming, he told the press that the American bombers had come from "Shangri-La," a mythical locale referenced in James Hilton's Lost Horizon, a popular novel of the day.

Since the Japanese had attacked Pearl Harbor on December 7, 1941, and plunged the United States into World War II, Roosevelt and his senior military commanders had looked for a means to strike back at the enemy in a meaningful way and bolster the morale of the American public. Within weeks, a plan was hatched. It was the brainchild of Captain Francis S. Low, operations officer on the staff of Admiral Ernest J. King, commander-in-chief of the US Navy.

Low proposed a bombing raid on Tokyo using carrier-based aircraft, however, there were no conventional types with the range to deliver a payload across the estimated distance and offer even a remote chance that the crews might survive the daring operation. Even as President Roosevelt endorsed the idea, the search for a suitable bomber concluded with the twin-engine North American B-25 Mitchell, an Army Air Forces medium bomber that seemed to fit the bill in many respects.

The planners of this risky enterprise reasoned that B-25s could be transported across the Pacific Ocean aboard an aircraft carrier to within striking distance of Tokyo and that their pilots and crews could be trained to take off from the pitching carrier deck – a function for which the bomber was never intended – deliver their bombs, and then fly on to bases in China. The plan was both far-fetched and brilliant, and just the right man was found to command the intense training effort and fly the lead bomber on the historic mission.

Lieutenant Colonel Jimmy Doolittle had been a reservist in the Army Air Corps. A veteran of World War I, he had served as an aviation instructor, and then performed as a stunt pilot and barnstormer between the wars. He was

No. 23 *Nitto Maru* burns to the waterline after being shelled by the light cruiser USS *Nashville*. *(Public Domain US Navy via Wikimedia Commons)*

also a champion air racer, winning both the Schneider and Thompson trophies in 1931. In winning the Thompson Trophy he set a world speed record of 252.68 miles per hour while piloting the 800-horsepower GeeBee Super Sportster plane. For good measure, Doolittle was a proficient bantamweight boxer and a former oil company executive.

In March 1942, Doolittle met his volunteer air crews at Eglin Air Base, Florida, and weeks of training ensued. A stretch of runway was painted to resemble the outline of a flight deck, just 500 feet long and with little margin for error in the critical moments of take-off. Meanwhile, the targets were confirmed. The B-25s would hit Tokyo, as well as the cities of Nagoya, Osaka, Yokohama, Yokosuka, and Kobe. Although only 16 bombers would take part and damage would probably be minimal, each city would at least, hopefully, receive a calling card from the United States armed forces.

The B-25s would carry only a modest payload of three 500-pound general purpose bombs and a cluster of incendiaries. The planes were stripped of any unnecessary equipment to lighten their weight, and every available space was crammed with extra containers of aviation fuel. If all went well, the bombers would be transported to a distance of 400 miles from the coast of the home islands, make their bomb runs, and fly on to safety in China.

On April 3, 1942, the aircraft carrier USS *Hornet* weighed anchor from Alameda Naval Air Station in San Francisco Bay and passed beneath the famed Golden Gate Bridge in company with two cruisers, four destroyers, and a fleet oiler. Only after every airman was aboard the carrier did Doolittle divulge the nature of the mission. "For the benefit of those who have been guessing," he said, "we are going

A B-25 Mitchell medium bomber lifts off the flight deck of the USS *Hornet* on April 18, 1942. *(Public Domain US Army Air Force via Wikimedia Commons)*

A Doolittle Raider pilot climbs skyward from the deck of USS *Hornet* in adverse weather conditions. *(Public Domain US National Archives and Records Administration US Navy via Wikimedia Commons)*

ELITE FORCES OF WORLD WAR II

Lieutenant Colonel Jimmy Doolittle attaches a medal given to him by the Japanese government before World War II to a bomb that will be dropped on Tokyo. *(Public Domain US Navy via Wikimedia Commons)*

Shown with the rank of lieutenant general, Jimmy Doolittle received the Medal of Honor for the daring raid on Tokyo.
(Public Domain US Air Force via Wikimedia Commons)

to bomb Japan. The Navy will get us as close as possible and launch us off the deck." He finished by asking if any of the men wished to opt out of the hazardous mission. They all stayed.

A second Navy task force including the carrier USS *Enterprise*, two cruisers, four destroyers, and an oiler, left San Francisco on April 8. The two groups made rendezvous in the open sea on the 13th, and formally designated as Task Force 16, the Americans headed for hostile waters.

The weather was far from perfect on the morning of April 18, and to make matters worse it appeared the critical element of surprise had been lost when a Japanese patrol boat, the 70-ton No. 23 *Nitto Maru*, was spotted at a distance. The light cruiser *Nashville* sank the enemy craft quickly, but it was quite likely that the picket vessel had radioed the contact with the US task force. For Doolittle, Admiral William F. "Bull" Halsey, commanding the Task Force 16, and Admiral Marc Mitscher, skipper of the Hornet, it was decision time.

The B-25s were more than 200 miles away from their optimal launch point, while wind and rain swept the Hornet's flight deck. The three officers conferred and chose to launch the bombers anyway. At 8:20 a.m., Doolittle gunned his B-25's engines. The bomber roared down the flight deck, dipped precipitously toward the wavetops, and finally clawed its way into the air. Doolittle circled overhead as the others joined up, repeating the harrowing take-off procedure.

The Americans flew toward Japan at 225 miles per hour, first at low level and then climbing to 1,200 feet as they skirted the coast of Honshu. Although the Imperial Palace, residence of Emperor Hirohito, schools, hospitals, and other civilian locations were off limits, there were plenty of military targets. As the B-25s swept toward Tokyo, surprise was complete. The streets were crowded, but scarcely anyone glanced up toward the incoming planes. Virtually no antiaircraft fire was encountered, and schoolchildren waved at the Americans from the ground.

At 12:15 local time, Doolittle's plane was the first to release its bombs. One by one, the others followed, over Tokyo and elsewhere. As the Americans sped away, they attempted to form up for the flight to China amid high winds. Smoke billowed from oil storage tanks and other facilities set ablaze, and one American bomb hit the Japanese aircraft carrier *Ryuho* in drydock at Yokosuka. The damage was slight, but the impact on the mindset of the Japanese military leadership proved seismic.

After nearly 13 hours in the air, the American aircrews individually met their fate. One B-25 landed at Vladivostok, Russia, and its crew was interned for the duration of the war. Others ditched in the sea with empty fuel tanks. Doolittle crashed into a rice paddy. Of the 80 US airmen who participated in the raid, only one was killed in action. Eight were captured and tried in a Tokyo kangaroo court. Three of these were beheaded, and a fourth died in prison. With the help of friendly Chinese civilians, Doolittle and other survivors made their way to safety. Doolittle went on to high command with the Twelfth, Fifteenth, and Eighth Air Forces during the war. He received the Medal of Honor, and each Raider was decorated with the Distinguished Flying Cross.

As for the Japanese, their immediate consternation at being bombed gave way to a fundamental change in their prosecution of the war in the Pacific. The belief that their island nation was impregnable to enemy attack evaporated. The decision was made to extend their defensive perimeter across the Pacific, leading directly to the tactical defeat at the Battle of the Coral Sea as their efforts to capture Port Moresby in New Guinea and threaten Australia were thwarted. In June 1942, the Japanese met disaster at the Battle of Midway, the turning point of the Pacific War.

From there, Japan was obliged to fight a defensive war, one of attrition which it could not hope to win. ■

Blindfolded Doolittle Raider Lieutenant Robert L. Hite is led away by his Japanese captors. Hite was liberated from a prison camp on August 20, 1945. *(Public Domain US Air Force via Wikimedia Commons)*

US MARINE RAIDERS

Marine Raiders and their war dogs traverse a jungle trail in the Pacific. *(Public Domain US National Archives and Records Administration via Wikimedia Commons)*

From the beginning there had been some grousing among officers of the US Marine Corps. The Marines, after all, were an elite force in themselves. There was no real need for another elite force within their beloved Corps.

Nevertheless, the Marine Raiders were authorised in February 1942, by order of Lieutenant General Thomas Holcomb, Commandant of the Marine Corps. And there was plenty of support even higher in the chain of command. President Franklin D. Roosevelt was in favour of the concept, and not much else was required to make the idea a reality.

That idea had originally been put forth by Lieutenant Colonel Evans F. Carlson, a veteran of the US Army who had joined the Marines in 1939, left the service, and then returned after adventures that included a stint in China where he had observed the communist forces under Mao Tse-tung and admired their esprit de corps, as well as their fighting efficiency. When Carlson returned to the service, he advocated the formation of hard-hitting battalions of specially trained Marines who had demonstrated exceptional fighting ability through rigorous training, including parachute qualification, to take on the most difficult of tasks in the looming war with Japan. He also brought back the motto of Mao's guerrillas, "Gung-ho!" which loosely translates into English as "Work together!"

Eventually, the Marine Raiders would be authorised to a strength of four battalions, but the most famous of these by far were the 1st and 2nd Battalions, whose exploits during their brief existence became the stuff of Marine legend and controversy. Lieutenant Colonel Merritt A. "Red Mike" Edson commanded the 1st Battalion, while Carlson took the 2nd Battalion. By the summer of 1942, US ground forces were staged for their first offensive action in the Pacific theatre of World War II, and the Raiders were there.

When the 1st Marine Division stormed ashore on the island of Guadalcanal in the Solomons archipelago, Edson's 1st Raider Battalion took part in securing the nearby island of Tulagi, just across Sealark Channel from Guadalcanal and later dubbed Ironbottom Sound. The Raiders and other Marine units encountered stiff resistance on Tulagi and more than 150 were killed or wounded, but the Japanese garrison was virtually annihilated with only three prisoners taken as the island was secured by the afternoon of August 8.

By early September, the Marines on Guadalcanal were fighting hard to hold the island's vital airstrip they had named Henderson Field, and Major General Alexander Vandegrift, commander of the 1st Marine Division, consolidated his infantry strength with the transfer of Edson's Raiders and other troops to a defensive line that had to be held at all costs against an expected Japanese onslaught. Edson was keenly aware that a desperate battle faced the defenders and ordered his men to dig in along the forward slope of a long ridge. The Raiders dug and then waited.

US Marine Raiders were featured in this 1943 advertisement for Chesterfield cigarettes. *(Public Domain Carolina Magazine 1943 Liggett and Myers Tobacco Company via Wikimedia Commons)*

A machine-gun crew of the 2nd Raider Battalion occupies a flooded foxhole on the island of Bougainville. *(Public Domain US Signal Corps Archives via Wikimedia Commons)*

62 ELITE FORCES OF WORLD WAR II

ELITE FORCES OF WORLD WAR II

After fighting the Japanese at Bougainville, a group of Marine Raiders poses in 1944. *(Public Domain US National Archives and Records Administration via Wikimedia Commons)*

During rigorous training a Marine Raider leaps a barbed wire obstacle. *(Public Domain US Marine Corps via Wikimedia Commons)*

On September 12, the Japanese launched a desperate nocturnal attack, hitting the Raiders' left flank hard. They were repelled just as another wave of attackers hit the right flank. Hand-to-hand fighting ensued, and the enemy was again driven back. A third Japanese assault failed, and after nearly six hours of combat Edson informed the senior commander that the line would hold. However, he was sure that the enemy would strike again.

The next night, a torrent of Japanese troops hit the ridge, but the Marines held in one of the most stirring episodes of courage on the battlefield in the history of the Corps. Since that terrible engagement, the otherwise nondescript high ground has been known as "Bloody Ridge" or "Edson's Ridge." A few Japanese troops fought their way to the edge of Henderson Field but were cut down by Marine engineers, and by 4 a.m. on September 14, the enemy onslaught had blown itself out.

A month later, Edson's Raiders were still in the fight, and the intrepid officer had also taken command of the 5th Marine Regiment. Resuming the offensive to eject the Japanese from Guadalcanal, Vandegrift ordered an advance along the Matanikau River. Edson responded by sending two battalions across the mouth of the river, and when elements of the Japanese 4th Infantry Regiment attempted to establish artillery and machine-gun positions to take the advancing Marines under fire, a Raider company hit their exposed flank, nearly surrounding the enemy soldiers and hurling them back with heavy losses.

Meanwhile, Carlson and the 2nd Raider Battalion executed a high-risk raid on the island of Makin in the Gilberts. They landed in small boats launched from the submarines Argonaut and Nautilus on the night of August 17-18, 1942, but rough surf and confused orders complicated the situation for the 211 Raiders of the battalion's six rifle companies. Heavy Japanese resistance was encountered, and the Raiders beat back a pair of fanatical suicide Banzai charges. They also shot up a Japanese flying boat intending to insert reinforcements after sunrise on the 17th.

Still, the Raiders' situation was beginning to deteriorate. That night an evacuation got underway, but by the morning of the 18th dozens of Raiders were still on Makin. Carlson considered surrender and wrote a note intended for the Japanese commander asking for terms, but the Japanese soldier sent with the communication was killed by Raiders who were unaware of his mission. Subsequently, the remaining Raiders reached safety aboard the submarines after paddling their small boats nearly four miles.

Nineteen Marine Raiders were killed in action during the Makin Raid, and rumours of Carlson's possible intent to surrender dogged him for the rest of his career. Despite the fact that they had killed roughly half of the Japanese garrison at Makin, the Raiders had not fulfilled all of their objectives, including intelligence gathering and the capture of prisoners for interrogation.

By November, Carlson's 2nd Raider Battalion had joined Edson's 1st Battalion on Guadalcanal. The 2nd Battalion landed a full 30 miles beyond the Marine perimeter and undertook a month-long campaign of search and destroy against the Japanese that were left on the island, inflicting more than 500 casualties on the enemy in exchange for 16 Raiders dead and 18 wounded. The so-called "Long Patrol" was a masterpiece in tactical warfare behind enemy lines.

In the autumn of 1942, the two additional Marine Raider battalions were constituted, and the Raider formations were later consolidated into two regiments. Nevertheless, the Raider concept remained unpopular within the Marine Corps establishment, particularly considering the rumours of Carlson's possible surrender at Makin and concerns that his political beliefs were pro-communist.

By 1944, the character of World War II in the Pacific had changed. The need for mobile, light infantry that specialised in deep penetration missions and raids had waned. At the same time, Marine combat divisions were in need of manpower. In a somewhat ignominious end, the Marine Raiders were disbanded and their ranks absorbed into other combat units.

Although the Marine Raiders were in existence for a relatively short time, their combat record places them among the memorable formations of the US Marine Corps. ■

Weary Marine Raiders pause after reaching the safety of USS Nautilus following the Makin Raid. *(Public Domain United States Government via Wikimedia Commons)*

LIEUTENANT COLONEL EVANS F. CARLSON

Lieutenant Colonel Evans F. Carlson was a military man for most of his life, but much of that time was spent amid scepticism and mistrust, even though he had proven himself on the battlefield on more than one occasion.

The father of the US Marine Raiders, Carlson had come to the Marines after spending several years in and out of the US Army. During that period of service he was wounded in action in World War I and received a commission as a 2nd lieutenant. In the 1920s, he was commended for heroism in Nicaragua, leading 12 Marines against 100 militants and receiving the Navy Cross for heroism.

Between the world wars, Carlson travelled to China on three occasions. He came to appreciate the esprit de corps of the Chinese communist forces then engaged against the Japanese on the Asian continent. While he admired the Chinese and even took hold of their motto of "Gung-ho!" or "Work together!" he was wary of Japanese aggression, so much so that he felt compelled to spread the alarm.

Carlson left the Marines in 1939 to lecture across the United States on the topic of Japanese militarism. He urged preparedness and a resolute stand against the Japanese intent to expand their territory and influence across Asia and the Pacific. When he returned to the Marines in 1941, Carlson had nurtured the concept of the Marine Raiders and put forth his idea for the formation of these elite fighting men.

Although Carlson was already suspected of having a left-leaning political affinity due to his outspoken admiration of the Chinese communist army under Mao Tse-tung and the higher echelons of Marine Corps command frowned upon the constitution of an elite force within the Marines, who already considered themselves to be elite, Carlson had a powerful advocate.

In the early 1930s, the officer had served as a member of the Marine security detail for President Franklin D. Roosevelt during visits to the famed Little White House in Warm Springs, Georgia. He knew the Roosevelt family, and the President's son, James, had become a devotee of the rebel officer. When the concept of the Raiders was presented to FDR, Carlson found the support that he needed.

Major James Roosevelt served as Carlson's executive officer and participated in the Makin

Lieutenant Colonel Evans F. Carlson was the father of the US Marine Raiders. (Public Domain US Marine Corps via Wikimedia Commons)

Weary Lieutenant Colonel Evans F. Carlson is shown aboard the submarine USS Nautilus after the Makin Raid. (Public Domain US Navy via Wikimedia Commons)

Raid. While Carlson, aged in his mid-40s, led the raid as commander of the 2nd Raider Battalion, rumours of his possible intent to surrender to the Japanese at Makin undermined his credibility to an extent. Even after Carlson's Raiders executed the brilliant Long Patrol on Guadalcanal, other Marine officers were still intent on ending the Raider experiment.

After the Long Patrol, Carlson was ordered to return to the US and given a series of administrative assignments. Subsequently, the four Raider battalions were consolidated into a single unit, and then they were disbanded as their numbers were parcelled out to Marine combat divisions.

Although he was without a command, Evans Carlson wanted to return to combat duty. He was given that opportunity during Operation Galvanic in November 1943, when the US 2nd Marine Division assaulted the islet of Betio at Tarawa Atoll in the Gilbert Islands. Technically along as an observer, Carlson exhibited conspicuous bravery, often exposing himself to enemy fire to maintain communications during the desperate battle.

Carlson's tremendous courage prompted Colonel David Shoup, commander of the 2nd Marine Regiment, to remark, "He may be Red, but he isn't Yellow!" Carlson was again in the thick of the fighting on the island of Saipan in the Marianas in the spring of 1944. He was seriously wounded there, and the disability forced his retirement from the Marines in 1946.

Promoted to the rank of brigadier general on the retired list, Carlson died at the age of 51 on May 27, 1947. He remains one of the most innovative and committed officers in the history of the US Marine Corps. ■

Fleet Admiral Chester W. Nimitz decorates Lieutenant Colonel Evans Carlson on Guadalcanal in 1942. (Public Domain US Marine Corps via Wikimedia Commons)

ELITE FORCES OF WORLD WAR II

MAJOR GENERAL MERRITT A. EDSON

As the beleaguered Marines clung to their positions across the high ground defending Henderson Field at Guadalcanal, a stalwart presence seemed to be everywhere, encouraging his men to hold fast, bolstering their courage, and providing continuing support.

Colonel Merritt A. "Red Mike" Edson was a Marine's Marine. He had already led the 1st Marine Raider Battalion in the fight for the neighbouring island of Tulagi, and his command had been expanded when reinforcements were brought to Guadalcanal in September 1942 to hold the vital airstrip and defeat the Japanese in the first American ground offensive of World War II in the Pacific.

On the night of September 12, Edson was convinced that his Marines were directly in the path of a looming Japanese assault. He was right. The enemy stormed forward, into the teeth of Marine machine guns and rifle fire. The fighting was hand-to-hand, and in some areas the Japanese reached American foxholes, where they were killed with knives, shovels, and bare hands. After the enemy survivors had melted back into the jungle, Edson knew the battle was not over.

"They were just testing," Edson told his men as he moved among them. "They'll be back… You men have done a great job, and I have just one more thing to ask of you. Hold out just one more night. I know we've been without sleep a long time. But we expect another attack from them tonight and they may come through here. I have every reason to believe that we will have reliefs here for all of us in the morning."

The Japanese did come back the next night, and the stalwart defenders of "Bloody Ridge" or "Edson's Ridge" as the high ground was known ever after stood firm, repulsing the enemy and essentially sealing the fate of the Japanese on Guadalcanal.

Colonel Merritt Edson sits with a group of Marine officers at Tulagi in August 1942. *(Public Domain US Navy via Wikimedia Commons)*

Merritt A. Edson was 45 years old when his command presence stirred the Marines on Guadalcanal to such courage in the face of the enemy, and he received the Medal of Honor for his personal valour. He was a 25-year veteran of the Marine Corps and took command of the 1st Raider Battalion, the prototype for the three battalions that were soon organised, in early 1942. He was promoted colonel that spring, and following his exploits at Guadalcanal he was named chief of staff of the 2nd Marine Division, then preparing for Operation Galvanic and the invasion of Tarawa Atoll in the Gilbert Islands. For his service at Tarawa, he received the Legion of Merit and promotion to brigadier general.

During the conquest of the Marianas in 1944, Edson received the Silver Star for service on the islands of Saipan and Tinian. He was soon elevated to chief of staff of the Fleet Marine Force, and when World War II in the Pacific ended in September 1945, he had spent nearly four years overseas.

Promoted major general in August 1947, Edson retired from the Marines after 30 years of service in which he had also received the Navy Cross twice. He later served as commissioner of the Vermont State Police and as president of the National Rifle Association. Tragically, he ended his own life on August 14, 1955, at the age of 58. ■

Major General Merritt A. "Red Mike" Edson was the hero of the fight at Bloody Ridge. *(Public Domain US Marine Corps via Wikimedia Commons)*

Brigadier General Merritt A. Edson observes Japanese positions from the front line on the island of Tinian. *(Public Domain US Marine Corps via Wikimedia Commons)*

OFFICE OF STRATEGIC SERVICES

General William J. Donovan reviews graduates of OSS training before their deployment to China. *(Public Domain US Office Of Strategic Services via Wikimedia Commons)*

OSS operative 1st Lieutenant George Musulin poses as a Chetnik in this photo taken in German-occupied Serbia. *(Public Domain US Office of Strategic Services via Wikimedia Commons)*

In the summer of 1941, the road to war appeared inevitable for the United States. Engaged in an undeclared naval conflict with the Nazi Kriegsmarine in the Atlantic and aware that Britain, standing alone, was the great bulwark against Hitler's dream of world domination, President Franklin D. Roosevelt addressed an obvious weakness in his nation's defence apparatus.

American intelligence operations were fragmented and probably inefficient. In fact, there was some resistance in powerful circles to even pursuing a robust means of waging covert and overt intelligence operations in wartime. In fact, some years earlier Secretary of State Henry L. Stimpson had remarked, "Gentlemen do not read each other's mail."

Roosevelt's approach to intelligence gathering was somewhat more pragmatic, and he established the office of the Coordinator of Information (COI) on July 11, 1941. The purpose of the new agency was to collect information, coordinate research and analysis, develop training and operations for covert activities, organise guerrilla warfare efforts, distribute propaganda, and engage in combat operations. At the time, several organisations were engaged in some of these activities, including the US Army, US Navy, and the Federal Bureau of Investigation (FBI). And each of them guarded its turf jealously.

The president wanted to change all that with a centralised approach to such operations, and to lead the COI, he chose an old law school classmate, World War I hero, and something of a political opponent. Colonel William J. Donovan was a successful and influential Wall Street attorney, well connected in business and social circles. If anyone could overcome the inter-agency rivalry that had existed and mould US intelligence and black operations into an effective, cohesive effort, Donovan could.

At first, there was minimal support, but Donovan saw the looming shadow war and recruited intelligent, educated and willing men to the great undertaking. In the midst of it all, the Japanese attack on Pearl Harbor – one of the greatest intelligence failures in US history – brought a renewed sense of urgency to the program. On June 13, 1942, President Roosevelt signed another executive order, expanding Donovan's role and renaming his enterprise the Office of Strategic Services (OSS).

This aerial view of Camp X near Toronto, Ontario, Canada, was taken in 1943. *(Public Domain Lynn Hodgson – Camp X via Wikimedia Commos)*

Donovan had developed ties to the British intelligence community and solicited the help of acknowledged experts. The British were quite willing to assist, and representatives of the Special Operations Executive (SOE) and Secret Intelligence Service (SIS) became involved with the quiet support of William S. Stephenson, the leader of the British Security Office in New York City.

The OSS apparatus soon included a framework of a dozen major components. The Administrative Services and Personnel Procurement branches handled the day-to-day activities of OSS headquarters in Washington, DC, while the Communications branch (Commo), Maritime Unit (MU), Research and Development (R&D), and Morale Operations (MO) offices were established. The Special Operations (SO) group was responsible for paramilitary activities, and the Operational Groups (OG) engaged in direct action. X-2

The OSS supplied false identity documents like these for agents in Italy. *(Creative Commons Baminvestor via Wikipedia)*

OSS men relax in the lounge at their forward base on the island of Ceylon. *(Public Domain US Office of Strategic Services via Wikimedia Commons)*

was responsible for counter-intelligence, while Research and Analysis (R&A) engaged in espionage and intelligence evaluation. By 1943, a separate Schools and Training (S&T) organisation was established to accommodate a growing number of recruits.

The British provided access to an existing training facility administered by the SOE in Toronto, Canada. Known as Camp X, it was already operating when dozens of American recruits, the first of their kind, were admitted to complete the four-week training course that covered a myriad of intelligence related topics. The participants learned fieldcraft, survival techniques, hand-to-hand combat techniques, the use of codes and ciphers, and surveillance. They underwent a strenuous program of physical fitness. Most of all, they were strictly schooled in keeping their mouths shut. Giving away information or letting down their guard would mean certain death, or death for others.

Donovan was provided an almost unlimited budget, and he set about identifying the people that could build a sophisticated and efficient apparatus. He also located two areas that would serve as training and educational facilities. One of these was the Catoctin Recreational Demonstration Area in the mountains of central Maryland, and the other was the Chopawamsic Recreational Demonstration Area in Virginia. Both were just a short distance from the headquarters of the OSS In Washington, DC.

The sites had been developed by the Civilian Conservation Corps in the 1930s, and there were barracks, mess halls, and thousands of acres for field exercises. At Catoctin, a section was set aside as the presidential retreat. Roosevelt called it Shangri-La, and it later became Camp David, still guarded by a detachment of US Marines and serving the same function today. Chopawamsic was adjacent to the expansive Marine Corps base at Quantico, Virginia. Catoctin became Area B, receiving its first recruits in April 1942, and these men eventually became the nucleus of Detachment 101, which trained Kachin guerrillas to fight the Japanese in the jungles of Burma. Chopawamsic became Area A, where an advanced course was set up. In the spring of 1943, a communications school at Chopawamsic was designated Area C.

As the OSS program expanded, an espionage school was established at the Lothian Farm, a sprawling 100-acre estate in Clinton Maryland. It became simply known as "the Farm." Other facilities were expanded or acquired as the agency pursued its mission. The Congressional Country Club in Bethesda, Maryland, was even requisitioned for OSS training.

The earliest OSS operatives were sent on various missions with only a smattering of training. They had little introduction to the basics of surveillance and intelligence gathering, much less the conduct of raids against enemy installations or the training of local partisan and guerrilla bands to fight the Axis in Europe or the Pacific. However, as the war progressed, OSS training steadily improved. Many experts, both American and British, taught a broad array of subjects.

OSS trainees were at times sent on covert missions around the Maryland and Virginia countryside. Groups were tasked with setting dummy explosives beneath bridges under the noses of sentries. They were ordered to infiltrate supposedly secure facilities, including aircraft production plants. They were required to negotiate challenging obstacle courses, and future Central Intelligence Agency (CIA) Director William Casey suffered a broken jaw when an explosive detonated and he had failed to keep his head low while crawling through an area sown with booby traps.

As World War II progressed, the OSS deployed dozens of teams on missions in the European theatre from Scandinavia to the Mediterranean, the Balkans, and the Middle East. OSS operatives were active in the China-Burma-India theatre and elsewhere in the Pacific. More than 16,000 personnel served with the OSS, though a relative few of them were deployed in dangerous roles as spies, saboteurs, or guerrilla fighters.

Dozens of OSS operations, some conducted in partnership with the British SOE, became the stuff of legend.

President Harry Truman ordered the OSS to be dissolved after World War II ended; however, the requirement for a robust intelligence effort was fully recognised. The agency served as the forerunner for the modern CIA, which emerged in 1947. ■

OSS men meet with anti-Nazi guerrilla leaders in the Balkans. *(Public Domain reproduced from Novosti.rs via Wikimedia Commons)*

GENERAL WILLIAM J. DONOVAN

William J. Donovan, the man President Franklin D. Roosevelt chose to establish a coordinated intelligence gathering and clandestine operations program for the United States, was an extraordinary individual. Roosevelt had known Donovan while the two were students at Harvard Law School, and even though they were often at odds regarding political issues of the day, they found common ground in their shared commitment to training and deploying specialised operatives that would carry World War II to the Axis enemy.

In the summer of 1941, Roosevelt established the office of Coordinator of Information, and at the urging of intelligence officer William S. Stephenson, head of the British Security Coordination office in New York, the president's trust in Donovan was confirmed. Eleven months later, the burgeoning COI was provided with sweeping new authority and its name was changed to the Office of Strategic Services (OSS).

Donovan was no stranger to military matters and appreciated the need for intelligence coordination. He had been wounded in combat during World War I and received the Medal of Honor for action in the Argonne Forest in the autumn of 1918. As a young lieutenant colonel, Donovan led the US Army's 165th Infantry Regiment into an attack on October 14. Tanks had been assigned to provide support for Donovan's infantry, but when the armour failed to show up, the foot soldiers were ordered ahead anyway.

The situation deteriorated rapidly, and Donovan sent messengers to the rear to summon reinforcements. However, each man was killed. A few tanks finally arrived, but they were disabled by German artillery fire.

General William J. 'Wild Bill' Donovan, director of the OSS, confers with Colonel William Harding Jackson in 1945. *(Public Domain US Army Signal Corps via Wikimedia Commons)*

The shelling was accompanied by poison gas, which also took a terrible toll.

Showing no regard for his personal safety, Donovan displayed tremendous command presence. "I had walked to different units and was coming back to the telephone when smash, I felt as if somebody had hit me on the back of the leg with a spiked club," he wrote. "I fell like a log, but after a few minutes managed to crawl into my little telephone hole. A machine gun lieutenant ripped open my breeches and put on the first aid. The leg hurt, but there were many things to be done. Beside me three men were blown up, and I was showered with the remnants of their bodies."

Donovan remained in the hole, just yards from the enemy line. Slipping in and out of consciousness from loss of blood, he maintained command for five hours until wrapped in a blanket and evacuated. The German position finally fell on October 16, and Donovan recovered from his wound, returning to his prosperous New York law practice between the world wars.

In his role as Roosevelt's hand-picked OSS director, Donovan, who became known as "Wild Bill," wrote a top secret memorandum dated June 25, 1942. Titled "Primary Blueprint Memo," the document related his perspective on the intelligence organisation he was tasked to build. "...We face an enemy who believes one of his chief weapons is that none but he will employ terror. But we will turn terror against him – or we will cease to exist."

Recruiting talent wherever he could, Donovan capably led the OSS during the war years, rising to the rank of major general, and afterward he worked behind the scenes to establish the modern CIA, although President Harry S. Truman declined to appoint him as the director of the new intelligence agency in 1947.

Donovan continued to practice law, served briefly as U.S. Ambassador to Thailand, and died at age 76 on February 8, 1959. He remains the only individual in US history to have received the Medal of Honor, Distinguished Service Cross, Distinguished Service Medal, and National Security Medal. ∎

General William J. 'Wild Bill' Donovan led the Office of Strategic Services during World War II. *(Public Domain US National Archives and Records Administration via Wikimedia Commons)*

Lieutenant Colonel William Donovan is shown in uniform in France in the autumn of 1918. *(Public Domain US National Archives and Records Administration via Wikimedia Commons)*

ELITE FORCES OF WORLD WAR II

OSS DETACHMENT 101

General Joseph Stilwell, US commander in the China-Burma-India theatre, was reluctant to deploy the few men of OSS Detachment 101 when they arrived at his headquarters. In July 1942, he flatly told Captain Carl Eifler, the small group's leader, "I didn't send for you and I don't want you."

Stilwell was not initially a proponent of clandestine or guerrilla warfare, but Detachment 101 had come to the CBI to wage just that. Ultimately, Stilwell gained respect for the group and even authorised its enlargement from an early handful of only 120 men. Detachment 101 formed even as its parent organisation, the Office of Strategic Services (OSS), was being organised by its chief, General William "Wild Bill" Donovan, from the office of the Coordinator of Information.

Donovan was itching to get men into action in a meaningful way in the CBI, and in the spring of 1942 Detachment 101 was organised. Training took place at a facility in Canada operated by the British Special Operations Executive and at a camp located deep in the Catoctin Mountains of Maryland. By the summer Eifler and company were abroad. The primary task of Detachment 101 was to organise and train Kachin tribesmen, indigenous to northern Burma, in guerrilla tactics and to lead them in clandestine attacks on Japanese troops, supply routes, and installations behind enemy lines while also gathering intelligence. Detachment 101 became the first US force deployed behind Japanese lines in Asia for an extended period.

A base of operations was established in India's Assam Province, and the unit became steadily more active by 1943, although some sources relate that operations commenced quite a bit earlier. Nevertheless, Detachment 101 had established six bases by the end of the year and conducted missions against Japanese rail lines and other targets with varying degrees of success. The Kachins had proven themselves resourceful and effective in the guerrilla role, striking at the Japanese and inflicting heavy casualties, while also assisting downed Allied airmen in evading capture. By early 1944,

Officers of OSS Detachment 101 posed for this group photo in January 1945. *(Public Domain US Army via Wikimedia Commons)*

Major Bob Moore, Major Red Maddox, Colonel Ray Peers, Gen. Dan Sultan, Major Butch Brown, Major Rob Delaney, Major Dow Jones, Major Johnny Raiss

Stilwell authorised an increase in personnel to 3,000, anticipating its supporting effort in the advance on the city of Myitkyina by Galahad Force, which consisted of the famed Merrill's Marauders and two regiments of Chinese troops.

While the fight for Myitkyina extended into the summer, Detachment 101 provided critical intelligence and fire support, increasing its operational area more than 100 miles south and steadily increasing its strength to a peak of more than 9,000. Eifler had been wounded and was succeeded as Detachment 101 commander by Captain William Peers.

In the autumn of 1944, Allied forces began their drive from Myitkyina into central Burma.

OSS commander Carl Eifler celebrates his promotion to colonel in the field. *(Public Domain US Army via Wikimedia Commons)*

Detachment 101 expanded its operations in step with the advance, often screening the forward movements and providing information on enemy troop strength. After Mandalay and Lashio were occupied, Detachment 101 moved further south, engaging in its heaviest combat against the Japanese. During a three-month period of fierce fighting, the force killed more than 1,200 Japanese soldiers and lost approximately 300 men.

Disbanded in July 1945, Detachment 101 was credited with inflicting more than 15,000 casualties on the Japanese while destroying nine trains, 57 bridges, and 272 trucks, taking 78 prisoners, and rescuing 230 downed Allied airmen. Casualties were surprisingly low, 338 Kachin guerrillas and 27 American operatives.

President Dwight D. Eisenhower presented Detachment 101 veterans with the Presidential Unit Citation in 1956, and referred to the unit as perhaps the most effective force of its kind ever assembled. ■

A squad of Kachin Rangers recruited by OSS Detachment 101 prepares for action. *(Public Domain US Army via Wikimedia Commons)*

MERRILL'S MARAUDERS

The unit was conceived with a strength of 1,000 to 3,000 men to fight the Japanese in similar style to the British Army's Chindits, who conducted long range penetration raids deep behind enemy lines while under the command of their charismatic leader, Brigadier Orde Wingate.

When Prime Minister Winston Churchill, President Franklin D. Roosevelt, and Canadian Prime Minister William Mackenzie King met at Quebec in August 1943, that was the idea, and the US Army was charged with organising a formation that would become legendary in the China-Burma-India theatre (CBI). The 5307th Composite Unit (Provisional) also became better known by the nickname an enterprising reporter provided – Merrill's Marauders.

No time was wasted, and the 5307th was formed just as the Quebec Conference ended. Its commanding officer was hand-picked by General Joseph Stilwell, commander of US and Chinese forces in the CBI. Brigadier General Frank Merrill, whose command became his namesake, was chosen because he had endured, along with Stilwell, the humiliating defeat of Allied forces in Burma at the hands of the Japanese. Merrill had risen in rank from major to brigadier general in just a few months. He had virtually no experience in jungle warfare, nor in field command of a combat force. Nevertheless, Stilwell, a tough judge of character, had seen something in Merrill. He was proven correct, and Merrill turned out to be an excellent choice.

Merrill's Marauders were to be schooled in the art of deep penetration, survival for lengthy periods behind enemy lines in the inhospitable jungles of Asia, and in carrying the war to the enemy where he was most vulnerable. The 5307th actually trained with Wingate's Chindits for a time while in India, arriving in Bombay on October 31, 1943, and moving on to Deolali 125 miles distant.

Wingate's ambitious Operation Thursday provided Merrill's Marauders with their first opportunity to engage the enemy. Deployed in February 1944, the Americans entered the jungle and rapidly ran into the veteran Japanese 18th Infantry Division. The opposing forces made contact on March 1, and five days of incessant fighting ensued near the southern end of Burma's inhospitable Hukawng Valley. The Marauders proved their toughness from

Brigadier General Frank Merrill discusses a battle plan with two men of the 5307th in Burma. (Public Domain US Army via Wikimedia Commons)

Brigadier General Frank Merrill (left) confers with theatre commander Lieutenant General Joseph Stilwell. (Public Domain US Army via Wikimedia Commons)

the outset, killing, wounding, or capturing 800 enemy troops in their baptism of fire.

Weeks in the jungle followed, and by the end of May the Marauders had fought four more extended engagements against the Japanese. Coordinating with regiments of the Chinese Army, they advanced to capture the airfield outside the town of Myitkyina. During their movement punctuated by pitched battles, Merrill's Marauders covered a distance of 750 miles – all on foot. The jungle proved to be a worthy adversary as well as the Japanese. During their long ordeal, the Americans suffered 700 casualties, including combat killed and wounded, those suffering from rampant tropical diseases, and others who had simply reached the point of physical or mental exhaustion.

On March 31, Merrill was incapacitated when he suffered the second heart attack of his military career. While recovering in the hospital, Merrill received news that the Marauders had decisively defeated Japanese reinforcements headed for the 18th Division in a tough fight at Nhpum Ga. The news cheered him considerably. The victory

Merrill's Marauders move out along a jungle trail in Burma. (Public Domain US Signal Corps via Wikimedia Commons)

had been won while the Marauders were under the capable command of Merrill's executive officer, Lieutenant Colonel Charles Hunter.

After spending three months in the jungle fighting the enemy, the Marauders were exhausted. Rumours began to circulate of an impending withdrawal and an opportunity to rest and absorb replacements. However, these hopes proved false as General Stilwell called on the depleted command to join elements of the Chinese Army in an effort to capture the town of Myitkyina itself. The Marauders could muster about 1,500 men capable of carrying a rifle, and many of these were ill to varying degrees. But they followed orders and attacked eastward toward Myitkyina in a sweeping advance that was code named Operation End Run.

The Japanese clung desperately to the town. Their 3,500 defenders received sporadic resupply, allowing them to continue their determined fight. At the same time, the combat effectiveness of Merrill's Marauders eroded with each passing day. Only 200 of the original 5307th personnel were still with the unit by June 1944, and many of these men were so ill with various diseases that they could hardly function. An order was issued that every soldier was required to perform regular duty unless he had run a fever of 102 degrees Fahrenheit for at last three consecutive days, and even then his health was reviewed by a panel of doctors before he was withdrawn. Malaria, scrub typhus, and dysentery were everywhere, and some soldiers were simply unfit mentally for duty after the arduous experience they had endured.

In 1945, Captain Fred O. Lyons, an officer with the Marauders, told an interviewer of the horrors that were still fresh in his mind. "Every one of the men was sick from one cause or another," he commented. "My shoulders were worn raw from the pack straps, and I left the pack behind…The boys with me weren't in much better shape…A scout moving ahead suddenly held his rifle high in the air. That meant enemy sighted… Then at last we saw them, coming down the railroad four abreast…The gunner crouched low over his Tommy gun and tightened down. Then the gun spoke. Down flopped a half dozen Japs, then another half dozen. The column spewed from their marching formation into the bush.

General Joseph Stilwell presents medals to Merrill's Marauders at Myitkyina. *(Public Domain US Signal Corps via Wikimedia Commons)*

General Frank Merrill talks with Kachin scouts in the Burmese jungle. *(Public Domain US Army via Wikimedia Commons)*

Although plagued by a heart condition, General Frank Merrill became famous as the leader of Merrill's Marauders. *(Public Domain US War Department via Wikimedia Commons)*

We grabbed up the gun and slid back into the jungle. Sometimes staggering, sometimes running, sometimes dragging, I made it back to camp. I was so sick I didn't care whether the Japs broke through or not; so sick I didn't worry any more about letting the colonel down. All I wanted was unconsciousness."

Hunter knew his command had reached the breaking point and beseeched Stilwell for relief. But the fight dragged on until the overland supply route the Japanese had depended on was severed on August 4, 1944. The surviving defenders of Myitkyina finally surrendered. It had been a grim affair for the victors as well as the vanquished. Merrill's Marauders had lost another 570 men to disease alone. Nearly 1,250 Allied soldiers had been killed in action, and another 4,000 were wounded.

By mid-August, those who had served gallantly with Merrill's Marauders were reassigned to the 475th Infantry Regiment. Every man had received the Bronze Star medal and the Presidential Unit Citation for conspicuous bravery. In the future, the 475th Regiment was redesignated the 75th Regiment and then the 75th Ranger Regiment. Thus, the modern Rangers of the US Army may claim the fighting record of Merrill's Marauders as a portion of their heritage.

After recovering from his heart attack, Frank Merrill became a staff officer with Southwest Asia Command. He received a well-earned promotion to major general in September 1944 and was appointed chief of staff of the US Tenth Army, commanded by General Simon Bolivar Buckner, Jr. Buckner was killed in action at Okinawa, and Merrill stepped in briefly to lead the American forces on the island.

In the autumn of 1945, Merrill returned to the United States and held various staff appointments until retirement in 1948. He worked as the commissioner of roads and public highways for the state of New Hampshire until he suffered yet another heart attack and died at the age of 52 in 1955. ■

BLACK SHEEP SQUADRON

During the desperate air battles that raged in the Solomon Islands from 1942-1943, one of the legendary American air squadrons of World War II emerged with the reputation of a hard-hitting, risk-taking group of pilots that emulated the attitude of their legendary commander, Major Gregory "Pappy" Boyington.

Marine Fighter Squadron 214 (VMF-214) was established at Naval Air Station Ewa on the Hawaiian island of Oahu on June 1, 1942. The squadron was originally known as the Swashbucklers and completed a single tour of duty flying from Henderson Field on the island of Guadalcanal. The squadron then disbanded; however, it did not pass into obscurity.

In August, VMF-214 was reconstituted at the island of Espiritu Santo in the New Hebrides, and its 27 pilots came under the command of Boyington, a veteran of air combat in China with the American Volunteer Group, better known as the Flying Tigers. Boyington had shot down six Japanese planes over China, and his pilots nicknamed him "Pappy." At age 31, he was at least a decade older than most of the pilots of VMF-214. The pilots also settled on a new nickname, the Black Sheep, not because they had earned a rowdy reputation as some histories have speculated, but because of the somewhat roundabout way the squadron had come back together.

Boyington, though, had indeed already developed a reputation for mischief. In China, he had often found himself in the doghouse of Flying Tiger commander General Claire Chennault. He enjoyed a good drink and engaged in other escapades, but when it came to fighting the Japanese in the air, Boyington was a superb leader. His squadron was also given one of the outstanding aircraft of the war as its weapon. The Chance Vought F4U Corsair was an outstanding fighter plane, and the Japanese came to dread encounters with a Corsair and a skilled pilot at its controls. In grudging respect, they nicknamed the plane "Whistling Death."

The Black Sheep flew missions in the southern Solomons and then moved up to a forward base at Vella Lavella. Their short combat tenure lasted only from September 1943 to January 1944, but it produced spectacular results. During their first two weeks of operations, the Black Sheep shot down 23 Japanese aircraft and claimed another 11 probable kills. During the period only five VMF-214 pilots were lost.

Boyington was always aggressive. He instilled a combative spirit in his pilots, and during 84 days of air operations the Black Sheep shot down 100 enemy planes. In the autumn of 1943, Boyington made a much-publicised deal with the St. Louis Cardinals of major league baseball. He offered to shoot down a Japanese plane for every ball cap sent to the squadron. The cardinals sent 20 caps, and the Marine pilots flamed 20 Japanese planes, sending back 20 decals of Japanese flags that represented the kills.

Major Gregory "Pappy" Boyington briefs pilots of VMF-214 prior to a mission.
(Public Domain US National Archives and Records Administration via Wikimedia Commons)

Leading the Black Sheep, Boyington piled up an outstanding number of kills. While escorting dive bombers over Bougainville in October 1943, he shot down three Japanese Zero fighters in just one minute. He led VMF-214 into a brawl with 60 enemy fighters one day; outnumbered nearly three-to-one, the Black Sheep destroyed 20 enemy planes and incurred no losses themselves.

Boyington scored 28 air victories in the Pacific and received the Medal of Honor. He was shot down and captured on January 3, 1944, and liberated from a Japanese prison camp 20 months later. Five days after Boyington was shot down, VMF-214 was disbanded. Boyington subsequently retired from the Marines with the rank of colonel and died in 1988 at age 75.

A third incarnation of the Black Sheep Squadron took place at the end of January 1944. These pilots were assigned to the aircraft carrier USS *Franklin*, and 32 of them were among 800 killed when a pair of Japanese bombs hit the carrier in March 1945.

Chance Vought F4U Corsair fighters line an airstrip in the Pacific theatre.
(Public Domain US National Archives and Records Administration via Wikimedia Commons)

Pilots of the Black Sheep Squadron stand before a Corsair fighter at Espiritu Santo, New Hebrides. *(Public Domain National Museum of the US Navy via Wikimedia Commons)*

ELITE FORCES OF WORLD WAR II

US ARMY RANGERS

When the news of British Commando operations began to filter through the press and across the Atlantic Ocean, their successes caught the attention of American military men. Among them was Major General Lucian Truscott, then a liaison officer with the British.

Truscott became quite familiar with Commando operations and believed strongly that the US Army should develop its own version of these highly trained, hard hitting special forces. He broached the subject with Army Chief of Staff General George C. Marshall, urging the establishment of a force "along the lines of the British Commandos."

Eventually, five battalions of US Army Rangers were organised in the European theatre during World War II, and a sixth was established in the Pacific. On June 19, 1942, the 1st Ranger Battalion

US Army Ranger Colonel William O. Darby was killed in action in northern Italy in 1945. *(Public Domain US Army via Wikimedia Commons)*

This photo depicts German prisoners marching into captivity on June 8, 1944, at Pointe du Hoc after the 2nd Ranger Battalion has been relieved. *(Public Domain US National Archives and Records Administration via Wikimedia Commons)*

Soldiers of the 2nd Ranger Battalion rest atop the cliffs at Pointe du Hoc after D-Day. *(Public Domain US Navy via Wikimedia Commons)*

was activated under the command of Colonel William O. Darby, recruited from troops of the regular army stationed in Ireland. The earliest Rangers were trained by members of the British Commandos at facilities in Scotland.

Prior to his selection as the Ranger commander, Darby had been an artillery officer and held various staff positions. Within months, he was leading three Ranger battalions, the 1st, 3rd, and 4th, into action in North Africa and Sicily. During Operation Jubilee, the ill-fated raid conducted largely by Canadian forces at the port of Dieppe in Nazi-occupied France in August 1942, a force of 50 Rangers had participated. Darby's Rangers made their first attack against enemy forces at Arzew, Algeria, in the opening hours of Operation Torch, the Allied landings in North Africa on November 8, 1942. Darby led three Ranger companies against Vichy French troops holding a fortified position overlooking the harbour and captured its heavy guns in 15 minutes. Major Herman Dammer led two more companies that seized port facilities and captured scores of French prisoners. Darby received the Distinguished Service Cross for the operation.

When the Allied Fifth Army went ashore at Salerno on the Italian mainland in September 1943, Darby's Rangers drew the tough assignment of securing Chiunzi Pass and holding the surrounding heights, which towered to 4,000 feet above the highway to Naples. The Rangers quickly covered the 19 miles from the landing beaches to the pass, seized their objective, and held until relieved. Control of the pass also blocked German reinforcements from reaching the Salerno beachhead, which was nevertheless hotly contested. The Rangers fought off repeated German counterattacks and held Chiunzi Pass for three long weeks.

As the long slog up the Italian boot proceeded against heavy German resistance, Allied forces stalled before the formidable defences of the Gustav Line in central Italy. In January 1944, the Allies attempted a daring amphibious

US ARMY RANGERS

Members of the US Army's 6th Ranger Battalion move out during the Cabanatuan Raid in the Philippines. *(Public Domain US Army via Wikimedia Commons)*

manoeuvre dubbed Operation Shingle. The US VI Corps came ashore at the resort town of Anzio with orders to outflank the Gustav Line and advance rapidly on Rome, the capital of fascist Italy, approximately 35 miles to the northwest.

Major General John P. Lucas, commander of VI Corps, hesitated against initially light opposition. Eight days later as German resistance stiffened, he ordered the 1st and 3rd Ranger Battalions and a detachment from the 3rd Infantry Division to launch a two-pronged thrust to capture the town of Cisterna.

The Rangers moved out in darkness utilising the cover of an irrigation trench to hopefully conceal their advance. At first, everything seemed to go according to plan. However, when the Rangers emerged from the trench, they were greeted with a hail of German machine-gun and rifle fire. Enemy troops of the Hermann Göring and 715th Infantry Divisions had sprung a devastating trap. Only six Rangers of an original complement of 767 managed to escape the debacle.

Cisterna was a devastating blow to the Rangers, and Darby was detailed to briefly command the 179th Infantry Regiment and then held staff positions in Washington, D C. He longed to return to combat and finally was given the post of assistant commander of the 10th Mountain Division. He was killed by a shell fragment in northern Italy in April 1945 and posthumously promoted to brigadier general.

Meanwhile, the 2nd Ranger Battalion wrote a stirring chapter in the history of the US Army on D-Day, the June 6, 1944, invasion of Normandy. Colonel James E. Rudder led the Rangers in scaling the 100-foot cliffs at Pointe du Hoc, where it was believed a battery of German 155mm guns might enfilade two critical American landing beaches, Omaha to the east and Utah to the northwest.

Around 7 a.m. on the morning of the 6th, Rudder's 225 Rangers leaped from their landing craft onto a sliver of beach barely 33 feet wide and began their hazardous assault. Some of the craft had veered off course and delayed the attack more than half an hour, and the defenders were alert. Allied destroyers swept into the shallows to blast at the Germans atop the cliffs with their 5-inch naval guns.

The Rangers used 82-foot ladders borrowed from the London Fire Department and launched rockets with ropes and grappling hooks attached to establish climbing lines up the face of the rocks. Some of the ropes, however, had become waterlogged on the run-in to the beach and were too heavy to reach the heights. The Rangers clawed their way to the summit, taking heavy casualties. They put the defenders to flight but found to their consternation that the big guns were gone.

Moving inland, a pair of Ranger sergeants, Len Lomell and Jack Kuhn, noticed vehicle tracks and followed them across the landscape

Lieutenant Colonel Henry Mucci led the 6th Ranger Battalion during the Cabanatuan Raid. *(Public Domain US Army Signal Corps via Wikimedia Commons)*

scarred by craters from bombs and naval shells. They found the 155mm cannon under the canopy of an orchard, pointing toward Utah Beach. Strangely, they were neither firing nor being guarded. The Rangers smashed the sights with their rifle butts and dropped thermite grenades down the barrels, rendering the guns useless, right under the noses of 100 German soldiers sitting idle nearby.

Rudder consolidated his position at Pointe du Hoc, and his Rangers beat back three determined German counterattacks. When the Allied lodgement in Normandy was finally secured, only 90 of the original Ranger contingent could shoulder a rifle – the rest were killed or seriously wounded.

While the struggle at Pointe du Hoc continued, the American troops of the 1st and 29th Infantry Divisions were fighting for their lives on Omaha Beach. The 5th Ranger Battalion had also come ashore in the Dog White sector of Omaha. General Norman Cota of the 29th Division attempted to rally his troops and noticed the Rangers on his flank. Cota shouted to Major Max Schneider, commander of the 5th Rangers, "What outfit is this?"

When Schneider responded that his unit was the 5th Rangers, Cota delivered an expletive, "Well… it then, Rangers, lead the way!" On that bloody day, the motto "Rangers lead the way!" was born. Amid desperate fighting, the Americans moved off Omaha Beach and claimed a toehold on D-Day.

In the Pacific, the 6th Ranger Battalion executed a daring raid to free 500 British and American prisoners of war held in terrible conditions at Cabanatuan prison camp on the Philippine island of Luzon. Supported by Filipino guerrillas, the Rangers moved stealthily forward on the night of January 30, 1945, surprised the Japanese guards, and brought the prisoners, many of whom had survived the infamous Bataan Death March and been held in captivity for three years, to safety.

The Rangers were briefly disbanded after World War II but reconstituted during the Korean War. Today, the 75th Ranger Regiment continues the tradition of its forebears and serves as the US Army's premier direct action raiding force. ■

After Pointe du Hoc is secured on D-Day, a US Army Ranger climbs a ladder to the top. *(Public Domain US Navy Wikimedia Commons)*

ELITE FORCES OF WORLD WAR II

US AIRBORNE DIVISIONS

Through the course of World War II, the United States Army created five airborne divisions. After thorough examination of the burgeoning utility of airborne forces during the early months of the war in Europe, General George C. Marshall, Chief of Staff of the Army, approved the recommendation to form a dedicated airborne command.

That command came into being on March 23, 1942, and Lieutenant Colonel William C. Lee, rightly called the father of the US airborne, was given command. Lee had observed German airborne exercises first-hand in the 1930s, and his incessant pleas for a concerted airborne effort in the US military had driven superior officers to distraction. Although platoon and then battalion sized paratrooper units had been formed since 1940, only four battalions were in existence at the end of 1941.

When Lee received the call to lead the Airborne Command he was 46 years old. First, he headed the Provisional Parachute Group, but the real augmentation of the airborne supposedly began after a tense call from none other than President Franklin D. Roosevelt. Lee had recently received a dressing down from a superior officer and had been told to cease his advocacy. Sometime later, the office telephone rang. The caller asked, "What are you folks doing toward developing airborne warfare?" Roosevelt was on the other end of the line, and Lee handed the phone to the colonel who had recently berated him. From there, the race was on.

On August 15, 1942, the 82nd Infantry Division, which had fought with distinction in World War I, was redesignated the 82nd Airborne Division, and training began at Camp Claiborne, Louisiana.

General Dwight D. Eisenhower visits with paratroopers of the 101st Airborne Division prior to their D-Day jump.
(Public Domain Library of Congress via Wikimedia Commons)

On the same day, the 101st Airborne Division was activated at Camp Claiborne. The 11th Airborne Division was activated on February 25, 1943, at Camp Mackall, North Carolina, and the 17th and 13th Airborne Divisions followed at Camp Mackall on April 15, and August 13.

Each of these divisions was deployed overseas during World War II; however, the 13th Airborne did not see action. The 17th Airborne was engaged in the Battle of the Bulge, Operation Varsity, the airborne crossing of the River Rhine, and the fighting in central Europe during the final months of the war. The 11th Airborne was the lone division allocated to the Pacific theatre, operating extensively in the Philippines as elements executed the brilliant raid that freed prisoners from the hellish Japanese camp at Los Banos.

The combat sojourns of the 82nd "All American" and the 101st "Screaming Eagles" during the war have become the stuff of legend.

Troopers of the 101st Airborne Division retrieve supplies after an airdrop at Bastogne during the Battle of the Bulge. *(Public Domain US Army Center of Military History via Wikimedia Commons)*

General James M. Gavin led the 505th Parachute Infantry Regiment and later the 82nd Airborne Division during World War II.
(Public Domain US Army via Wikimedia Commons)

US AIRBORNE DIVISIONS

Troopers of the 504th Parachute Infantry Regiment accompany a tank during the Battle of the Bulge. *(Public Domain US Army via Wikimedia Commons)*

The 82nd Airborne Division, under General Matthew Ridgway, went into action in July 1943, during Operation Husky, the invasion of Sicily. Although the parachute drop scattered the airborne troopers over a wide area, they coalesced and took on enemy troops in pitched battles prior to linking up with infantry coming ashore.

Prior to their mission, Colonel James M. Gavin of the 505th Parachute Infantry Regiment issued a statement to his men. "…Tonight you embark on a combat mission for which our people and the free people of the world have been waiting for two years. You will spearhead the landing of American forces on the island of SICILY. Every preparation has been made to eliminate the element of chance. You have been given the means to do the job and you are backed by the largest assemblage of air power in the world's history. The eyes of the world are upon you…" Gavin went on to command the 82nd Airborne Division later in the war.

A follow-up airdrop unfolded in tragedy as American gunners mistook the transport planes overhead for enemy aircraft. Twenty-three planes were shot down, 37 damaged, and 81 troopers of the 504th Parachute Infantry Regiment were killed. During further operations in Italy, the 504th detached and fought at the Anzio beachhead. A German officer was impressed with the Americans' ferocity and called them "Devils in baggy pants."

After returning to England, the 82nd began preparations for Operation Overlord, the invasion of Normandy. Jumping into enemy-occupied territory in the predawn hours of June 6, 1944, the 82nd Airborne parachuted and landed in gliders on the western flank of the five Normandy invasion beaches. Jumping astride the River Merderet, the objectives of the 82nd included securing the area between the river and the English Channel, the capture of the town of Ste. Mere-Eglise, the establishment of crossings of the Merderet at La Fiere and Chef-du-Pont, and maintaining a defensive line with a linkup to the 101st Airborne's 502nd Parachute Infantry Regiment.

Meanwhile, the 101st was engaging in its first combat with the D-Day operation. Its objectives were securing four causeways, narrow routes off Utah Beach and across marshy ground for the advance of the 4th Infantry Division, the securing of locks at La Barquette on the River Douve, destruction of heavy German guns at St. Martin-de-Varreville, and the capture of bridges across the Douve.

Difficult weather conditions scattered the airborne troops widely, but Ste.-Mere-Eglise was captured and held against repeated German counterattacks. The causeways were taken and held for the advancing infantry, and casualties, though extensive, were below the estimates of some pessimistic senior officers.

The 82nd Airborne was withdrawn to England in early July following 33 days of intense combat. During that period the division lost 5,245 men killed, wounded, and missing in action. Its capture of Ste. Mere-Eglise, crossings of the Merderet,

Paratroopers of the 11th Airborne Division meet former Los Banos internees after the February 1945 raid. *(Public Domain US Signal Corps National Archives and Records Administration via Wikimedia Commons)*

and westward drive across the Cotentin Peninsula had been performed with elan.

The 101st Airborne wrested control of the crossroads town of Carentan from German paratroopers in a pitched battle, fighting to defend its gains through the end of June. When relief came, 4,670 casualties had been sustained, but General Maxwell Taylor, commanding the division, praised his men, "You hit the ground running toward the enemy. You have proved the German soldier is no superman. You have beaten him on his own ground, and you can beat him on any ground."

The 82nd and 101st Airborne Divisions rested and absorbed replacements prior to their next major combat experience during Operation Market Garden, a combined airborne and ground offensive to seize key bridges in the Netherlands and facilitate a potential war ending thrust into the Ruhr, the industrial heart of Germany. Both divisions were inserted on

Elements of the 82nd Airborne Division parachute into the vicinity of Grave, Netherlands, during Operation Market Garden. *(Public Domain US Army via Wikimedia Commons)*

September 17, 1944. The 101st was to seize the southernmost bridges at Son, St. Oedenrode, and Veghel and hold the single ground route open through the town of Eindhoven, a stretch of road later nicknamed "Hell's Highway."

The 82nd was to capture the bridge at Grave across the River Maas, four more over the Maas-Waal Canal, and another across the River Waal at Nijmegen. The route was secured by both divisions, and Major Julian Cook led the 3d Battalion, 504th Parachute Infantry Regiment, in a harrowing crossing of the Waal under intense German fire.

Market Garden ultimately failed, but the 101st held its ground in an embattled area known as the Island until late November. Withdrawn to Camp Mourmelon, France, it had suffered 1,682 casualties in 72 straight days of fighting. The 82nd Airborne was pulled out of the line at the Island on November 11, with losses of 1,912 men. As the trucks bearing the combat-hardened men of both divisions headed back toward France, Dutch civilians lined the roads and shouted "September 17!" in recognition of their valour.

Both the 82nd and 101st were engaged in the desperate fighting to contain the Nazi Ardennes offensive in December 1944 and January 1945. During the famed Battle of the Bulge, the airborne troopers were called from reserve positions as badly needed reinforcements. The 82nd Airborne bolstered the northern shoulder of the Bulge around Elsenborn Ridge, conducting an initial tactical withdrawal in the face of overwhelming enemy armoured strength and then holding fast against attacks by elements of three German divisions.

Meanwhile, the 101st reached the embattled crossroads town of Bastogne, Belgium, and defended it against strong German panzer and infantry attacks. Surrounded, General Anthony McAuliffe, in temporary command of the 101st, famously replied "Nuts!" to a German surrender demand. Along with elements of Combat Command B, 10th Armored Division, and other units, the Screaming Eagles held Bastogne until contact was made with the 4th Armored Division spearhead of General George S. Patton's Third Army counterattacking northward.

When the end of the war in Europe came, both the 82nd and 101st Airborne Divisions concluded operations fighting as infantry. The 82nd ended the war at Ludwigslust, Germany, near the River Elbe and accepted the surrender of 150,000

Men of the 511th Parachute Infantry Regiment evacuate a wounded man in the Philippines, autumn 1944. *(Public Domain US Army Signal Corps National Archives and Records Administration via Wikimedia Commons)*

Troopers of the 101st Airborne Division inspect the wreckage of a glider in the Netherlands, September 1944. *(Public Domain US Army Signal Corps / US Army Military History Institute / Photo Courtesy of U.S. Army via Wikimedia Commons)*

Prior to a jump, paratroopers of the 508th Parachute Infantry Regiment, 82nd Airborne Division, check their equipment. *(Public Domain US Signal Corps Archive via Wikimedia Commons)*

enemy soldiers. Elements of the 101st reached Hitler's Eagles Nest at Berchtesgaden.

In the Pacific, two battalions of the 503rd Parachute Infantry Regiment were airdropped on the island of Noemfoor on July 2, 1944, and participated in securing the island. The 503rd later came ashore in the Philippines aboard amphibious craft at Mindoro and parachuted into the island of Corregidor in February 1945.

General Joseph Swing's 11th Airborne Division reached the Philippines aboard landing craft at the island of Leyte on November 18, 1944. In February 1945, the paratroopers were engaged in heavy fighting with the Japanese south of the city of Manila. Swing and his staff were aware that 2,147 internees, including 1,575 Americans, were held at Los Banos prison and feared that the Japanese might massacre their prisoners.

Swing set to work on a daring plan to rescue the internees, and on February 23, one of the most audacious raids of World War II got underway. Working with Filipino guerrillas, a flying column of glidermen aboard trucks sped toward Los Banos while other attacks in the area diverted Japanese attention.

General Swing watched the progress of the raid from a Piper Cub artillery liaison aircraft, and one Army officer observed that the "...results were spectacular. Internees poured out and into the loading area. Troops started clearing the barracks... and carried out to the loading area over 130 people who were too weak or too sick to walk."

In just over six hours, the raid on Los Banos was concluded with every internee successfully evacuated. The raiders lost four men killed and six wounded, and the operation is studied in military classrooms around the world to this day as an exercise in precise tactical excellence. The 11th Airborne continued fighting in the Philippines until withdrawn at the end of August, days after World War II had concluded. ■

FLYING TIGERS

Since the Japanese believed they owned the skies over China, their pilots expected a routine mission on the morning of December 20, 1941. The 10 Mitsubishi Ki-21 bombers would cover the 300 miles from their base at Hanoi in French Indochina, drop their payloads on the Chinese city of Kunming, and then head for home.

On this day, however, that illusion was shattered. As they drew close to their target, several of the Japanese pilots noticed four tiny specks in the distance. Curious more than alarmed, they carried on, dropping their bombs and turning away. For a moment they remained unaware that the hunters had become the hunted.

Four Curtiss P-40 Tomahawk fighters led by American Lieutenant John V. "Scarsdale Jack" Newkirk ripped into the Japanese bombers, and soon they were joined by 10 more P-40s. In short order, the Ki-21s were pursued and massacred in the air, shot to pieces by these pilots of the American Volunteer Group (AVG). A single bomber crew escaped to report the incident, describing the attackers as fighters with insignia of the Chinese Air Force on their wings and snarling shark's mouths painted on their engine cowlings. The flamboyant pilots of the AVG, soon to be nicknamed the Flying Tigers, had flamed their first victims – and a legend was born.

The Flying Tigers had come into being under the command of Claire Chennault, a retired US Army Air Corps captain and former stunt flier then in the service of the Chinese Nationalist government of Generalissimo Chiang Kai-shek. Since the Japanese had been intent on expanding their territory into China as early as 1931, the fight had been desperate for the Chinese, and nowhere was the contest more unequal than

General Claire Chennault led the Flying Tigers of the American Volunteer Group to fame in the war-torn skies over China. *(Public Domain US Air Force via Wikimedia Commons)*

in the air. Chiang and his wife, the influential Soong Mei-ling, better known as Madame Chiang, set about a campaign of redress. Using her considerable charm and diplomatic capability, Madame Chiang convinced Chennault to come to the aid of the Chinese air arm.

The outbreak of the Second Sino-Japanese War in 1937 had brought renewed urgency to the situation, and Chennault came out of retirement in Louisiana to take up the challenge halfway around the world. He was asked initially to go to Washington, DC, to secure the purchase of the P-40 fighters from the US and the cooperation of the administration of President Franklin D. Roosevelt, which soon allowed trained pilots to quietly discharge from the American military to travel to China as "instructors" with the Central American Aircraft Company (CAMCO), a front for the raising of a skilled group of fighter pilots to take the air war to the marauding Japanese.

Chennault recruited 300 pilots, ground crewmen, and administrative personnel, and the first airmen reached China in the spring of 1941. Chennault installed his own method of aerial combat in the recruits. He had criticised the prevailing fighter tactics from World War I in his 1935 book titled The Role of Defensive Pursuit. "There was too much of an air of medieval jousting in the dogfights," he reasoned, "and not enough of the calculated massing of overwhelming force so necessary in the cold, cruel business of war."

Training first Chinese pilots and then the new arrivals of the AVG, Chennault pointed out the weaknesses and strengths of the Japanese fighters they would encounter, including the Nakajima Ki-27 Nate, and later the Nakajima Ki-43 Oscar and the formidable Mitsubishi A6M Zero, or Zeke. He told his students to avoid single air combat with the nimble Zero. "Never get into a dogfight with the Zero," he warned. "When you spot the Zeros, make one diving run with guns blazing, and then get the hell out of there!"

Before the US government allowed Chennault to recruit pilots and receive the Curtiss P-40s – fighters originally earmarked for the British Royal Air Force but deemed outmoded and rejected from Lend Lease

This Curtiss P-40 fighter painted in the Flying Tiger scheme resides at the National Museum of the US Air Force, Wright-Patterson Air Force Base, Dayton, Ohio. *(Public Domain National Museum of the US Air Force via Wikimedia Commons)*

ELITE FORCES OF WORLD WAR II

In this 1942 photo ground crewmen work to keep a Curtiss P-40 fighter of the Flying Tigers airworthy. (Public Domain Library of Congress via Wikimedia Commons)

Flying Tiger pilots run to their fighter planes in China. (Public Domain US Signal Corps via Wikimedia Commons)

Japanese invincibility in the air over China. Following those frenetic and dangerous few days, the Flying Tigers had destroyed 297 Japanese planes, 229 of them in aerial combat. Only 14 Flying Tiger pilots were lost, 10 of them in combat, and just 12 P-40s were shot down during the period.

Nineteen Flying Tiger pilots shot down five or more Japanese planes, achieving the status ace. Colonel David "Tex" Hill was credited with shooting down 12½ enemy planes with the Flying Tigers and ended the war with 18 aerial victories. Other top scoring pilots were Robert Neale with 13, Ed Rector 10½, and George Burgard, Robert Little, and Charles Older, each with 10 air-to-air kills. Major Gregory "Pappy" Boyington, who later received the Medal of Honor and led the famed Black Sheep Squadron in the Pacific shot down six enemy planes with the AVG and ended the war with 28 confirmed kills. Boyington was shot down, captured, and liberated from a Japanese prison camp in 1945.

On July 4, 1942, the Flying Tigers flew their last combat mission, shooting down four Ki-27s. On the same day, the AVG was disbanded and its personnel assimilated into the newly activated 23rd Fighter Group, US Army Air Forces, the China Air Task Force, and later the US Fourteenth Air Force. Some former Flying Tiger pilots returned to the US when their unit dissolved, while others continued to fight the Japanese. Chennault was recalled to service with the US forces and promoted colonel. He was soon given command of the China Air Task Force as a brigadier general, and later took command of the Fourteenth Air Force with the rank of major general. ■

Japanese bombers like this Ki-21 often fell victim to the aggressive pilots of the Flying Tigers. (Public Domain Asahi Shimbun via Wikimedia Commons)

Flying Tiger ace and flight leader Robert Smith stands next to his Curtiss P-40 fighter. (Public Domain Brad Smith US Air Force via Wikimedia Commons)

shipment – Madame Chiang and her brother, lobbyist and diplomat T.V. Soong, successfully brought the plight of the Chinese air forces to Roosevelt's attention, even as Chennault was doing all he could do.

When he finally got the green light to recruit American pilots and receive the P-40s that came across the Pacific in pieces, crated with nondescript legends marked on them to avoid attention, Chennault went to work. Six months before the December 7, 1941, attack on Pearl Harbor brought the US into World War II, he had 112 first-rate pilots recruited. There were training accidents, and some precious P-40s were lost in training at an airfield in Loiwing, China, but the pilots embraced Chennault's innovative tactics and began to refer to him affectionately as Old Leatherface.

The AVG pilots and their planes were organised into three squadrons, the Adam and Eves, Panda Bears, and Hell's Angels. For a time the group shared an airfield at Toungoo, Burma with RAF units, including No. 112 Squadron, and they were later based at Kunming. They borrowed the tiger shark motif from the British, who had in turn appropriated it from German Luftwaffe squadrons they had encountered in the Mediterranean theatre. Chinese civilians liked the look and began calling the AVG the Flying Tigers. Then a cartoonist from Walt Disney Studios drew a logo with a stylishly winged Bengal tiger flying through a V for victory, and it was emblazoned on the fuselages of many AVG fighters.

Although the Flying Tigers actually flew as a combat unit for only seven months, from December 1941 to July 1942, they performed exceedingly well. Combat attrition reduced effective aircraft to as few as 55 and available pilots dwindled as low as 70 at times, but the AVG's combat record put paid the notion of

FRENCH FOREIGN LEGION

General Charles de Gaulle reviews troops of the 13e Demi-Brigade in Rome. *(Licence Ouverte via Wikipedia)*

The French Foreign Legion is one of the world's most famous fighting forces, and at the outbreak of World War II it was well established as such. Formed in 1831, the Legion was known the world over, and its ranks were filled with adventurers and career soldiers of many nationalities.

In 1939, nearly 80 percent of the Legion's officer cadre was German, and many of its rank and file were as well. It was clear to the French government that German intelligence, the Abwehr, had infiltrated the Legion. Security concerns were address by sending Legion formations to the remote deserts of North Africa and the Middle East. A few were retained to man the static defences of the Maginot Line, and as new Legion units were activated, soldiers of 50 different nations populated these regiments.

The most famous and the most travelled Legion formation of World War II was the 13e Demi-Brigade. The unit was originally ordered to Finland to fight the invading Soviets in 1940, but the valiant Finns were compelled to sign a peace agreement with the Soviet Union before the force could deploy. From there, the 13e Demi-Brigade participated in the fighting in Norway, temporarily holding the port of Narvik. Meanwhile, when the Nazi blitzkrieg fell upon France and the Low Countries, the 11th Regiment held its positions in the Maginot Line for two weeks, losing more than 2,500 soldiers, 85 percent of its strength, before being transferred to North Africa.

With the fall of France, the Nazis pressed the Vichy government to disband the Foreign Legion, and about 1,000 German soldiers requested discharges. The Legion fractured into units loyal to Vichy and those who supported the Free French forces under General Charles de Gaulle. An entire battalion of the 13e Demi-Brigade was disbanded in Morocco, but the bulk of the unit pledged its loyalty to the Free French.

Subsequently, the 13e Demi-Brigade participated in the abortive Free French expedition that failed to occupy the port of Dakar, Senegal, in June 1940, never leaving its transport ships. Months were spent in the Cameroons, and later the unit was shipped to Eritrea to support British campaigns against the Italians. The 13e Demi-Brigade became the core of a French force in the Middle East and fought the Vichy 6th Regiment, Legionnaire against Legionnaire, in the summer of 1942. When Damascus fell to the Free French in late July, some of those who surrendered with the 6th Regiment elected to join the 13e Demi-Brigade.

The most celebrated combat of the 13e Demi-Brigade occurred during the Battle of Gazala, when elements of the unit fought under General Pierre Koenig and the 1st Free French Brigade in defending their position at Bir Hacheim, the southernmost strongpoint in a series of defensive posts in the Libyan desert. Axis forces of Panzerarmee Afrika under General Erwin Rommel were thrusting toward Tobruk, but the defenders held their position for two weeks and two days, May 26 to June 11, 1942, causing a tremendous delay in the timetable for the capture of the Libyan port.

When Allied forces hit the beaches at Oran, Algiers, and Casablanca in Operation Torch, November 8, 1942, some Vichy Legion forces briefly opposed the landings but then switched to the Allied side after successful peace negotiations were concluded. The 13e Demi-Brigade had already joined with the British Eighth Army under General Bernard Montgomery, pursuing the Axis enemy following the tremendous victory at El Alamein in October 1942.

A legionnaire of the 13e Demi-Brigade drinks water from a canteen in the desert, 1942. *(Public Domain OWI United States Government via Wikimedia Commons)*

By 1944, scattered elements of the French Foreign Legion, including the 13e Demi-Brigade, were combined into a single regiment that took part in the Italian campaign, landed at Toulon in southern France, and crossed the River Rhine into Germany. By war's end, the Legion regiment had crossed the River Danube and entered Austria. ■

Soldiers of the French Foreign Legion rush forward during the defence of Bir Hacheim, June 12, 1942. *(Public Domain Collections of the Imperial War Museums via Wikimedia Commons)*

ELITE FORCES OF WORLD WAR II

1ER BATAILLON DE FUSILIERS MARINS COMMANDOS

Among the first Frenchmen to volunteer to carry on with the fight against the Nazis after his country capitulated, Sub Lieutenant Philippe Kieffer, a naval officer, took command of only 16 patriotic men determined to get into the fighting.

In April 1942, Kieffer brought his small contingent to Camp Camberley along with his second, Lieutenant Jean Pinelli, for training in Commando operations. Further instruction took place at the Commando facilities at Achnacarry, Scotland. The little band grew to 23 men the following month and received the designation 1er Company de Fusiliers Marins, or 1st Company of Naval Rifles. As the numbers grew, the unit reached battalion strength and three troops were formed along with a headquarters company.

On Bastille Day, July 14, 1942, the French Commandos took part in a parade commemorating the national holiday. Soon afterward, the formation was attached to No. 10 Inter-Allied Commando. Its complement had risen to 81 men, and as its strength increased, the newly designated Troop 1 was augmented by a second formation, Troop 8, and another detachment responsible for the use of the K-Gun depth charge projector in the event of naval deployment. Overall at peak strength the battalion numbered 177 men. Troop 8 took shape in the spring of 1943 with 75 men under Lieutenant Charles Trepel. These expatriates had come from occupied France and the country's colonial dominions in North Africa and the Middle East.

In the beginning, the men wore the distinctive cap with its red pompom, indicative of the French Navy, and the shoulder flash "FRANCE" was proudly visible.

The battalion's first combat experience loomed with Operation Jubilee, the raid on the French coastal town of Dieppe, in August. Assigned to work with No. 3 and No. 4 Commando, the French forces were tasked with gathering documents and intelligence located at the Dieppe city hall, distributing cash to members of the French Resistance forces they encountered to finance further guerrilla operations, functioning as interpreters, and persuading Frenchmen to return to England with them and enlist in the Free French military.

French naval officer Philippe Kieffer led Commandos of the 1er Bataillon de Fusiliers Marins Commandos. *(Public Domain United Kingdom Government via Wikimedia Commons)*

The badge of the 1er Bataillon de Fusiliers Marins features a dagger and the Cross of Lorraine. *(Creative Commons BrunoLC via Wikipedia)*

The abortive operation ended in tragedy. Although the No. 4 Commando effort to silence a German battery at Varengeville was successful, the landings of No. 3 Commando were disrupted early. Most of these men were captured, and the French suffered one killed and two missing.

In November 1942, elements of the battalion took part in Operation Fahrenheit, a raid on the Nazi communications centre at Pointe de Plouezec on the northern coast of Brittany. The objectives were to gather intelligence, take prisoners for interrogation back in Britain, and destroy the signals apparatus. Only a few men from No. 6 Commando and a couple of French Commandos were involved in the raid, which ended in failure. Split into three groups, the

Abandoned Canadian and Commando equipment lies on the beach at Dieppe after the August 1942 raid. *(Creative Commons Bundesarchiv Bild via Wikipedia)*

1ER BATAILLON DE FUSILIERS MARINS COMMANDOS

Commandos were discovered by sentries, and an attempt to breach barbed wire obstacles was abandoned with casualties on both sides.

By the autumn of 1943, Troops 1 and 8 were sharing a base of operations at Eastbourne, Sussex. Training continued amid a series of raids involving small numbers of Commandos. From July 1942 to February 1944, a total of 10 such operations were mounted. Some of these were successful in assessing the strength of Hitler's Atlantic Wall defences, while others ended in tragedy.

One such dismal outcome occurred on February 27-28, 1944, as French Commandos participated on Operation Premium, a small raid on launching sites for the V-2 rockets that were then terrorizing population centres in Britain. Trepel led the six Frenchmen, who boarded the Motor Torpedo Boat *MTB 682* at Great Yarmouth bound for the coastal town of Wassenaar, Netherlands, and were lost during the operation. No word of the circumstances was immediately available until graves were discovered after the area was liberated by Allied troops. Some sources say that the entire complement drowned, their bodies washing up on the beach to be interred by the Germans as "unknown English airmen."

Even as the tragedy of Operation Premium unfolded, preparations were underway for Operation Overlord, the Allied invasion of Nazi-occupied northwest France on June 6, 1944. In May, the battalion, along with the rest of No. 10 Inter-Allied Commando, was assigned to the 1st Special Service Brigade under Brigadier Lord Lovat, becoming its 5th and 6th Troops. While training for the Normandy landings was underway, some of the French Commandos were known to be from the coastal region of France. When they recognised the landing beaches and environs depicted in intelligence photographs, security concerns were raised. For a brief period, the Frenchmen were confined to barracks in the days leading up to the invasion.

On the eve of Operation Overlord, Kieffer was promoted lieutenant commander. Kieffer led the French Commandos ashore at 7:30 a.m. on Sword Beach, the easternmost of the five Allied invasion beaches on D-Day. The landing craft carrying the bulk of No. 4 Commando allowed the Frenchmen to pass ahead to become the first ashore in the homeland.

Launch sites for the V-2 rocket were the targets of the failed Operation Premium. *(Creative Commons AElfwine via Wikipedia)*

British Commandos, joined by their French comrades, move off Sword Beach toward Pegasus Bridge on D-Day. *(Public Domain Collections of the Imperial War Museums via Wikimedia Commons)*

Supporting the 3rd Infantry Division, the Commandos were to open a 1,600 foot breach in the German defences at Sword Beach. They took casualties initially but fought their way forward, capturing a large German strongpoint that housed a 50mm anti-tank gun just after the weapon had disabled one of the landing craft bringing a Commando troop to the beach.

One of the prominent structures at Sword Beach was a local casino, and the Commandos rooted out German defenders from the building before proceeding between Coleville and Saint-Aubin-d'Arquenay. Along with the full complement of No. 4 Commando, the Frenchmen proceeded to relieve British glider troops at Pegasus Bridge and occupied a section of the defensive line, warding off German counterattacks until infantry of the 3rd Division arrived to relieve them. Kieffer was wounded twice on June 6, and by the end of the day the small French Commando force had sustained 27 killed in action and many others wounded, approximately 25 percent of its original fighting strength.

After fighting in Normandy through August, the battalion returned to England for rest and to absorb replacements. By the autumn of 1944, the Frenchmen were in action on the island of Walcheren in the estuary of the River Scheldt. Operations to clear the Germans from the estuary were costly but necessary as control of the waterway was essential to opening the deep water port of Antwerp, Belgium, 40 miles inland along the river's course, to Allied supply traffic. With the end of World War II, the battalion reverted to the control of the French armed forces. It exists today and carries the heritage of its predecessors in its uniform and unit badge featuring the Cross of Lorraine.

Kieffer, who had been among the first Frenchmen to enter the liberated city of Paris in August 1944, led the attacks at Walcheren and other points during the opening the River Scheldt to merchant shipping. He remained active with the French Navy after the war and was promoted commander in 1954. He received numerous commendations for bravery, including his country's Commander of the Legion of Honour and the Order of the British Empire. He died at age 63 in 1962 after a lengthy illness. ■

Plouezec was the sight of the ill-fated Operation Fahrenheit on the coast of Brittany. *(Creative Commons Rüdiger Wölk via Wikipedia)*

ELITE FORCES OF WORLD WAR II

THE BRANDENBURGERS

German covert operations were underway even prior to the first day of World War II in Europe. Well before the Wehrmacht spearheads rolled across the Polish frontier on September 1, 1939, a group of nondescript men had infiltrated border villages.

Posing as coal miners, they went about their business, blending in with the local population – until they received word to spring into action, disrupting communications and impeding the progress of any Polish military response to the Nazi invasion. German military intelligence, the shadowy Abwehr, had ordered the men of the Kampf-Truppen to move on vital infrastructure as well. So, they seized the power station at Chorzow in Upper Silesia and cut the supply of electricity to a vast area of Poland. The efforts of the Kampf-Truppen threw the Polish Army into confusion and facilitated the rapid advance of the Wehrmacht.

Though the work of the Kampf-Truppen was quite successful, the unit was intended for a short lifespan. After the conquest of Poland, it was to be disbanded. However, one insightful officer refused to watch the elite covert unit go by the wayside. Abwehr Captain Theodor von Hippel saw the value of such a unit in future operations and petitioned Admiral Wilhelm Canaris, chief of the intelligence agency, to maintain the Kampf-Truppen as the nucleus of a permanent special forces group under the control of the Abwehr.

Although Canaris was less than enthusiastic about the prospects, he agreed to Hippel's proposal. On October 25, 1939, the 800th Special Duties Construction Company came into being. The name of the group was intended as a cover for its true purpose, but those who joined its ranks quickly began to refer to themselves as Brandenburgers, a reference to the German city located near their barracks and training facilities.

German soldiers exit a ferry while moving forward in Denmark, April 1940.
(Creative Commons Karl Marth via Wikipedia)

The Brandenburgers drew their recruits from a variety of backgrounds, expatriate Germans who had heeded Hitler's call to come home and serve the Third Reich, raw soldiers brand new to the military, older veterans of the army, and adventurers. They spoke many different languages and brought varied cultural backgrounds with them, which enhanced the opportunities for successes later to be realised. The Brandenburgers participated in intense physical training and specialised in the art of stealth and deception to carry out their assigned tasks.

Admiral Wilhelm Canaris served as Abwehr chief and approved the creation of the Brandenburgers.
(Creative Commons Bundesarchiv Bild via Wikipedia)

Often preceding organised conventional forces, the Brandenburgers laid the foundation for swift movement with the capture of key objectives such as road networks, bridges, and airfields. When the Germans invaded Denmark in April 1940, the Brandenburgers wore Danish Army uniforms and captured every objective assigned to them.

On May 10, 1940, Hitler unleashed Case Yellow, the Nazi invasion of France and the Low Countries. The Brandenburgers preceded the Blitzkrieg once again. Dressed as Dutch policemen purportedly escorting a group of prisoners through the town of Gennep, they came to the town's border bridge. On the proper signal, both policemen and prisoners threw off their disguises, pulled out their weapons, and rushed the span, capturing it intact.

There was little organised resistance at the Gennep border bridge, but as the German columns crossed into the Netherlands a doctor stopped to bandage a Brandenburger's slight wound.

"There isn't much of your company left," the doctor remarked. The wounded man replied, "Company? There were nine of us." The response was an incredulous, "Impossible!" But the retort came quickly, "We are the Brandenburgers!"

As the German juggernaut advanced into Belgium, the Brandenburgers took control of several locks that held back floodwaters, preventing Belgian soldiers from unleashing such an obstacle to the German line of march. More than 100 Brandenburgers participated in the opening hours of Case Yellow, some of them dressed as women and pushing baby carriages. With precision, they rushed forward and took control of the tunnel at the estuary of the River Scheldt, as well as the bridges across

Adolf Hitler watches German troops march into Poland in September 1939.
(Creative Common Bundesarchiv Bild via Wikipedia)

SS chief Heinrich Himmler sought Hitler's approval for his own special forces. (Creative Commons Bundesarchiv Bild via Wikipedia)

German soldiers cross the border into the Soviet Union on June 22, 1941. (Public Domain Johannes Hähle WW2 Photo Archive via Wikimedia Commons)

the Rivers Meuse and Dender. In the aftermath of the successful clandestine infiltration, more than 90 Iron Crosses were presented to the men of No. 3 Brandenburger Company.

By mid-May 1940, the authorised strength of the Brandenburgers was increased to a full regiment. While preparations were made for covert operations to support Operation Sea Lion, the anticipated Nazi invasion of Great Britain, and for the ambitious Operation Felix, the assault on the British bastion of Gibraltar on the tip of the Iberian Peninsula, both offensive actions were called off – to the great disappointment of the highly motivated men and officers.

In the spring of 1941, Hitler's panzers rolled into the Balkans intent on conquering Yugoslavia and later Greece. Posing as boatmen plying the River Danube, the Brandenburgers preyed on the crews of unsuspecting Yugoslav barges and watercraft. They captured numerous vessels and confiscated cargoes and supplies while preventing others from being sunk in an attempt to block the important waterway.

On June 22, 1941, Hitler launched Operation Barbarossa, the Nazi invasion of the Soviet Union. The Nightingale Group, a small unit of Brandenburgers composed of ethnic Ukrainians who despised Soviet dictator Josef Stalin, crossed into their homeland on the first day of the offensive. While wearing German uniforms, these men were convincing enough to dupe a Red Army patrol into believing that they were actually Soviet special operations troops returning from a secret mission against the invaders. The patrol provided an escort into the village of Przemysl, which the Nightingale men controlled until they were relieved.

While the Germans enjoyed widespread successes in the early days of Barbarossa, SS Sturmbannfuhrer (Major) Adrian von Folkersam led 60 Brandenburgers dressed as men of the Soviet Secret Police, the dreaded NKVD, and joined a column of Red Army soldiers in retreat. For several days, the Brandenburgers played their individual roles to perfection, even gaining the confidence of the Red Army general who commanded troops in the area. He gave the Brandenburgers a tour of Soviet positions, including prepared defences against the oncoming Germans at the city of Maikop.

One of the Brandenburgers boldly suggested that an artillery battery should be reoriented in a different direction. The guns were moved. They had been sighted previously along the actual route of advance which the German vanguard was marching. To further assist the offensive, the Brandenburgers issued fictitious orders, rendered the area communications network inoperable, and seized several oil fields that the Soviets had intended to put to the torch.

By the autumn of 1942, the fortunes of war were beginning to turn against the Third Reich. Although the Brandenburgers had earned high praise and grown to division strength, their further usefulness came into question. The German Army was no longer conducting large-scale offensive actions that benefitted from clandestine activities such as the Brandenburgers were known to perform. Complicating the situation was Hitler's growing mistrust of Canaris. The Fuhrer decided to place greater emphasis on future covert operations with the SS. Reichsführer SS Heinrich Himmler was perhaps Hitler's most trusted subordinate, and he had made overtures for the formation of SS special operations units for months.

As they were marginalised, some Brandenburgers chose to transfer to army panzergrenadier units. Others were allowed to join the newly-formed SS commandos. By February 1944, the Brandenburgers were officially dissolved, and the unit was designated a panzergrenadier division of the German Army. ∎

Members of the Brandenburger Nightingale Group infiltrated their native Ukraine. (Public Domain Центр досліджень визвольного руху Українська повстанська армія: Історія Нескорених. — Львів : ЦДВР, 2007. — с. 28 via Wikimedia Commons)

Adolf Hitler reviews troops of the 1st SS Leibstandarte, which became a Waffen SS combat division. *(Creative Commons Bundesarchiv Bild via Wikipedia)*

1ST SS LEIBSTANDARTE ADOLF HITLER AND 12TH SS HITLER JUGEND

T he founding fathers of the Waffen SS, the armed combat wing of the paramilitary organisation, were Reichsführer SS Heinrich Himmler and Oberstgruppenführer (Colonel General) Paul Hausser. They were given permission to form fighting units by Adolf Hitler himself and over the furious objections of Wehrmacht senior officers.

SS combat formations began as small infantry units and progressed to motorised formations, panzergrenadier divisions, and then to fully equipped panzer divisions. The SS, or Schutzstaffel, was a separate entity from the traditional German Army, a fanatically loyal body of Nazi men inculcated with ideology and willing to fight and die for the Führer and the advance of their Aryan doctrine.

When the Waffen SS came into being in the spring of 1933, its purpose was to establish elite combat formations that would lead the Nazi conquest of Europe. The Waffen SS attracted young Nazis who were willing to endure a rigorous training regimen in which one in three recruits failed to pass. In the beginning they were required to exhibit the physical characteristics

Troops of the 1st SS Leibstandarte advance across Polish territory. *(Public Domain Collection Narodowe Archiwum Cyfrowe via Wikimedia Commons)*

An armoured vehicle of the 1st SS Leibstandarte SS makes its way through the streets of Kharkov. *(Creative Commons Budesarchiv Bild via Wikimedia Commons)*

Panzer General Heinz Guderian inspects a heavy Tiger tank of the Leibstandarte in the spring of 1943. *(Public Domain Ohlemacher Government of Poland via Wikimedia Commons)*

of Aryan ancestry as well. The Waffen SS men enjoyed a camaraderie that was not traditional in the German Army, officers and men eating meals together and addressing one another familiarly rather than with the stiff "Herr" or "Sir."

Although early combat performance was disappointing, the Waffen SS grew into a formidable body of battle-hardened combat divisions. During the Polish campaign of 1939, a lack of combat experience was punctuated with Nazi zeal and recklessness to produce heavy casualties among the formations. However, over time the SS divisions became disciplined fighters known for ferocity – and for many atrocities – on the battlefields of the Eastern and Western fronts during World War II. Subsequently, Waffen SS divisions were utilised as superb shock troops in attack and stalwart soldiers in defence. They were reported to have received the best equipment and burnished a reputation for brutality that overshadowed their accomplishments on the battlefield.

Two of the most famous SS panzer divisions were the 1st SS Leibstandarte Adolf Hitler and the 12th SS Hitler Jugend. These divisions became legendary in combat and exemplify the fanatical devotion to the Führer inherent in all organically German SS fighting formations.

The 1st SS Leibstandarte Adolf Hitler was originally formed in the 1920s as Hitler's personal bodyguard. Evolving and growing in strength to a motorised regiment and then to a panzer combat division, the Leibstandarte fought in campaigns throughout the conflict, including the invasion of Poland, the conquest of France and the Low Countries, Operation Barbarossa, the occupation of Greece, the fighting in Italy and Normandy, the Ardennes offensive, and the final defence of the Nazi capital of Berlin. The remnants of the Leibstadarte surrendered to US Army forces at Steyr, Austria, on May 8, 1945.

The 12th SS Hitler Jugend, or Hitler Youth, is remembered as perhaps the most blindly loyal to Hitler of any Waffen SS formation. The 12th SS was formed in early 1943 around a cadre of experienced officers from the Leibstandarte. Its rank and file consisted of young dedicated Nazis of the Hitler Youth born in the first six months of 1926. The first combat of the 12th SS occurred during the tenacious defence of Normandy in response to the Allied D-Day landings.

The evolution of the Waffen SS units into full panzer divisions was accomplished by 1943, but well before that time the Leibstandarte, 2nd SS Division Das Reich, 3rd SS Division Totenkopf, 5th SS Division Wiking, and others fought as infantry formations. During Operation Barbarossa, the invasion of the Soviet Union on June 22, 1941, the Leibstandarte and Wiking Divisions were components of Army Group South under the command of Field Marshal Gerd von Rundstedt, charged with the conquest of Ukraine.

During five months of bitter fighting, the Leibstandarte drove 600 miles into Soviet territory and sustained heavy casualties, losing much of its combat strength. The division was relieved on the front in June 1942, after a full year. One-third of the Waffen SS troops that participated in Barbarossa were killed, wounded or missing. The Leibstandarte retired to the west for refitting and received full panzer formations before returning to the crucible of the Eastern Front.

The Leibstandarte took part in a major German counteroffensive against the Red Army in the winter of 1943. Divided into ad hoc battle groups, the division drove on Kharkov, and an aggressive young officer stepped to the forefront. Brigadeführer (brigadier general) Kurt "Panzer" Meyer led his command into the centre of the city, fighting house to house to subdue the Red Army defenders. Although his unit suffered heavy casualties, Meyer's men captured the entire command element of a Soviet division. Soon, however, the intrepid officer found his battle group surrounded. In the ensuing hours, the Waffen SS men hung on grimly until relieved by another battle group under the infamous Standartenführer (Colonel) Joachim Peiper.

When Kharkov was finally captured, the Nazi flag was raised in Dzerzhinsky Square, and the location was ceremonially renamed in honour of the Leibstandarte.

The Leibstandarte went on to fight at the epic tank battle of Kursk. On July 7, 1943, a single heavy Tiger tank of its 13th Panzer Company, commanded by Unterscharführer (sergeant) Franz Staudegger, took on 50 Soviet T-34 medium tanks. The Tiger's 88mm main gun allowed Staudegger to attack

Kurt 'Panzer' Meyer was a foremost commander of Waffen SS forces and a convicted war criminal. *(Creative Commons Bundesarchiv Bild via Wikipedia)*

Grimly determined soldiers of the 12th SS Division Hitler Jugend are shown near Caen in the summer of 1944. *(Creative Commons ZarKroZ via Wikipedia)*

out of range of the enemy, and he wreaked havoc on the formation, destroying 22 T-34s and compelling the survivors to retreat. Staudegger received the Knight's Cross for the action.

During the Battle of Prokhorovka, the decisive armoured clash at Kursk, Obersturmbannführer (lieutenant colonel) Rudolf von Ribbentrop, son of Nazi Foreign Minister Joachim von Ribbentrop, led seven PzKpfw. IV tanks of the 1st SS Panzer Regiment into battle. Approximately 100 German tanks took on waves of Soviet T-34s. Ribbentrop remembered, "…Soon the first shell was on the way and with the impact a T-34 began to burn. It was only 50 to 70 metres from us… The avalanche of enemy tanks rolled straight toward us – tank after tank."

Ribbentrop survived the harrowing battle, and the battered Leibstandarte was withdrawn to France in April 1944 after heavy fighting in the Balkans and Ukraine around the capital of Kiev had reduced its armoured strength to just three tanks.

After refitting, the Leibstandarte was ordered to the Pas de Calais, where the Allied invasion of northwest Europe was expected. However, the main landings occurred in Normandy on June 6, 1944. Hitler retained operational control of the available panzer divisions and held the Leibstandarte north of the River Seine until late in the month, its leading elements only arriving in Normandy on the night of the 27th, well after the Allied lodgement was established.

Meanwhile, the 12th SS Hitler Jugend was committed to Normandy at 5 p.m. on D-Day, too late to strike a preemptive blow. The division, complete with more than 20,000 troops and 229 tanks, set out to cover the 65 miles from Lisieux to Normandy, but the advance was agonisingly slow. Refugees clogged the roads, and Allied air power played havoc with troop and vehicle movement during daylight hours.

Panzer Meyer led the vanguard of the Hitler Jugend, and his 25th Panzergrenadier Regiment came up alongside the army's 21st Panzer Division to oppose the Canadian 3rd Division, which had come ashore at Juno Beach. Meyer had three infantry battalions and a battalion of PzKpfw. IV tanks at his disposal, and he climbed to the top of the tower at the Abbey of Ardenne on the outskirts of the tactically vital crossroads town of Caen and surveyed the approaching Canadian columns of tanks and infantry.

Brimming with confidence, Meyer shouted, "Little fish! We'll throw them back into the sea in the morning!"

Just after 10 a.m. on June 7, the Canadians topped a ridgeline barely 200 yards from the hidden positions of the 25th Panzergrenadier Regiment. A ferocious battle ensued, and the Canadians were thrown back two miles before concentrated naval gunfire and artillery stopped the Hitler Jugend counterthrust. In their baptism of fire, the young ardent Nazis had destroyed 28 Canadian tanks. However, the commander of the division was killed in action, and Meyer was elevated to lead the entire 12th SS.

Both the 12th SS and the Leibstandarte fought like lions in Normandy. The divisions were instrumental in denying Caen to British forces for a solid month. The city had been a D-Day objective. But in their fanatical defence, the combat efficiency of both was steadily drained. Casualties ran high, and day by day the German position in Normandy became

A Canadian soldier pauses with a wounded prisoner of 12th SS in Normandy. *(Public Domain Public Archives of Canada via Wikimedia Commons)*

more precarious. In late July, the Allies launched Operation Cobra, carpet bombing and the subsequent unleashing of fresh divisions of the US Third Army to exploit a breakout from the Normandy hedgerows into open country.

The Germans formed a new defensive line around the town of Falaise, and Meyer personally rallied a panicked infantry division of regular army troops. Still, the situation was deteriorating, and roughly 100,000 German soldiers were in danger of being encircled. The Hitler Jugend and Leibstandarte sacrificed themselves to keep the only escape route open. Sixty men of the 12th SS held the northern shoulder at Argentan for three days, and only four of them were captured alive. The Leibstandarte held the southern shoulder, allowing 40,000 Germans to evade the Allies' clutches, and executing a fighting withdrawal. On the evening of August 16, the last remnants of the Leibstandarte reached safety across the River Orne.

The ordeal of the Leibstandarte and Hitler Jugend in Normandy was reflected in their losses. The former suffered 5,000 casualties and was forced to abandon much of its equipment inside the Falaise Pocket. The latter could muster only 300 soldiers and 10 tanks according to a report from Army Group B high command on August 22.

The 12th SS received replacements and some new tanks and equipment and went on to fight in the Ardennes offensive and Hungary, surrendering in Austria at war's end.

Although their heroism and fanatical loyalty to Hitler cannot be denied, the reputation of the Waffen SS combat divisions in World War II is tarnished irretrievably by their record of horrific war crimes. Meyer, for example, was convicted of murder in the execution of Canadian prisoners in Normandy. He was also involved in other atrocities. A death sentence was later commuted to life in prison, and Meyer was released in 1954. He died seven years later at age 51. ■

German losses during the retreat from Falaise in Normandy were considerable. *(Public Domain Polish Government Ministry of Information Photo Service via Wikimedia Commons)*

Soldiers of the 12th SS Hitler Jugend man a machine-gun position in Normandy in 1944. *(Public Domain Narowode Archiwum Cyfrowe via Wikimedia Commons)*

GERMAN COMMANDOS

GERMAN COMMANDOS

Reichsführer SS Heinrich Himmler prevailed upon Adolf Hitler to allow his henchmen to form special operations units of their own, and in early 1942 the Sonderlehrgang zbV Oranienburg came into being. Through the course of World War II, the organisation experienced a series of name changes, but its purpose was always to conduct covert operations under the control of the SS. Meanwhile, the Luftwaffe had organised its first special operations division prior to the outbreak of the war. The 7th Flieger Division was the first operational parachute unit in the German armed forces and was originally composed of elite airborne troops.

German special forces conducted numerous operations and gained fame under the command of SS Obersturmbannführer Otto Skorzeny, who came to be known as the "most dangerous man in Europe." Skorzeny led both SS and Luftwaffe commandos in the daring raid to rescue deposed Italian fascist leader Benito Mussolini from imprisonment at the Gran Sasso in the Abruzzi Mountains of central Italy on the afternoon of September 12, 1943.

Days earlier, Mussolini had been ousted from power by the Fascist Grand Council in Rome and placed under arrest. A long-time ally and friend of Adolf Hitler, he was moved to the Campo Imperiale Hotel and held there at the direction of the new government. Hitler was intent on rescuing Mussolini, and Skorzeny was the man with the stout resolution to carry off one of the most hazardous operations of World War II.

The rescued Benito Mussolini poses with Commando Otto Skorzeny at Gran Sasso. *(Creative Commons Bundesarchiv Bild via Wikipedia)*

Skorzeny and a force of glider-borne SS and Luftwaffe commandos pulled off their rescue of Mussolini flawlessly, swiftly exiting their aircraft, overcoming the guards and spiriting the former dictator to a waiting Fieseler Storch light aircraft. The weather had deteriorated, and every second counted as commandos cheered. Skorzeny personally helped Mussolini aboard the small plane and then abruptly climbed in himself. The added weight exceeded the safe limit for the Storch, but the pilot revved the engine and rolled toward the edge of a cliff.

Plunging earthward at first, the plane clawed for altitude, and the pilot was barely able to stay airborne. Eventually, Mussolini was delivered to a German airfield, where the rescued dictator climbed aboard a Heinkel He-111 bomber for transport to Berlin. Upon arrival, he was embraced by Hitler. Skorzeny received the Iron Cross for the mission. The commandos accomplished their task, springing Mussolini from captivity and seeing him off in the small plane, in just 12 minutes.

By mid-1943, Skorzeny's SS commando force had grown to battalion strength and supplanted the Abwehr-controlled Brandenburgers as the premier German special forces unit. In the spring of 1944, Skorzeny led his force during Operation Rosselsprung, a major counter-insurgency offensive to eradicate Yugoslav partisans, many of them communist under the leadership of the charismatic Yosip Broz, popularly known as Tito. The SS men came within a hair of taking

This knocked out German Panther tank has been disguised as an American M10 tank destroyer. *(Public Domain US Department of Defense via Wikimedia Commons)*

A sturmgeschütz self-propelled assault gun is adjacent to an American halftrack during preparations for deception during the December 1944 Ardennes offensive. *(Creative Commons Bundesarchiv Bild via Wikipedia)*

Adolf Hitler and Miklos Horthy ride together during a period of cooperation in 1938. *(Creative Commons Marecek2000 via Wikipedia)*

Yugoslavian partisan leader Josip Broz, better known as Tito, was a target of SS commando operations in the Balkans. *(Public Domain Digital Library of Slovenia via Wikimedia Commons)*

Hungarian regent Miklos Horthy was outfoxed by SS Commandos who kidnapped his son. *(Public Domain Cserlajos via Wikimedia Commons)*

Tito alive. That summer, Skorzeny exhibited force of personality and command presence in restoring order after the July 20 assassination attempt on Hitler at his Wolf's Lair headquarters in East Prussia. The commando leader moved to Berlin to assist with quelling any lingering opposition to the Führer after the failed attempt, cementing his loyalty to the Nazi regime.

In late 1944, Hitler became convinced that the Hungarian government, led by Regent Miklos Horthy, was wavering in its commitment to the Axis. Concerned that Hungary might conclude a separate peace with the Allies, the Führer sent Skorzeny and his SS commandos to Budapest in October to assess the situation. Coincidentally, the Hungarians were in the midst of negotiations with the Soviet Union. When Skorzeny and his band kidnapped Horthy's son and carried him off to Berlin, the talks were abruptly concluded. The regent was taken into custody by the commandos the following day, and the threat of Hungarian duplicity was quickly erased.

Within a week of the Hungarian operation, Skorzeny was given command of Panzer Brigade 150, a unit that he was ordered to train in covert operations. These men were to dress as Allied soldiers and sow confusion behind the lines during Hitler's desperate offensive in the West that came to be known as the Battle of the Bulge.

Hitler told his commando chief, "I want you to command a group of American and British troops and get them across the Meuse and seize one of the bridges. Not, my dear Skorzeny, real Americans or British. I want you to create special units wearing American and British uniforms. They will travel in captured Allied tanks. Think of the confusion you could cause! I envisage a whole string of false orders which will upset communications and attack morale."

As ordered, Skorzeny trained the men thoroughly, and their mission was code named Operation Greif. Time was of the essence, and the preparations began immediately. Skorzeny asked for a complement of 3,300 men, and captured vehicles were procured for the ruse. As the hour approached, however, the requests fell short of expectations. Only two American Sherman tanks were available, and they were in poor condition. Other vehicles were few in number, and some Soviet equipment – obviously of no use – was sent. Only a handful of men who were fluent in English could be found, and those who had some knowledge of American slang and idiomatic expressions were even fewer.

Nevertheless, Operation Greif went forward. Skorzeny's men infiltrated American lines and began to stir confusion. As the German spearheads of the Ardennes offensive rolled ahead in mid-December 1944, frontline American units were taken by surprise and many were overrun. Their retreat was complicated by the work of the commandos, who switched road signs, set ambushes, sent traffic in the wrong direction while posing as US military police, and committed acts of sabotage. These efforts also crippled the American response to the offensive, causing delays in reinforcing and holding ground as the main German thrusts advanced toward the River Meuse.

Rumours of Germans dressed in American uniforms and operating behind the lines spread rapidly through the Allied ranks and accounts of their prowess grew with each retelling. One concern was the implication that German agents were afoot and intent on kidnapping General Dwight D. Eisenhower, commander of Allied forces in Europe. Eisenhower spent Christmas in seclusion but emerged after several days, annoyed by the circumstances. General Omar Bradly, well known as the commander of the US 12th Army Group, was stopped numerous times at Allied roadblocks and questioned extensively before he was allowed to pass. In the end, Skorzeny's commandos were rounded up. As many as 17 of the Germans were shot as spies, and as the episode ended, Hitler's great offensive ground to a halt and was eventually repulsed.

Panzer Brigade 150 was disbanded shortly after Operation Greif. Skorzeny continued to fight until the end of the war, finally surrendering at Salzburg, Austria in the spring of 1945. ■

SUBSCRIBE

FlyPast is internationally regarded as the magazine for aviation history and heritage.

shop.keypublishing.com/fpsubs

Britain at War is dedicated to exploring every aspect of the involvement of Britain and her Commonwealth in conflicts from the turn of the 20th century through to the present day.

shop.keypublishing.com/bawsubs

ORDER DIRECT FROM OUR SHOP...
shop.keypublishi

OR CALL +44 (0)1780 480404
(Lines open 9.00-5.30, Monday-Friday GMT)

TODAY

SAVE UP TO £43 WHEN YOU SUBSCRIBE!

Aeroplane is still providing the best aviation coverage around. With focus on iconic military aircraft from the 1930s to the 1960s.

shop.keypublishing.com/amsubs

Classic Military Vehicle is the best-selling publication in the UK dedicated to the coverage of all historic military vehicles.

shop.keypublishing.com/cmvsubs

OBERSTURMBANNFÜHRER OTTO SKORZENY

He cut the figure of an adventurer, a buccaneer, and a fearless fighter. SS Obersturmbannführer Otto Skorzeny's face bore the 'schmisse" or dueling scars that were a badge of honour for those of his warrior class. He became a legend in covert operations in World War II and earned the nickname of "the most dangerous man in Europe" during the conflict.

Skorzeny was born in Austria in 1908 and became a follower of Adolf Hitler, joining the Nazi Party in 1931. Throughout his life, he apparently remained loyal to his Fuhrer, first literally and then in memory as he never publicly renounced Nazism. In 1939, Skorzeny attempted to join the Luftwaffe and qualify as a pilot. He was denied on the basis of his age and physical stature. He was too old at 31, and he stood a burly six feet, four inches tall.

Instead, the enthusiastic Nazi was lured into the Waffen SS and served in the Fuhrer's elite bodyguard, the 1st SS Leibstandarte Adolf Hitler. He saw combat in France and the Low Countries during the early months of World War II. After transferring to the Eastern Front, he was seriously wounded. When he had recovered, Skorzeny was given command of his first elite unit, two battalions of troops that were moulded into his commando force. Four months later, Skorzeny's men executed the rescue of Mussolini at the Gran Sasso.

Throughout the remaining years of the conflict, Skorzeny was actively engaged in or planning further covert operations, including a counter-insurgency offensive in Yugoslavia, the kidnapping of Hungarian Regent Miklos Horthy's son to flatten the possibility of Hungary concluding a separate peace with the Allies, his personal effort to maintain stability in Berlin in the wake of the failed July 20, 1944, assassination attempt against Hitler, and the

SS Obersturmbannführer Otto Skorzeny led ambitious commando raids across Europe. *(Public Domain Republic of Poland via Wikimedia Commons)*

organisation and deployment of Panzer Brigade 150 personnel in Operation Greif behind American lines during the Battle of the Bulge.

Skorzeny fought to the end, and after Panzer Brigade 150 was dissolved he moved to the Eastern Front, commanding troops that defended a vital bridge across the River Oder in a vain attempt to slow the Soviet Red Army's advance that eventually reached Berlin. He approved an operation to send frogmen into the River Rhine to plant explosives on the Ludendorff Bridge at Remagen after the span was captured by American troops and the first Allied lodgement on the east bank of the Rhine was consolidated. His reputation firmly established, Skorzeny received the oakleaves to the Knight's Cross as the war neared its end. He surrendered to American troops in Salzburg, Austria, on May 19, 1945.

Skorzeny was implicated in war crimes committed at the Dachau concentration camp but was acquitted at trial. He was also tried on charges of misuse of American uniforms and other crimes but was cleared. Remaining in prison until 1948, he escaped with the help of loyal former SS men. He emerged in Western Europe and was photographed in Paris in 1950, then ventured to Spain and opened an engineering firm. All the while, he remained interested in clandestine operations, probably assisting other former SS officers and soldiers to escape the clutches of the Allied courts, spiriting them to South America or other destinations via the famed Odessa network.

Skorzeny also worked as an advisor to the Egyptian and Argentine governments. He died of lung cancer in Madrid, Spain, in 1975 at the age of 67. His funeral services were reportedly well attended by former members of the SS, who paid tribute to one of their leaders and gave the Nazi salute. ■

Otto Skorzeny, the most dangerous man in Europe, greets German soldiers in February 1945. *(Creative Commons Bundesarchiv Bild via Wikipedia)*

The Fieseler Storch that whisked Benito Mussolini to safety waits at the Gran Sasso. *(Creative Commons Bundesarchiv Bild via Wikipedia)*

Klingenberg tours a concentration camp with Reichsführer SS Heinrich Himmler and other Nazis. (Creative Commons Bundesarchiv Bild via Wikipedia)

HAUPTSTURMFÜHRER
FRITZ KLINGENBERG

The tankers and grenadiers of the 2nd SS Division Panzer Division Das Reich expected a fight as they approached the stately old city of Belgrade. The German invasion of Yugoslavia had begun on April 6, 1941, as Hitler sought to bail out his Fascist cohort Benito Mussolini, whose Italian army had been roughly handled in Greece, and to secure his own southern flank for Operation Barbarossa, the upcoming invasion of the Soviet Union.

The Nazi juggernaut rolled forward, advancing swiftly toward the Yugoslav capital city. However, expectations of battle were quickly quelled as the vanguard of Das Reich reached Belgrade on the night of April 13. More than a day earlier, an audacious SS officer had captured the city with only six men. While all SS formations were considered elite by most observers, Hauptsturmführer (Captain) Fritz Klingenberg displayed exceptional initiative and seized an opportunity that presented itself.

Commanding a company, Klingenberg was ordered to perform reconnaissance, secure bridges, and establish roadblocks along the River Danube. The tasks were completed, but the officer noticed that little enemy activity appeared to be happening across the waterway. He concluded that Belgrade was ripe for conquest. Disobeying orders, Klingenberg assembled his small force and found an abandoned boat. After rowing to the far bank of the Danube, he sent the boat back to ferry more troops across. However, it sank en route, leaving the officer and half a dozen men stranded.

Undeterred, the seven German soldiers pushed ahead. They encountered some Yugoslav troops riding in British-made vehicles and bagged 20 prisoners. Among them was a drunken German tourist who was caught in the wrong place when the invasion commenced. The Yugoslavs believed he was a spy and intended to execute him. When he sobered up, he was grateful for the rescue, and his working knowledge of the Croatian language made him useful as an interpreter.

Pressing on, Klingenberg's contingent passed several Yugoslav checkpoints, capturing the sentries along the way. Their good fortune took a temporary turn on the outskirts of Belgrade, and a brisk two-hour gun battle broke out with a few stalwart defenders. When it was over, none of the Germans had been wounded, and the audacious group continued into the centre of the city. Eerily, the local population took little notice. There was no further resistance. The Nazi flag

Fritz Klingenberg led the intrepid group of SS soldiers that captured Belgrade in 1941. (Creative Commons Bundesarchiv Bild via Wikipedia)

replaced the Yugoslav national banner up the nearest flagpole on the afternoon of April 12, and the mayor of Belgrade and his entourage came forward to inquire about terms of surrender.

Klingenberg bluffed that Luftwaffe air attacks would commence if his advance patrol did not check in shortly and informed the officials that his small unit was the vanguard of a host of SS tanks and troops. At the time, the Germans' radio was broken, and they were out of ammunition. But the ruse worked. Within an hour the details of the surrender were complete. Klingenberg and his associates took up residence in a luxury hotel after instructing 1,300 Yugoslav soldiers to lay down their arms.

More of Klingenberg's company managed to reach Belgrade during the next day, and when the bulk of Das Reich arrived, control of the city of 200,000 people was handed over.

Klingenberg received the Knight's Cross of the Iron Cross for his stunning feat. He was subsequently promoted to standartenführer (colonel) and later commanded the 17th SS Panzer Division Götz von Berlichingen. He was killed in action at age 32 on March 23, 1945. ■

German panzer troops pause during their drive into Yugoslavia in the spring of 1941. (Creative Commons Bundesarchiv Bild via Wikipedia)

FALLSCHIRMJÄGER

FALLSCHIRMJÄGER

The demonstration that Reichsmarschall Hermann Göring witnessed as a guest of the Soviet Union left a lasting impression. Red Army parachutists had exited a Tupolev TB-3 transport aircraft through a hatch in the roof and then crawled along a wire to the wings to jump when the order was given.

When the airborne soldiers came to earth, they formed up and drew their light artillery and machine-gun support units together to complete an exercise in light infantry attack. Altogether 1,000 men had parachuted, while another 2,500 had come in via air-landing with gliders.

Göring was convinced that these manoeuvres he witnessed in the mid-1930s meant another aspect of modern warfare was in the offing. And so, in October 1938 he sanctioned the formation of the first Fallschirmjäger, parachute and glider troops, of the Luftwaffe. The new formation was christened the 7th Flieger Division, and Göring personally selected the man who would lead it. Like the Reichsmarschall, General Kurt Student was a veteran fighter pilot of World War I. He had been wounded in combat but recovered to pioneer the airborne formations of the Nazi Wehrmacht.

The 7th Flieger Division was later named the 1st Parachute Division, and the German airborne participated in the fighting on every front during World War II in Europe. An American pamphlet assessing the elite Nazi formations noted, "After proper physical conditioning, the candidate works from a jumping tower, practicing landing methods under different conditions. The school also requires and develops fearlessness; to illustrate, in a transport plane any sign of hesitation at the command 'Jump!' may cost the candidate his membership in a parachute company.

A determined Fallschirmjäger wears the distinctive rounded helmet and shoulders a machine gun. *(Creative Commons Bundesarchiv Bild via Wikipedia)*

"However, parachute jumping is only a small part of the candidate's training, inasmuch as the German Army hopes to make him a useful member of a crack combat organisation," the brochure continued, "he must know how to take part in what is called a 'vertical envelopment' – that is, the capture of an area by airborne troops."

Considering the evaluation, the US observations were accurate. The rigorous three-month training course produced airborne soldiers of excellent morale and strong commitment. The average age of the Fallschirmjäger was only 18, and the airborne soldiers wore distinctive rounded and rimless helmets and long blue-gray smocks over their parachute webbing to prevent entanglements with parachute shrouds or static lines of transport planes. They wore a distinctive airborne badge depicting a plunging Nazi eagle clutching a swastika. With the earliest campaigns in the West, the airborne troops were deployed, and expectations were high.

Two battalions of Fallschirmjäger completed assignments to capture airfields in Poland during the 1939 campaign. After the Sitzkrieg, or Phony War, heated up once again, large-scale airborne operations contributed to the swift capitulation of Denmark and Norway. A single parachute battalion, the first to ever participate in combat, seized airfields at Oslo and Stavanger, announcing to the world that the Fallschirmjäger were indeed elite. The following month during Case Yellow, the invasion of France and the Low Countries that commenced on May 10, 1940, Fallschirmjäger opened the conquest of the Netherlands with the lightning seizure of bridges at Moerdijk, Dordrecht, and Copenhagen, and again with the capture of a tactically vital airfield. One airborne thrust was defeated, and the assault on The Hague, seat of the Dutch government, initially failed with 1,200 German prisoners taken. Still, the entire country was under the Nazi heel in one week.

One of the most spectacular feats of World War II was accomplished on the opening day of

A Fallschirmjäger crew services a mortar from a camouflaged position. *(Creative Commons Bundesarchiv Bild via Wikipedia)*

The Fallschirmjäger badge features the plunging Nazi eagle. *(Creative Commons Ken modified by Gunnar.offel via Wikipedia)*

the offensive as Fallschirmjäger were inserted into Belgium by parachute and glider to seize key objectives. On that first day, 70 glider troops were whisked to pinpoint landings on the roof of Fort Eben Emael, a formidable strongpoint situated on a rocky bluff just 15 miles from the German-Belgian frontier and guarding the important Albert Canal. Most military tacticians believed Eben Emael was impregnable, studded with heavy artillery and machine-gun positions atop a sheer 130-foot precipice above three bridges. If the fort was neutralised and the three bridges over the Albert Canal were captured intact, German forces would move rapidly to the southwest and across Belgium.

The glider landings were accomplished with astonishing accuracy, and the small force overran 14 gun emplacements in the first 20 minutes as

Junkers Ju-52 transport planes, set afire during operations in the Netherlands in 1940, burn furiously.
(Creative Commons Bundesarchiv Bild via Wikipedia)

German airborne troops parachute into Crete. Operation Mercury was a pyrrhic victory.
(Creative Commons Bundesarchiv Bild via Wikipedia)

German paratroopers question villagers during operations on Crete, May 1941.
(Creative Commons Bundesarchiv Bild via Wikipedia)

they took the Belgian garrison of 800 soldiers completely by surprise. The Belgians retreated to underground defensive positions, but by noon the following day Eben Emael was in German hands. As reinforcements arrived, a total of 424 German airborne soldiers had defeated the Belgians, who surrendered with 25 dead and 59 wounded. A total of 42 gliders were delivered at intervals, towed behind Junkers Ju-52 transport aircraft. Hitler personally awarded the Knight's Cross to the officers who led the assault on the fortress, and every soldier who took part in the operation was advanced one rank.

Although the German plan for Operation Sea Lion, the invasion of Great Britain, was called off, the Fallschirmjäger were to have played a key role in the seizure of numerous objectives during the opening hours. Nevertheless, there were further missions for which to prepare. In the spring of 1941, the German focus switched to the Balkans, partly to assist Axis partner Benito Mussolini whose invasion of Greece was foundering and also to secure the German southern flank in preparation for Operation Barbarossa, the invasion of the Soviet Union.

German forces quickly took charge in Greece, forcing the British and Commonwealth defenders on the mainland to retire to the island of Crete. Student persuaded Hitler that his airborne forces could subdue the resistance on Crete and demonstrate their superior fighting qualities once again. Hitler agreed to Operation Mercury, the insertion of more than 7,000 parachute and glider-borne troops into Crete at key locations. The result was at best a pyrrhic victory and nearly meant the demise of the Fallschirmjäger.

The Germans were overconfident due to erroneous intelligence reports and found the defenders of Crete, 40,000 strong, to be stubbornly resistant. When Operation Mercury was launched on May 20, a near-disaster unfolded. Gliders and Ju-52 transports were shredded by antiaircraft fire. Some aircraft burst into flames and crashed, their bellies still full of fighting men, killing everyone aboard. After 10 days of heavy combat, the Germans finally gained the upper hand. Although Crete was conquered and 14,000 casualties had been inflicted on the Allies prior to their evacuation, 2,000 German airborne soldiers were killed in

FALLSCHIRMJÄGER

General Kurt Student led the formation and operations of the Fallschirmjäger during World War II. *(Creative Commons Bundesarchiv Bild via Wikipedia)*

action, and 220 of the 500 Ju-52s involved had been shot down, a staggering rate of loss.

Hitler was appalled and forbade the use of Fallschirmjäger in large-scale operations for the remainder of the war. In a face-saving display of Nazi nationalism, a great production was made of the award of the Iron Cross to Max Schmeling, a Fallschirmjäger and former heavyweight boxing champion of the world.

For the duration of World War II, the Fallschirmjäger fought as elite light infantry, engaging in only small-scale parachute operations from time to time. On the Eastern Front, they were deployed in the battle for Leningrad, which devolved into a 900-day siege. Before the stalemate consolidated, they blunted Red Army counterattacks effectively. In February 1944, the Fallschirmjäger tenaciously clung to the town of Monte Cassino, which anchored the defences of the Gustav Line on the Italian front. In one instance, the 2nd Battalion, 1st Parachute Division, ensconced in strong positions along the mountainous terrain, denied high ground at Hill 593 to the US 34th Division for the duration of the fight.

When Allied commanders feared that the ancient Benedictine abbey that crowned the heights surrounding Monte Cassino was being used as an observation post by the defending Germans and that the enemy had heavily fortified the surroundings, waves of bombers levelled the structure. Although they had not been holed up in the abbey prior to the air raids, the airborne troops did occupy the ruins. From their highly defensible positions, they inflicted heavy casualties during multiple Allied attempts to dislodge them. Finally, they pulled out when the Gustav Line was breached during Operation Diadem in the spring of 1944.

After the Allied landings in Normandy on D-Day, June 6, 1944, two battalions of the 6th Regiment, 2nd Fallschirmjäger Division, clung stubbornly to the crossroads town of Carentan. The US 101st Airborne Division reached Carentan on June 11, and a pitched battle ensued. The Germans finally retired as their ammunition was nearly exhausted. During the weeks that followed, the 6th Regiment further contested the American advance on the town of St. Lo and was virtually destroyed in the cauldron of the Falaise pocket in August.

At peak strength, the Fallschirmjäger numbered more than 160,000 soldiers. Student was elevated to the command of an army group prior to war's end. He was tried and convicted of war crimes but never served a day in prison, dying at age 88 in 1978.

The Fallschirmjäger earned the grudging respect of their adversaries on all fronts. One Briish officer who had confronted them at Monte Cassino asserted that they were the most determined enemy troops he encountered in the entire war. The German airborne soldier was inculcated with Nazi fervour and fearless in battle. A document confiscated from a prisoner taken in Crete exemplified the Fallschirmjäger perspective on combat. Titled *The Parachutist's Ten Commandments*, it read:

"1. You are the elite of the German Army. For you, combat shall be fulfilment. You shall seek it out and train yourself to stand any test.
2. Cultivate true comradeship, for together with your comrades you will triumph or die.
3. Be shy of speech and incorruptible. Men act, women chatter; chatter will bring you to the grave.
4. Calm and caution, vigour and determination, valour and a fanatical offensive spirit will make you superior in attack.
5. In facing the foe, ammunition is the most precious thing. He who shoots uselessly, merely to reassure himself, is a man without guts. He is a weakling and does not deserve the title of parachutist.
6. Never surrender. Your honour lies in Victory or Death.
7. Only with good weapons can you have success. So, look after them on the principle – First my weapons, then myself.
8. You must grasp the full meaning of an operation so that, should your leader fall by the way, you can carry it out with coolness and caution.
9. Fight chivalrously against an honest foe; armed irregulars deserve no quarter.
10. With your eyes open, keyed up to top pitch, agile as a greyhound, tough as leather, hard as Krupp steel, you will be the embodiment of a German warrior." ■

A burning Ju-52 transport plane streaks earthward as German airborne troops land on Crete. *(Creative Commons Arthur Conry via Wikipedia)*

Fallschirmjäger execute small unit tactics in ground combat. *(Creative Commons Bundesarchiv Bild via Wikipedia)*

ELITE FORCES OF WORLD WAR II

JAPANESE AIRBORNE

Impressed with the early successes of their German cohorts' airborne forces early in World War II, the Japanese were motivated to develop their own such elite formations. General Hideki Tojo, his nation's war minister, is believed by some historians to have played a significant role in the pursuit of airborne forces, but true to form an interservice rivalry emerged between the Imperial Army and the Imperial Navy.

The Army organised the First Raiding Squadron in December 1940, led by Lieutenant Colonel Keigo Kawashima and a cadre of 10 officers. After physical training and the use of an amusement park tower near Tokyo and testing with dummies, the initial jumps by paratroopers were made in February 1941, as 250 volunteers qualified as parachutists. Subsequently, a base in Manchuria was established for additional training, and the airborne force grew to two regiments under Colonel Seiichi Kume.

Meanwhile, the Navy authorised a testing unit at Yokosuka Naval Station on Tokyo Bay in November 1940. Live jumps began just two months later, and two battalions were organised as elements of the Yokosuka Special Naval Landing Force. In mid-November 1941, the 1st and 3rd Yokosuka were activated under Commander Toyoaki Horiuchi.

The naval airborne were first into action, jumping into Manado in the northern Celebes Islands, while troops of the Sasebo Special Naval Landing Force made amphibious landings. The island was defended by 1,500 Dutch troops, mostly reservists and militia. The island's airfield was secured, and reinforcements parachuted in as the invaders took control of Manado. A second operation occurred on the island of Timor. Jumps were executed at mid-day on February 20, 1942, and the operation was successfully completed within two days.

Army paratroopers of the 2nd Raiding Regiment and other units were transferred to Cambodia to mount airborne assaults on the island of Sumatra, targeting oil fields and refineries that were vital to the Japanese war effort. The air insertion began on February 14, 1942, and British and Dutch troops fought bravely in defence of the island's principal airfield but were forced to retreat, yielding it to the Japanese. The fighting at the refineries lasted several hours, continuing into darkness before the defenders fell back. Just after midnight, demolition charges left by the Dutch detonated and rendered roughly 80 percent of the refinery in ruins.

The Japanese airborne troops claimed to have killed 530 Allied soldiers for the loss of 29 dead and 48 wounded, one supporting bomber shot down, and two transport planes lost to crashes. They returned to Cambodia when Sumatra was secured.

Japanese ground forces were overrunning Burma at the time, and the airborne forces

Paratroopers of the Imperial Japanese Army deploy near the city of Palembang on the island of Sumatra. *(Public Domain Imperial Japanese Army Air Service via Wikimedia Commons)*

A Japanese naval paratrooper is in full kit ready for an airborne mission while carrying the ashes of a fallen comrade. *(Public Domain Imperial Japanese Navy via Wikimedia Commons)*

were initially tabbed to lend support. However, deteriorating weather curbed the opportunity for parachute operations. And so, the paratroopers returned to Japan and were proclaimed as heroes, "Soldier Gods of the Sky." Although planning for further operations in the Aleutians and New Guinea were drawn up, these were shelved with the ebbing need for offensive airborne capability.

In the autumn of 1944, an airborne raid against American forces in the Philippines ended in confusion and great loss. Some of the survivors joined Japanese ground troops on the island of Leyte. In a second mission, intended to coordinate with a ground offensive on Leyte, 18 of 35 transport planes were shot down. Others dropped their parachutists in the wrong place. A handful of paratroopers did manage to attack an airfield and destroy a few parked planes, but American mechanics and supply clerks fought back until relieved by combat engineers and artillerymen fighting as infantry.

Further airborne operations were either cancelled due to bad weather or logistics issues, including the final proposed missions of the war against US forces on the island of Okinawa. Even as the war came to an end, a plan for combined Army and Navy paratroopers to strike in late August 1945 was approved. However, the atomic bombs put an end to the initiative. ■

Japanese Special Naval Landing Forces paratroopers pose for a group photo. *(Public Domain Uruguay Round Agreements Act via Wikimedia Commons)*

SPECIAL NAVAL LANDING FORCES

Japanese SNLF troops don gas masks during heavy fighting in the Chinese city of Shanghai. (Public Domain Ministry of the Navy via Wikimedia Commons)

Trained as light infantry, the Japanese Special Naval Landing Forces (SNLF), or Kaigun Tokubetsu Rikusentai, emerged as components of the Imperial Japanese Navy personnel complement aboard operating warships. At a startling pace, Japan had evolved from an inward looking feudal state to a world power by the turn of the 20th century.

Japanese warships operated extensively along the coast of the Asian mainland and in the Pacific in the decades prior to World War II, and the Special Naval Landing Forces became active as shore parties and occupation troops, first seeing action in the Russo-Japanese War of 1904-1905.

These units proliferated and saw extensive service in China, particularly in Shanghai, and their clash with Chinese troops in 1932 is seen as a watershed moment in the history of these elite soldiers. Comparisons to US Marines are erroneous, as the SNLF were later organised into battalion size units and remained under the control of the Navy throughout their existence rather than functioning as a semi-autonomous entity.

In response to the Shanghai Incident, the Navy authorised the formation of two SNLF battalions. Four more were organised in 1936, one in each of the primary naval districts, Yokosuka, Sasebo, Kure, and Maizuru. Each of these was conceived with 539 officers and two rifle companies. However, through the next decade the numbers of each SNLF battalion varied from 200 to 3,000 personnel. By the end of 1937, a dedicated SNLF headquarters and two more battalions were authorised, and at the time of the Pearl Harbor attack in December 1941, there were 12 battalions. These were elite troops known for their physical stamina and training in amphibious landings. In 1941, the 1st and 3rd Yokosuka SNLF were converted to airborne units.

During World War II, the SNLF formations were involved in offensive action in China, the Philippines, and islands across the Pacific along with occupation assignments until the tide of the conflict turned against Imperial Japan. From that point they were deployed as defensive troops and proved formidable adversaries in that role as Allied forces advanced across the Pacific. In June 1942, the Maizuru 3rd SNLF occupied the island of Kiska in the Aleutians. The SNLF was reinforced with troops of the Imperial Japanese Army, but the entire force evacuated in July 1943 in the face of an upcoming US landing.

In August and September 1942, the two-week Battle of Milne Bay in Papua, New Guinea, was the first land action in which the Japanese were defeated in World War II. The SNLF 3rd and 5th Kure, 5th Sasebo, and 5th Yokosuka Battalions suffered 625 killed and more than 300 wounded in action with Australian and US troops. These units had been inadequately trained for the specific task of capturing the area to prevent Allied interference in the upcoming effort to occupy Port Moresby. Faced with determined opposition, they depleted their ammunition, chose death or surrender, and lost heavily in close quarter combat.

As the US Marines embarked on their series of amphibious operations in the island road to Tokyo, their first landing on a contested beachhead occurred at Tarawa Atoll in the Gilbert Islands. Five thousand Japanese troops defended Betio, the principal islet at Tarawa, and among these were 1,700 men of the 7th Sasebo SNLF along with 1,100 of the 3rd Special Base Force. Betio was a mere spit of land only two miles long and 500 yards across at its widest point. However, these defenders had fortified the islet with concrete blockhouses, and bunkers were dug deep into the sand and reinforced with steel and concrete roofs that were further protected by coconut logs. Machine-gun positions with interlocking fields of fire studded the shoreline.

Rear Admiral Keiji Shibasaki expected an American assault, but he was confident, asserting, "A million men cannot take Tarawa in a hundred years!"

The SNLF battalion at Tarawa was prepared to fight to the death when the US 2nd Marine Division launched the largest amphibious component of Operation Galvanic on November 20, 1943. A heavy pre-invasion naval bombardment was thoroughly ineffective, and as the Marines churned toward the designated landing beaches they were obliged to cross a wide lagoon in full view of the defenders. Compounding the issues they faced at the outset, the Marines encountered a coral reef, which impeded the progress of the flat-bottomed Higgins boats being used as landing craft. The Marines aboard the Higgins boats were obliged to exit the craft and

The battle flag unfurled, Japanese SNLF troops stand aboard a ship of the Imperial Navy. (Public Domain the Japanese Pictorial Weekly Magazine, Asahigraph, vol. 31 No. 1 via Wikimedia Commons)

ELITE FORCES OF WORLD WAR II

Australian soldiers such as these turned back the SNLF at Milne Bay, Papua, New Guinea. *(Public Domain Begnall, Frank N Government of Australia via Wikimedia Commons)*

US Marines fire on Japanese positions at Tarawa, where SNLF troops proved tenacious in defence. *(Creative Commons USMC Archives via Wikipedia)*

A wrecked US Marine LVT lies derelict on a beach at Tarawa strewn with the wreckage of war. *(Public Domain US Marine Corps via Wikimedia Commons)*

wade more than a mile ashore amid withering enemy fire. Some of the Marines embarked aboard LVTs (Landing Vehicle, Tracked), which were capable of negotiating the reef obstacle.

Struggling ashore on the beaches designated Red 1, 2, and 3, the Marines clung to a toehold and crouched behind a seawall little more than three feet high and running the length of the lagoon. A 34-man Scout-Sniper platoon under Lieutenant William Hawkins fought desperately to oust Japanese defenders from a long pier that jutted into the water, where they had spewed small-arms fire into the Marines from a flanking position.

The Japanese held firm through the night, and Marine reinforcements arrived the following morning – still under heavy fire. An unscheduled landing on Green Beach, a relatively quiet sector that had been designated as a contingency area, helped turn the tide at Tarawa as Marines pushed across Betio. Individual acts of heroism were repeated many times. A lone Marine would sprint toward a Japanese bunker occupied by fanatical SNLF troops and throw an explosive satchel charge through a firing slit. Flamethrowers were unleashes on the confined spaces. When exits were flung open and the defenders rushed out, Marine riflemen gunned them down.

Admiral Shibasaki died in his command blockhouse on November 23 after it came under heavy attack, Marine bulldozers covering exits with sand while gasoline was poured down ventilators and set alight. His final communiqué was broadcast: "Our weapons have been destroyed, and from now on everyone is attempting a final charge. May Japan exist for 10,000 years."

Although the 2nd Marine Division had conquered the "unconquerable" in a mere 76 hours, the price the SNLF exacted at Tarawa was extremely high. More than 1,000 Americans had been killed, and twice that number were wounded. In turn, the defenders of Tarawa were virtually annihilated. Only 17 Japanese naval infantrymen and soldiers were captured alive along with 129 Korean forced labourers who had been shipped to Betio to work on the fortifications.

The ordeal of Tarawa and the tenacity of its SNLF defenders taught the Americans hard lessons in amphibious warfare. Naval bombardment was later conducted with greater arcing fire to penetrate reinforced bunkers, while aerial bombing was stepped up as well. Larger numbers of tracked LVTs were made available, and the reliance on old charts that had not revealed the hazard of the coral reef had proven inadequate.

In September 1944, the US War Department issued a booklet titled Technical Manual: Handbook On Japanese Military Forces. Its description of the SNLF noted the transition from offensive to defensive posture and warned of an increasing presence of these naval ground troops. In subsequent operations, the SNLF battalions continued to prove their mettle. ■

Five Japanese prisoners captured at Tarawa sit in the sand with their hands raised. *(Public Domain US Navy via Wikimedia Commons)*

KAMIKAZE AND KAITEN

As the fortunes of war turned against Imperial Japan, the empire's military establishment concluded that desperate times called for desperate measures. Therefore, the formation of suicide squadrons was sanctioned for both air and sea, and the most committed of recruits stepped forward, willing to die for their Emperor Hirohito.

The idea for the Kamikaze, or Divine Wind, air squadrons came to Admiral Takajiro Onishi, newly appointed commander of the Imperial Navy's First Air Fleet, in the autumn of 1944. Onishi had received word of a courageous naval officer and his willing sacrifice in the face of a growing American military presence in the Pacific. The US Navy had wrested the initiative in World War II from Japan, and American forces were steadily advancing toward the home islands.

On October 15, 1944, Admiral Masafumi Arima, the 50-year-old commander of the 26th Air Flotilla based at Manila, Philippines, had come to the conclusion that he would sacrifice his own life in a suicide mission. Arima climbed into the cockpit of a Mitsubishi G4M Betty bomber. He had led many missions before, but this time he was alone and intended to die by deliberately crashing his aircraft into an American warship.

As he approached the massive US task force off the coast, Arima chose an aircraft carrier as his target and began his final run. Antiaircraft fire shook the plane. Shells exploded and showered the Betty with shrapnel. And then, before Arima could fulfil his mission, his plane was blasted from the sky.

Onishi reasoned that men like Arima would be emboldened by their adherence to the Japanese warrior code, Bushido. He had relatively few frontline aircraft that were combat worthy and knew that those airmen assigned to fly outdated types would likely be killed anyway.

Kamikaze pilot Ensign Kiyoshi Ogawa crashed his suicide plane into the aircraft carrier USS *Bunker Hill*. *(Public Domain Government of Japan via Wikimedia Commons)*

The aircraft carrier USS *Bunker Hill* blazes after being struck by Kamikazes on May 11, 1945. *(Public Domain US National Archives and Records Administration via Wikimedia Commons)*

Japanese Kamikaze aircraft prepare to take off on their one-way missions in early 1945. *(Public Domain Government of Japan via Wikimedia Commons)*

Why shouldn't these brave men be given the opportunity to die a hero's death while inflicting the maximum damage on the enemy?

The admiral gathered 23 non-commissioned officers who were pilots and asked them to volunteer for his new Tekko, or Special Operations, Squadrons. All 23 enthusiastically volunteered, and a squadron called Shimpu was quickly formed. A second followed, and it was dubbed Kamikaze. Both names were in reference to a great storm that destroyed an invading Mongol fleet as it approached the Japanese coastline in 1281. These early squadrons and those that followed are collectively known to history as Kamikaze.

Onishi hoped that a modern Divine Wind might inflict enough damage on the US Navy to turn the tide of the war in the Pacific, and just 10 days after the death of Arima a group of Japanese pilots attacked at the American fleet off the Philippine island of Leyte. One Mitsubishi A6M Zero fighter, armed with a bomb, struck the escort carrier Santee, while a second suicide plane hit the escort carrier Suwanee. A third managed to crash into the escort carrier St. Lo, which was devastated by secondary internal explosions and sank within half an hour.

Subsequently, American warships became wary of the Kamikaze, altering their antiaircraft fire and manoeuvre tactics to defend against them. American fighters stepped up combat air patrols to ward off the suicide attacks and shoot down as many Japanese planes as possible.

Meanwhile, another suicide program was undertaken. Ensign Sekio Nishina and Lieutenant (j.g.) Hiroshi Kuroki were midget submarine pilots of the Imperial Navy. Frustrated at their own inability to take the war to the Americans, the two officers came up with an idea. The Type 93 Long Lance torpedo had already been proven a

ELITE FORCES OF WORLD WAR II

A Kamikaze is caught seconds before making impact with the battleship USS Missouri in April 1945. (Public Domain US Navy via Wikimedia Commons)

deadly weapon in naval action, and the thought was to modify the Type 93 into a human torpedo. Released from a conventional submarine, the pilot would steer the Kaiten directly into its target, the hull of an American ship.

By January 1943, plans were completed, and the proposed weapon would carry an explosive charge of 3,000 pounds. Fifty-four feet long, the torpedo would have a range of 40 miles and travel at a maximum speed of 40 knots. Among other interpretations, the chosen name of Kaiten translates literally from the Japanese as the "heaven shaker." In the summer of 1944, students at two naval air training facilities were assembled and presented with the opportunity to volunteer for Kaiten missions. Roughly 200 men were accepted.

The first Kaiten missions occurred in late 1944, and the results, according to the US Navy, had minimal impact on the continuing American war effort. The fleet tanker Mississinewa was sunk in the harbour at Ulithi in the Caroline Islands, while the destroyer escort USS Underhill was lost northeast of the Philippines, and a small landing craft was also sunk. A total of 96 Japanese pilots lost their lives in Kaiten operations, 80 of these in combat sorties and the remainder in training accidents.

The Japanese also developed small suicide boats and enlisted a few suicide frogmen who carried explosives; however, the most destructive suicide weapon of World War II was by far the Kamikaze. Its devastating capability came into sharp focus during the battle for the island of Okinawa, roughly 330 miles from the home islands. During the 82 days of fighting before the island was secured,

the Japanese launched 10 waves of Kamikaze planes against the assembled US fleet offshore. These waves were called Kikusui, or Floating Chrysanthemums. A total of 29 US Navy ships were sunk and more than 120 damaged with the loss of more than 4,900 sailors killed or missing.

Standard Kamikaze pilots, though brave, were young and had undergone only minimal training. They were lauded as heroes and drank toasts with sake, Japanese rice wine, prior to taking off on their one-way missions. They often wrote poignant farewell letters to loved ones and left locks of hair, fingernail trimmings, or even an entire finger, for interment. They sometimes posed for final photographs.

At Okinawa nearly 1,500 Japanese aircraft were committed to the Kikusui, each wave consisting of as many as 350 planes. US Navy destroyers manned an anti-Kamikaze defensive cordon called the picket line off Okinawa and suffered mightily. The ordeal of the destroyer USS *Laffey* is one of heroism and terrible suffering.

Just before 8:30 a.m. on April 16, 1945, multiple Kamikaze attacked the little ship simultaneously. *Laffey's* guns, even the 5-inch main batteries, blazed away, and at one time the shipboard radar identified roughly 50 hostile blips on its screen. For an hour and 20 minutes, the crew of *Laffey* fought for their lives and withstood attacks from 22 Japanese planes. Six Kamikaze struck the destroyer, which also absorbed four bomb hits. Miraculously, the *Laffey* survived with only four 20mm guns still able to fire. The little ship eventually reached port at Guam with 31 sailors killed or missing and 72 wounded.

Through the end of World War II in the Pacific, approximately 2,800 Kamikaze sorties were flown, sinking 45 US ships and damaging an astonishing 368. At Okinawa, despite the terrible losses suffered, the US Navy remained on station and earned the nickname of the "fleet that came to stay."

For Japan, the sacrifice of its Kamikaze was most unsettling – too little and too late – a tragic exercise in futility. ■

A Kaiten human torpedo is launched from a light cruiser during trials. (Public Domain Government of Japan Rekishi Gunzō, History of Pacific War Vol.36 Kairyu and Kaiten via Wikimedia Commons)

The fleet tanker USS Mississinewa burns in the harbour at Ulithi after being struck by a Kaiten. (Public Domain US Navy via Wikimedia Commons)

SPECIAL AIR TORPEDO UNIT

Benito Mussolini, fascist dictator of Italy known to his people as Il Duce, fancied that the Mediterranean Sea was an Italian lake. The forces of the Royal Navy, Royal Air Force and Allied militaries put that notion paid early in World War II.

However, one elite unit of the Regia Aeronautica, the Italian Air Force, did its mightiest to make Mussolini's vision come to pass. The Special Air Torpedo Unit, or Reparto Speciale Aerosiluranti, came into being in August 1940, and within a year the original 278th Squadriglia Quattro Gatti, "Four Cats," was joined by several others that flew nearly 250 sorties and executed more than 100 aerial torpedo attacks against Allied shipping in the Mediterranean while flying from airfields in Italy, Sicily, and Libya.

The special torpedo squadrons flew the Savoia Marchetti SM-79 bomber, an aircraft that was considered obsolete by most standards even before the outbreak of war. The SM-79 Sparrowhawk, or Sparviero, was a tri-motored hunchback of a plane, constructed in large part of canvas and wood. Although particularly vulnerable to Allied fighters and anti-aircraft fire, its top speed of 290 miles per hour was more than adequate given light construction, and its range of 1,180 miles was suitable for the great distances missions were flown across open expanses of water.

The most famous Italian aircraft of World War II, the SM-79 was first flown in combat during the Spanish Civil War of the mid-1930s. With a crew of up to six, the plane was easily recognisable for its open dorsal hump that accommodated a machine-gunner for rear defence against

A flight of four SM-79 Sparrowhawks is shown during a Mediterranean mission. (Creative Commons Andrea Nicola via Wikipedia)

SM-79s fly over open water. Note the fasces present in the wing insignia, emblematic of fascist Italy. (Creative Commons Andrea Nicola via Wikipedia)

Carlo Emanuele Buscaglia was the most successful SM-79 pilot of World War II. (Public Domain State Treasury of Poland at www.audiovis.nac.gov.pl via Wikimedia Commons)

attacking enemy planes. The aircraft mounted three 12.7mm (.50-calibre) machine guns in dorsal and nose positions, as well as an optional location on the underside. A pair of 7.7mm (.303-calibre) machine guns were also located in waist positions. A total of 1,240 SM-79s were manufactured between 1936 and 1945.

The SM-79 was, in the hands of a capable pilot, quite the stable platform for delivering one or two aerial torpedoes packing warheads of 440 pounds. The aircraft was versatile in a bombing role as well, but as a torpedo plane it claimed 72 Allied warships of various size and 196 merchant vessels sunk along with another 500 damaged from 1940 until 1943, when Italy formally switched sides and fought the remainder of the war with the Allies.

The Special Air Torpedo Unit was instrumental in the Axis effort to bomb and starve the British bastion of Malta into submission. Strategically located in the Mediterranean, Malta was a key base for British aircraft, submarines and surface ships that operated across the expanse of the sea. They were particularly troublesome in interdicting convoys of supplies and reinforcements to German and Italian forces in North Africa, including those under the command of General Erwin Rommel, the Desert Fox, that were locked in a death struggle with General Bernard Montgomery's British Eighth Army.

In concert with German air assets in the summer of 1942, the SM-79s ravaged two convoys of resupply to the embattled island of Malta, sinking 10 ships, damaging five others, and allowing only two merchantmen to reach the Grand Harbour of Valletta. The largest Allied convoy, code named Pedestal, was savagely attacked, losing nine vital ships. During a period of three harrowing days, the convoy was set upon by German and Italian submarines and aircraft. The aircraft carrier HMS *Eagle* was sunk, and another, HMS *Indomitable*, was seriously damaged. The cruiser HMS *Manchester* was damaged so badly that it was later scuttled by its own crew. Although the massive tanker Ohio was hit repeatedly by bombs and set afire, its efficient damage control effort kept the ship afloat, reaching Malta while under tow by other vessels. Only nine

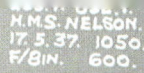

The battleship HMS *Nelson* was damaged by Italian SM-79 pilots in 1941.
(Public Domain Collections of the Imperial War Museums via Wikimedia Commons)

ships of the Pedestal convoy made port. During the swirl of battle that summer, the Sparviero squadrons lost 50 aircraft and 180 airmen.

The people of Malta persevered and outlasted the enemy air assault, which was finally halted after the Pedestal convoy got its trickle of supplies through. King George VI bestowed the George Cross on the entire population in recognition of their heroism. He proclaimed, "To honour her brave people I award the George Cross to the island fortress of Malta, to bear witness to a heroism and devotion that will long be famous in history."

The most successful SM-79 pilot of the Special Air Torpedo Unit was Captain Carlo Emanuele Buscaglia. A volunteer for service in the 240th Squadron, Buscaglia went to war in July 1940 and soon proved his courage in seriously damaging the cruisers HMS *Kent* and HMS *Glasgow* in torpedo attacks on September 17 and December 3. The cruiser HMS *Liverpool* was damaged by an Italian torpedo in October and put out of action for a year. In January 1941, Buscaglia and other torpedo pilots were joined by German dive bombers based in Sicily to damage the aircraft carrier HMS *Illustrious*. The light cruisers HMS *Phoebe* and HMS *Arethusa*, as well as the battleship HMS *Nelson*, were also damaged by SM-79 torpedo attacks.

Buscaglia was recognised with promotion to major and command of both the 281st Squadron and the 132nd Torpedo Group. He received the German Iron Cross 2nd Class and his own country's Silver Medal for gallantry five separate times. During the abortive Italian naval confrontation with the Royal Navy in the Battle of Cape Matapan, Buscaglia flew combat missions, but on November 12, 1942, he was shot down by a British Supermarine Spitfire fighter as he prepared to press home an attack against Allied shipping off the coast of North Africa during Operation Torch. After he failed to return to base, Buscaglia was presumed dead. He received a posthumous award of the Golden Medal for valour.

Actually, Buscaglia had been seriously wounded and rescued by the Allies. He recovered and was transferred to the United States, where he spent 10 months in prison at Fort Meade, Maryland. After Mussolini's fascist regime was deposed and the new government of Italy surrendered to the Allies in September 1943, Buscaglia was repatriated. He volunteered to serve with the air force of the new pro-Allied Italian government, while ironically the new fascist puppet state formed under Mussolini in northern Italy named a squadron of is meagre air force after the hero.

Buscaglia was appointed commander of the 28th Bombing Wing in July 1944. He was seriously injured during the take-off of his Martin Baltimore bomber and died a day later in hospital in Naples. The Third Wing of the modern Italian Air Force is named in his honour.

The wreckage of an SM-79 appears to have been stripped of usable material as it lies in the North African desert.
(Creative Commons whatsthatpicture via Wikipedia)

The dorsal hump of the SM-79 bomber is visible in this image from the war years. (Creative Commons Private collection of the Riggio family via Wikipedia)

10TH ASSAULT VEHICLE FLOTILLA

The men of the Decima Flottiglia MAS, or the Italian 10th Assault Vehicle Flotilla, were among the daredevils of World War II, and they recorded some of the conflict's most spectacular successes. Daring raiders, they were responsible for sinking 80,000 tons in Royal Navy warships by late 1943 and 148,000 tons of Allied merchant shipping during the same period.

The personnel of the 10th Assault Vehicle Flotilla of the Italian Navy, or Regia Marina, were highly trained frogmen, skilled in the art of underwater operations, the use of anti-ship explosives, and the operation of two innovative weapons of war, the Siluro a Lenta Corsa (SLC) and Motoscafa da Turismo (MTM) motorboat.

The SLC was a manned torpedo, roughly 22 feet long and powered by a weak electric motor, that travelled at a slow rate of speed and carried two pilots externally. Its range was only 15 miles, and the craft were capable of functioning on the surface or submerged if necessary. The SLC pilots, wearing wetsuits and breathing apparatus, would set their explosives, limpet mines or other types, with time-delay fuses, sink their craft, and then make good their escape. The SLC could also be used as a torpedo, its bow fitted with an explosive warhead. The frogmen nicknamed the SLC "Maiali," or pig.

The MTM was 18.4 feet long and powered by a 95-horsepower Alfa Romeo engine with a top speed of 33 knots. It carried a single raider who was armed with up to 10 pounds of explosives that could be attached to a target, while the bow of the motor boat was loaded with a 660-pound warhead. The frogmen who operated the MTM were designated the Gamma Group.

Early operations were unsuccessful and resulted in numerous casualties. The 10th Flotilla attempted its first use of the SLC on August 21, 1940. The submarine Iride, transporting

Italian human torpedoes such as this example were utilised during the raid on Alexandria harbour.
(Attribution Giovanni Dall'Orto via Wikipedia)

four human torpedoes en route to attack Gibraltar, was spotted by British aircraft and sunk. A month later, the submarine Gondar was attacked by British destroyers and heavily damaged while sailing from La Spezia with three SLCs aboard, their pilots intent on attacking Alexandria. The crew surfaced during the fight at sea and then scuttled Gondar. Two more missions fizzled, one of them with Maiali managing to enter the harbour at Gibraltar but failing to locate any targets.

Then, on March 25, 1941, a pair of Italian destroyers carried six MTMs within 10 miles of the harbour at Suda Bay on the island of Crete. Two MTMs struck the heavy cruiser York, and the British soon scuttled the seriously damaged warship prior to evacuating all forces from the island. Another MTM hit the Norwegian tanker Pericles, which was heavily damaged and sank while under tow for Alexandria, Egypt. Another MTM later damaged the destroyer HMS Eridge at El Daba, Egypt.

In July 1942, the Gamma frogmen set up a base of operations under the noses of the British, using the hulk of the old Italian freighter Olterra resting in Algeciras Bay adjacent to Gibraltar. From there, they damaged or sank 11 ships totalling 55,000 tons during just over a year of operations.

On September 10, 1941, SLCs attacked the British anchorage at Gibraltar and sinking the tankers Fiona Shell and Denbydale and the freighter Durham.

The Italian Navy scored its most spectacular success of World War II when frogmen of the 10th Flotilla assaulted Royal Navy warships anchored in the great harbour of Alexandria on the night

The battleship HMS *Valiant* was severely damaged by Italian frogmen at Alexandria, Egypt, in December 1941. *(Public Domain US Navy via Wikimedia Commons)*

104 ELITE FORCES OF WORLD WAR II

ELITE FORCES OF WORLD WAR II

Luigi Durand de la Penne participated in the Alexandria raid and rose to the rank of admiral in the Italian Navy after World War II. (Public Domain Marina Militare Italiana via Wikimedia Commons)

This SLC human torpedo is on exhibit at a museum in Rome. (Creative Commons Myrabella via Wikipedia)

The battleship HMS *Queen Elizabeth* was put out of action for months after the Italian raid on Alexandria. (Public Domain Collections of the Imperial War Museums via Wikimedia Commons)

of December 18, 1941. That evening, six frogmen boarded three Maiali and slipped away from the Italian submarine Scire just off the harbour entrance. The frogmen waited, and soon three British destroyers approached. When the protective boom was raised, the Italians followed the British inside. Moments later one submersible experienced motor failure, and frogman Emilio Bianchi passed out when his breathing equipment failed. The other diver, Luigi Durand de la Penne, pushed the human torpedo along, and a limpet mine was successfully attached to the World War I-vintage battleship HMS *Valiant*.

The two Italians were captured and locked up in a compartment aboard Valiant quite near the spot where the mine had been attached. They feared for their lives, and de la Penne confessed to Captain Charles Morgan, commanding officer aboard the battleship, that an explosive device would detonate soon. He would provide no other details and was returned to the same space. When the mine exploded, the ship was disabled, but neither prisoner was badly hurt. Valiant was out of action for six months.

Antonio Marceglia and Spartaco Schergat planted their limpet mine against the hull of another old battleship, HMS *Queen Elizabeth*. When that mine exploded at 4:30 a.m. on December 19, eight Royal Navy ratings were killed and the blast raised Admiral A.B. Cunningham, commander of the Royal Navy in the Mediterranean, five feet out of his chair. Queen Elizabeth was out of action for nine months.

The third Italian team, Mario Marino and Vincenzo Martelotta, blew the stern off the Norwegian tanker Sagona and badly damaged the destroyer HMS *Jervis*, which was refuelling at the time. Jervis was repaired and returned to service in January 1943, but the tanker was not repaired until 1946. These two frogmen remained fugitives for a day before they were arrested by Egyptian police and turned over to the British.

Although all six intrepid Maiali pilots were captured, their fortunes enjoyed a reversal when the fascist government of dictator Benito Mussolini was overthrown in the summer of 1943. The new Italian government negotiated with the Allies as landings were about to commence on the Tyrrhenian coast at Salerno. Italy formally switched sides and declared war on Germany. The prisoners were repatriated in 1944, and the raiders were presented their country's Gold Medal for bravery during the daring mission to Alexandria.

In an ironic twist of fate, the honoured presenter of the medals was none other than Admiral Morgan, former commander of the battleship Valiant. Morgan was heard to quip, "This is ridiculous, but all war is ridiculous. Congratulations on destroying my ship."

The British admired the courage of the elite Italian frogmen and the success of their SLC craft. In response, they developed their own brand of human torpedo, christening the new weapon the Chariot. In January 1945, the former enemies teamed up as Italian and British raiders sank the unfinished aircraft carrier Aquila at Genoa before the Germans were able to relocate the ship to the mouth of the harbour and sink her to block it.

Some members of the 10th Flotilla remained loyal to Mussolini and apparently joined him in northern Italy late in the war. Rather than continuing with naval operations, they were primarily involved with Nazi SS troops in activities to suppress Italian partisans. Reports of their participation in war crimes surfaced in the years following the end of World War II. ∎

This MTM explosive motorboat is located in the Naval Museum, Venice, Italy. (Creative Commons Gaius Cornelius via Wikipedia)

RED ARMY SNIPERS

The Soviet Red Army is believed to have maintained the sharpest perspective on the training and deployment of military snipers between the world wars, and for two good reasons. First, their snipers had fought with Republican forces during the Spanish Civil War and gained valuable experience. Second, and probably more important, during the Winter War with Finland the Finnish snipers had taught them a bitter lesson, taking a heavy toll.

Even before embarking on the costly invasion of Finland, the Red Army had boasted in 1938 that six million soldiers had earned the coveted Voroshilov Sharpshooter badge.

The first Soviet sniper schools were organised in 1924, and the Red Army concept of military sniping evolved somewhat differently from that of the armed forces of Western nations, including proficiency in sharpshooting, fieldcraft, intelligence gathering, stalking, and of course the nerve to carry out a mission and pull the trigger. Consequently, some analysts believe that many of the millions who claimed the designation of sharpshooter may not have been actual snipers in the truest sense. Nevertheless, there is little doubt that the vast number of sharpshooters provided a substantial pool of talent from which to select the very best.

When World War II began, two types of snipers were prevalent within the Soviet ranks. These included regular army personnel and soldiers who were identified as reserves of the supreme high command, or RVGK. The RVGK snipers were usually organised in brigades and assigned to armies or fronts (army groups) in formations ranging from platoon size to battalion strength. At the outset of the war, a single sniper squad was allocated to each infantry division, but division sniper schools were formed, and as they turned out graduates the number steadily increased. By the end of the war, a standard infantry or rifle battalion included 18 snipers, and two snipers were organic to each platoon.

Detailed Red Army sniper doctrine was developed and led to qualified personnel being assigned to the lowest operational level. The snipers were also ordered to hunt in pairs. Officers, particularly those at junior levels, were required to have some idea of how to properly utilise the sniper on the battlefield as an integrated component of ground combat. Throughout the war on the Eastern Front, Soviet snipers took their toll on the German invaders, both literally and in the psychological realm. Substantial formations of German soldiers were often completely immobilised by only a handful of Red Army snipers, and no Wehrmacht personnel felt absolutely safe, particularly in a static environment such as at Stalingrad.

One memorable incident occurred when the German 465th Infantry Regiment was ordered to attack through a dense forest in September 1941. Reports of the action reveal that German casualties at the hands of so-called "tree snipers" were horrendous, 75 confirmed killed and 25 missing. These resourceful and elusive Soviet marksmen were seldom seen, and the Germans were unable to mount any significant response to the threat. In another action, a single Soviet sniper was said to have paralysed a German

Vasili Zaitsev moves a group of Red Army snipers into position at Stalingrad. *(Public Domain Georgy Zelma Russian Federation via Wikimedia Commons)*

Many Soviet snipers plied their craft in the rubble of embattled Stalingrad 1942-1943. *(Public Domain Сергей Струнников Russian Federation via Wikimedia Commons)*

Wary of Red Army snipers, German soldiers keep their heads low during the fight for Stalingrad. (Public Domain Propaganda-Kompanie Geller Berliner Illustrierte Zeitung 1 ottobre 1942 via Wikimedia Commons)

Sniper Lyudmila Pavlichenko became a Hero of the Soviet Union. (Public Domain Russian Federation via Wikimedia Commons)

Sniper Roza Shanina was killed in action in 1945. She accounted for more than 50 enemy soldiers. (Public Domain Неизвестен Russian Federation via Wikimedia Commons)

panzer unit with harassing fire for five long days. When his rifle cracked, another report of a dead or wounded German soldier shortly followed.

The Soviet sniper remained concealed inside a disabled T-34 tank until one morning a wisp of smoke was seen to curl from the turret. When the Germans investigated, they found the sniper and took him prisoner. He had lived among the dead crewmen and eaten their frozen rations. Water was obtained by thawing their frozen canteens with his body heat. Although the fate of the intrepid sniper is unknown, he was likely executed within a short time in retribution for his tally.

Soviet snipers primarily used the Moisin Nagant Model 1891/30 rifle, standard Red Army issue, enhanced with the addition of Zeiss telescopic sights made available when the Soviet Union purchased the famed optics company in the 1930s. Semiautomatic Tokarev rifles were allocated to snipers twice, in 1938 and 1940, in the hopes of improving the user's rate of fire. However, both experiments were abandoned after disappointing results. Snipers often carried a backup weapon, usually a 7.62mm (.30-calibre) PPSh submachine gun, which was particularly useful in the event of close combat.

With the continuing stream of propaganda that accompanied the heroics of the Red Army in the field, the "cult of the sniper" emerged during the war. According to sources, several snipers amassed incredible numbers of kills. The most famous of these was Senior Sergeant Vasili Zaitsev, with at least 242. However, others were said to have exceeded that total considerably, including master snipers Nikolai Ilyin with 496, Ivan Kulbertinov 487, Mikhail Budenkov 427, Fyodor Okhlopkov 429, and Fyodor Djachenko 425. Ivan Sidorenko, a junior lieutenant with a mortar company, claimed the highest number of kills at 500 and was said to have taught himself sniping skills during the fighting around Moscow in late 1941.

Sidorenko survived the war and died at age 74 in Chelyabinsk in 1994. Ilyin was killed in action on August 4, 1943, during the epic battle of Kursk. Little is known of Kulbertinov other than his ominous nickname – Siberian Midnight. Okhlopkov was seriously wounded in the chest on June 23, 1944, just days after receiving the Order of the Red Banner. It was his 12th wound of the war and the end of his career as a sniper. However, he marched in the great Moscow Victory Day parade in 1945 and went on to hold numerous political offices for the next quarter century, including chief of the military department of the Tattinsky District Communist Party committee.

Female snipers were quite productive as well, and it is believed that more than 2,000 saw action during the war. According to Soviet records, the top female Soviet sniper was Lyudmila Pavlichenko with 309 kills. Natalia Kovshova reportedly shot 167 Germans, and Nina Petrova 122. Aliya Moldagulova was only 16 years old when she withdrew from technical school to join the Red Army and train at the Women's Sniper Training School in Veshnyaki outside Moscow. A soldier of the 64th Rifle Brigade, she reportedly killed 91 Germans before she lost her life in combat on January 14, 1944.

Zaitsev established a sniper school amid the rubble of Stalingrad, and one of his pupils, Tania Chernova, was believed by some to be her instructor's lover. During only three months

An instructor at the women's Central Sniper School encourages graduates as they head for the front. (Creative Commons RIA Novosti via Wikipedia)

of fighting in Stalingrad, she was credited with shooting 80 enemy soldiers and earned the nickname of the "Blond Sniper." She was wounded in the explosion of a land mine but recovered. Unconfirmed reports speculate that she lived until 2015 and well into her 90s.

Of course, there are many who doubt the veracity of the Soviet sniper records in World War II. Captain Clifford Shore, who fought in Europe in the West and penned the postwar classic With British Snipers to the Reich, devoted an entire chapter of the book to the Soviets and titled it "Russian Sniping...and the Great Myth."

Nevertheless, there is no doubt that Red Army snipers were members of an elite class of Soviet soldier. They certainly made their presence felt throughout the conflict. ■

VASILI ZAITSEV

The most celebrated sniper of World War II, or the Great Patriotic War, as it is remembered in the Soviet Union, was a shepherd born in the village of Elininski in the foothills of the Ural Mountains on March 23, 1915.

Senior Sergeant Vasili Zaitsev claimed at least 242 sniper kills against the Germans on the Eastern Front, many of them during the prolonged Battle of Stalingrad as the Red Army and the Wehrmacht were locked in a death struggle at the city on the great River Volga. Zaitsev grew up with a rifle in his hands, and his skills were honed protecting his flock against roaming wolves and hunting game in the deep forest. His grandfather taught him the basics of the stalk and told the boy, "The man of the forest is without fear."

When the Germans launched Operation Barbarossa, the invasion of the Soviet Union, on June 22, 1941, Zaitsev was serving as a bookkeeper in the Soviet Navy and posted to the far eastern port of Vladivostok. He volunteered for service with the army, and as every man and woman who could carry a weapon was needed at Stalingrad, he arrived there in September 1942 with the 284th Rifle Division. Zaitsev had already impressed his comrades with his proficiency with the 7.62mm (.30-calibre) Moisin Nagant Model 1891/30 rifle.

In just four weeks at the front, Zaitsev killed 40 Germans, and by December his total was said to have increased to an incredible 225. He swiftly became a national hero, grist for

Vasili Zaitsev greets soldiers of the Red Army. Zaitsev was credited with 242 sniper kills. *(Public Domain Russian Federation via Wikimedia Commons)*

Vasili Zaitsev was the most celebrated Red Army sniper of World War II. *(Creative Commons Mil.ru via Wikipedia)*

the robust Soviet propaganda mill that was desperately in need of heroes to bolster the morale of the people. Zaitsev became the scourge of the German Army at Stalingrad, and the story of his deadly encounter and dispatch of a German master sniper, known as Major Konigs, Colonel Heinz Thorwald, or Colonel Erwin Konig – whether thoroughly factual or embellished by propagandists – has become the stuff of legend.

Only the January 1943 blast of a mortar shell that temporarily blinded the hunter from Urals could halt Zaitsev's amazing string of sniper kills. He recovered and became an instructor of other snipers at a makeshift training centre in Stalingrad.

After the war, Zaitsev wrote a memoir of his experiences titled Notes of a Russian Sniper. He commented, "As a sniper I've killed more than a few Nazis. I have a passion for observing enemy behaviour. You watch a Nazi officer come out of a bunker, acting all high and mighty, ordering his soldiers every which way, and putting on an air of authority. The officer hasn't got the slightest idea that he only has seconds to live."

Zaitsev ended the war with the rank of captain and later became the manager of a textile factory in Kiev. He died in the city on December 15, 1991, at the age of 76. He was originally buried in Kiev, but later his remains were reinterred in Stalingrad (now Volgograd) at the massive memorial of Mamayev Kurgan.

During the course of his wartime service, Zaitsev was honoured as Hero of the Soviet and received four awards of the Order of Lenin, two of the Order of the Red Banner, and other recognition. The 2001 feature film Enemy at the Gates featured actor Jude Law as Zaitsev and was based in part on William Craig's 1973 book Enemy at the Gates: The Battle for Stalingrad. ■

Wearing white camouflage, Vasili Zaitsev, Red Army master sniper, prepares to take aim. *(Creative Commons Mil.ru via Wikipedia)*

ELITE FORCES OF WORLD WAR II

SOVIET NAVAL INFANTRY

Tracing its heritage to 1705 and the reign of Emperor Peter the Great, the Soviet naval infantry had dwindled to a single brigade in the Baltic Fleet on the eve of World War II. However, that strength was augmented during the conflict and increased to 350,000 personnel in 40 brigades, five of which were honoured for their service with the elite "Guards" designation as well as two battalions.

The new naval infantry formations were raised from across the Soviet Union, from the Black Sea to the Baltic and the Pacific, and the Soviet experience during the brief but costly Winter War with Finland in 1939-1940 prompted an increase in amphibious capability. After the German invasion of the Soviet Union in June 1941, the Soviet navy assumed a defensive posture and primarily supported coastal land operations. This focus allowed the military establishment to transfer a large number of naval personnel to units that would ultimately function as light infantry.

On June 22, the first day of the Nazi invasion, an existing naval infantry company of the Danube Flotilla counterattacked into neighbouring Romania. During four days of heavy fighting, this company, along with elements of the 25th Infantry Division and a detachment of border guards, held a substantial stretch of the River Danube on the Romanian side, withdrawing only after they were threatened with encirclement by rapidly advancing enemy forces on their flanks.

Although there was relatively little formalised training for the naval infantry units in the beginning, a more formalised program developed by 1942. Naval infantry formations were often led by army officers, and two naval infantry brigades fought at Stalingrad. Four naval infantry brigades drawn from Pacific Fleet personnel served under Marshal Georgi Zhukov in halting the German advance on Moscow in the winter of 1941.

During the course of the war, the need for more troops trained in amphibious warfare and the production of adequate numbers of landing craft became greater priorities for the Soviet military, and by 1945, the naval infantry had participated in 122 amphibious landing operations and participated in the defence of Odessa, Leningrad, Novorossiysk, Kerch, and Sevastopol in addition to Moscow and Stalingrad.

At Sevastopol, naval infantry units were supported by gunfire from warships and a handful of tanks in repulsing the first German drive against the Crimean port city in the autumn of 1941. A renewed enemy assault in December overran the 8th Naval Infantry Brigade, which withdrew from perimeter defences into the city itself. After months of siege warfare, a German assault in late June 1942, decimated the 7th Naval Infantry Brigade and 775th Rifle Regiment as they fought side by side. Troops of the 83rd Naval Infantry Brigade sustained serious losses in the amphibious operations that spawned the Battle of the Kerch Peninsula, a failed attempt to break the siege of Sevastopol in December 1941. Although the city finally fell to the Nazis, the occupiers found themselves conversely trapped inside as the Red Army rallied and advanced on the Eastern Front later in the war.

A total of 122 naval infantrymen were honoured with the title Hero of the Soviet Union for their actions in combat during World War II. The naval infantry brigades were disbanded in 1947, but sometime later the concept of amphibious warfare capability was revived. Today, the Russian armed forces include naval infantry, sometimes referred to as marines, as a component of the Coastal Troops of the Russian Navy. ■

Soviet naval infantry hoist their red banner at Port Arthur in Manchuria, 1939. *(Creative Commons RIA Novosti via Wikipedia)*

Soviet naval infantrymen man a machine gun during the siege of Leningrad. *(Creative Commons RIA Novosti via Wikipedia)*

Soviet naval infantrymen stand in ranks in Red Square during the 1945 World War II victory parade. *(Creative Commons Mil.ru via Wikipedia)*

ILYUSHIN IL-2 SHTURMOVIK SQUADRONS

The panzer formations were the mailed fist of the Nazi juggernaut that launched Operation Barbarossa, the invasion of the Soviet Union, on June 22, 1941. German armoured spearheads struck deep into Russia and spread chaos among opposing Red Army units.

But as the Great Patriotic War was prolonged and Soviet resistance stiffened, the panzer met its match on land with the introduction of the formidable T-34 medium tank and in the air with a flying tank, the Ilyushin Il-2 Shturmovik. The Il-2 and its improved variant, the Il-10, were the most successful ground attack and anti-armour aircraft of World War II, and the men and women who flew them were possessed of steeled nerve and burning resolve to strike back at the invaders.

During the course of the war, more than 36,000 Shturmovik aircraft were constructed, and its production in such great numbers is a testament to the type's success in its specified role. Designed by Sergey Ilyushin in 1938, the Il-2 made its first appearance in combat just days after the Nazi invasion. Losses were high in the beginning as the 4th Ground Attack Regiment, the first air unit to deploy the Il-2, lost 55 of 65 aircraft in combat with Luftwaffe fighters and antiaircraft batteries. Tactics were reviewed and refined in the wake of the disappointing results, and soon the Il-2 was becoming a deadly adversary.

The Ilyushin Il-2 Shturmovik was a workhorse ground attack aircraft of the Soviet Air Force. *(Public Domain Russian Federation via Wikimedia Commons)*

Variants of the Shturmovik, which translates from the Russian literally as ground attack aircraft, were armed in numerous configurations. Cannon ranging from 20mm to 37mm were affixed to the wings, and the primary such anti-tank weapon was the 23mm Volkov-Yartsev Vya-23. The aircraft was also capable of carrying a bombload of four 220-pound bombs or a single bomb of up to 1,320 pounds. Some models were fitted with 82mm rockets. For air defence or ground strafing the Il-2 mounted a

With cannon firing, Il-2 ground attack aircraft dive on German targets on the Eastern Front. *(Creative Commons RIA Novosti via Wikipedia)*

Senior Lieutenant Anna Yegorova flew 277 missions at the controls of an Il-2 Shturmovik. *(Public Domain USSR Information Bulletin, volume 4, number 98. September 1, 1944 via Wikimedia Commons)*

pair of forward-firing 7.62mm machine guns and a rear-facing single 12.7mm machine gun.

With weaponry capable of defeating the thick German armour of the PzKpfw. V Panther medium tank and even the PzKpfw. VI Tiger heavy tank, the Il-2 earned the grudging respect of the enemy. The Germans nicknamed the plane the "Black Death" and "Iron Gustav." The Luftwaffe fighter pilots who attempted to shoot it down found it stubbornly survivable. They called it the "Concrete Aircraft." Western Allied airmen who saw the Il-2 in action christened it the "Flying Tank." Effective against German tanks, convoys, troop concentrations, and artillery emplacements, the Shturmovik became the scourge of the Wehrmacht.

Although their sturdy planes were difficult to shoot down, protected by up to 13mm of steel surrounding the vital areas of the cockpit and

ELITE FORCES OF WORLD WAR II

Il-2 Shturmoviks fly over the Nazi capital of Berlin in 1945. (Public Domain LA gran guerra patria de la unión soviética. 1975 Government of Ukraine via Wikimedia Commons)

This Il-2 mounts 37mm cannon in underwing pods. The Il-2 also carried bombs and rockets. (Public Domain via Wikimedia Commons)

the engine, the pilots who flew the Il-2 were of superior constitution. They swept in low, exposing themselves to intense enemy ground fire, to deliver their payloads against exposed targets. Like birds of prey, they often circled and then assaulted the enemy in screaming dives, blasting their victims, and then clawing for altitude. It was common practice to make multiple passes, which only heightened the possibility of a crash or fatal damage from flak.

Lieutenant Ivan Grigorevich was the most successful Il-2 pilot of the war. A Hero of the Soviet Union, he was one of four individuals to receive the Order of Glory three times. After joining the Red Army in 1941, Drachenko transferred to the air force two years later and experienced his first combat during the epic Battle of Kursk in the summer of 1943. He was seriously wounded months later and taken prisoner by the Germans only to escape from captivity and return to the air with the 140th Guards Ground Attack Regiment, even though he had lost an eye.

During the bitter fighting of mid-1944, Drachenko and his rear gunner fought off an attack by no fewer than nine enemy fighters, limping back to base with their Il-2 badly shot up. Soon, he was back in the air and strafed a German train while shooting down an enemy fighter in the same mission. A few days later, he commanded a flight of six Il-2s on the hunt for enemy tanks. Pressing home their attacks, the Soviet pilots destroyed three Tiger tanks that had opposed Red Army ground troops, opening the way for a rapid advance.

Drachenko proved remarkably adept in all aspects of aerial warfare. During the course of the war, he shot down five German planes and became an air ace. He is believed to have killed more than 1,600 enemy soldiers and destroyed four bridges, 76 German tanks and armoured vehicles, six trains, and an incredible 600 automobiles.

Soviet reports of Il-2 activity are nothing short of astounding. In one case, three waves of 30 Shturmoviks ravaged a German armoured concentration, destroying 34 tanks and forcing the enemy to fall back. Another report states that the 9th Panzer Division was assailed by waves of Shturmoviks and lost at least 70 tanks in less than 30 minutes of intense action.

Attrition took its toll of operational Il-2s, and even late in the war as the Red Army drove relentlessly toward Berlin, Soviet Premier Josef Stalin wrote to the workers who produced the Il-2. "You have let down our country and our Red Army. You have not manufactured Il-2s until now. The Il-2 aircraft are necessary for our Red Army now, like air, like bread. Shenkman produces one Il-2 a day, and Tretiakov builds one or two MiG-3s daily. It is a mockery of our country and the Red Army. I ask you not to try the government's patience and demand that you manufacture more Il-2s. I warn you for the last time. Stalin."

At the same time, the Il-2 pilots who took to the air did everything in their power to carry the war to the Nazis. Lieutenant Anna Timofyeyevna Yegorova flew 260 missions with the 305th Ground Attack Regiment. She was decorated for bravery three times and proclaimed a Hero of the Soviet Union. When she was shot down, it was assumed that the last of her honours were posthumous; however, after the war she emerged from a German prison camp very much alive.

After joining the Red Army in 1940, Talgat Yakubekovich Begeldinov transferred to aviation training and became a pilot in 1942. He flew more than 300 sorties and rose to command the 144th Guards Ground Attack Regiment. Twice honoured as a Hero of the Soviet Union, he ended the war with the rank of colonel. Begeldinov was particularly skilled in strafing and regularly led missions against German airfields, destroying numerous enemy planes on the ground. In addition to his ground attack prowess, Begeldinov shot down four German Messerschmitt Me-109 fighters and a Junkers Ju-87 Stuka dive bomber during the war.

Begeldinov was shot down in enemy territory on May 6, 1943, and though both he and his gunner, P.V. Yakovlenko, survived the crash, Yakovlevenko was drowned when the two men attempted to swim across the River Seversky Donets. Begeldinov managed to reach safety on the opposite side and was rushed to a hospital with wounds to his leg and shoulder. Within a month, he was back in action. He remained in the Soviet Air Force until 1956, retiring with the rank of major general. ■

An Ilyushin Il-2 takes off at a modern air show. Il-2 pilots destroyed many German armoured vehicles. (Creative Commons Dmitry Terekhov via Wikipedia)

13TH GUARDS RIFLE DIVISION

Soviet soldiers attack during the lengthy Battle of the Dniepr in 1943.
(Public Domain Government of Ukraine via Wikimedia Commons)

"I am a Communist! I have no intention of abandoning the city!" Such were the stirring words of Colonel General Aleksandr Rodimtsev as his 13th Guards Rifle Division was charged with sacrificing everything in defence of the embattled city of Stalingrad, the industrial centre on the River Volga that bore the name of Soviet Premier Josef Stalin.

Stalingrad had been a focus of the German offensive against the Red Army in 1942 for months, but eventually the tables turned and the invaders were surrounded in the city by determined Soviet forces that compelled them to surrender in early 1943. Until then, however, the 13th Guards Rifle Division fought with distinction, holding the enemy fast at critical ground between the heights of the Mamayev Kurgan and the Tsaritsa Gorge and elsewhere.

On September 14, 1942, the division forced a crossing of the Volga and shored up defensive positions that were held by only a handful of beleaguered tanks and troops. Heavy casualties were sustained in the battle, but a German assault was repelled. In other fighting around Stalingrad, Lieutenant Anton Dragan and fewer than 50 men of the 13th Guards held the city's railroad station against repeated enemy attacks. Fighting the Germans room to room and even working their way underneath the building to pop up from beneath the floor, Dragan and his valiant men resisted until their ammunition was nearly depleted and most of their number killed or wounded. Dragan eventually slipped away with only five other men still alive.

By the time the 13th Guards Division entered combat at Stalingrad, it was already recognised as an elite formation of the Red Army. Formed in January 1942 as a redesignation of the 87th Rifle Division, the 13th earned the designation "Guards" in recognition of its previous fighting spirit. The 13th Division was thrown into the Second Battle of Kharkov in the spring of 1942 and suffered more than 50 percent casualties in repelling German counterattacks that quelled a Soviet offensive. Narrowly escaping encirclement, the division was withdrawn in mid-July, reinforced, and deployed to Stalingrad. Rodimtsev was placed in command of the 87th Division in November prior to the name transition. At Stalingrad the intrepid officer earned his second designation as Hero of the Soviet Union.

While it is believed that only about 300 men of the 13th Guards Division survived the fighting at Mamayev Kurgan, the Red October Tractor Plant, and other critical sectors at Stalingrad, the remnants of the unit were withdrawn, refitted and replenished once again, and then assigned to the 5th Guards Army.

The Battle of Kursk, the greatest clash of opposing armour in World War II, followed in July 1943, and the 13th Guards Rifle Division was moved from reserve into a defensive line at Oboyan, contributing to the eventual blunting of German attacks against the Soviet perimeter. From there, the division participated in the liberation of Ukraine, taking control of the town of Poltava after a fierce fight in September 1943. From that time, the division was known as the 13th Guards Rifle Division, Poltava. The long struggle during the Battle of the Dniepr followed, and its capture of the rail junction at Pomoshnaya and the town of Novoukrainka resulted in the award of the Order of Suvorov at the end of March 1944. Days later, the capture of Pervomaysk led to a second unit award of the Order of the Red Banner. By war's end the division had driven into Germany and captured the city of Dresden.

During the course of the Great Patriotic War, more than 20,000 soldiers who served with the 13th Guards Rifle Division received decorations for bravery, and 19 of them were honoured with Hero of the Soviet Union designation. Rodimtsev retired from the Red Army in 1977 after 50 years of service. ∎

Soviet soldiers advance through a trench during the heavy fighting at Stalingrad.
(Public Domain via Wikimedia Commons)

General Aleksandr Rodimtsev confers with soldiers of the 13th Guards Rifle Division.
(Creative Commons mil.ru via Wikipedia)

ELITE FORCES OF WORLD WAR II

ELITE FORCES PERSPECTIVE

On land, sea, and air, they were distinguished with acts of incredible bravery amid situations fraught with danger. Ordinary men and women would shrink from the call to such duty. But for these exceptional individuals there was no other response but to step forward.

The elite forces of World War II fought for king and country, for freedom and justice. They also served evil dictators, fighting for their Führer, Il Duce, and the empire. Committed to their cause, they exhibited extraordinary prowess in combat. From a handful of Commandos using the element of surprise or the art of deception to the quick strike of the determined airborne and armoured division, elite forces exerted tremendous influence on the course of the conflict.

Prime Minister Winston Churchill called for elite forces to "set Europe ablaze." And they did. President Franklin D. Roosevelt pushed for the creation of parachute divisions. And it

Motor launches of this type took part in Operation Chariot, the daring raid on the Normandie lock at St. Nazaire in March 1942. *(Public Domain Collections of the Imperial War Musuems via Wikimedia Commons)*

Royal Marine Commandos come ashore at Juno Beach on D-Day, June 6, 1944. *(Public Domain Collections of the Imperial War Museums via Wikimedia Commons)*

was done. Premier Josef Stalin called for the production of decisive weapons of war. And they were built. Adolf Hitler, twisted megalomaniac that he was, sought fanatical followers "as hard as Krupp steel." And his misguided devotees answered. Death in the service of the Japanese emperor, so many young men believed, was an end to be desired. And the Divine Wind of the Kamikaze left a poignant but destructive legacy.

World War II was a proving ground for the structure and implementation of elite forces. Never before in the history of armed conflict had such a commitment been made to the formation of units that specialised in certain aspects of warfare and those who might contribute to final victory in the shadows. The elite forces parachuted into battle, drove four-wheel drive trucks at breakneck speed across the barren desert, piloted midget submarines in death defying operations, rode human torpedoes, splashed onto

A heavy four-engine Avro Lancaster bomber of No. 617 Squadron RAF waits for the order to take off with its bombload. *(Public Domain Collections of the Imperial War Museums via Wikimedia Commons)*

ELITE FORCES PERSPECTIVE

Merrill's Marauders trek along a jungle trail in Burma during a long-range deployment. *(Public Domain US Signal Corps via Wikimedia Commons)*

Commandos of the 1st Special Service Brigade pause beside a Jeep on D-Day. *(Public Domain Collections of the Imperial War Museums via Wikimedia Commons)*

Officers of the 1st SS Leibstandarte Adolf Hitler pose for a photographer in Russia. *(Creative Commons Bundesarchiv Bild via Wikipedia)*

distant shores to gather intelligence and strike blows, and remained at their posts to the end.

Theirs was a breed apart.

Alexander the Great once remarked, "There has been a constant war, a war with fear. Those who have the courage to conquer it are made free and those who are conquered by it are made to suffer until they have the courage to defeat it."

The elite forces of World War II first waged the personal war against fear and conquered it. In turn, they were compelled to fight the determined foe, never shrinking from their task. They turned toward the enemy when lesser military men and women might turn away and run. In doing so, they established the foundation of the modern elite forces, those formations that carry the battle streamers, the unit citations, the heraldry, and the tradition of the warrior of World War II in today's military organisations across the globe. They find in their predecessors, qualities worthy to be remembered and emulated.

Throughout World War II, elite forces were present in all theatres. Orde Wingate's Chindits and Merrill's Marauders slashed through dark jungle, Commandos dashed into the harbour at St. Nazaire to disable the Normandie Dock, the Special Air Service and Long Range Desert Group roared across the wasteland to attack enemy installations, the British 1st and 6th Airborne Divisions and the US 82nd and 101st fought epic fights on D-Day and at Arnhem and Bastogne and elsewhere. The Commandos rushed ashore at Dieppe and in Normandy. The men of the X-Craft pressed home their attacks against Tirpitz. Intrepid Il-2 Shturmovik pilots struck hard at the Nazi panzers, and the Soviet sniper stalked. Otto Skorzeny earned the nickname of the "most dangerous man in Europe" while leading covert missions across the continent. And, of course, there were many more.

Exploring the triumphs and tragedies of the elite forces of World War II offers an appreciation of the strategic as it blends with the tactical. The men who made ideas become reality and set the great raids, remarkable missions, and sustained battles of the conflict in motion were often ready and willing to risk their own lives in the execution.

The motto of the Special Air Service, "Who Dares Wins," puts the performance of elite forces in perspective. Audacious, resolute and irrepressible, even in desperate situations, these units large and small carved their names in the annals of modern warfare and left an indelible mark on the future of armed conflict. Without hesitation, these warriors accepted the challenge presented. They understood that lives would be lost and that it would, in the end, be necessary to count the cost. ■

Soldiers of the Red Army's 13th Guards Rifle Division find a moment to relax during fighting on the Eastern Front. *(Public Domain aloban75.livejournal.com/564228.html Russian Federation via Wikimedia Commons)*

Troopers of the 101st Airborne Division trudge through snow toward the town of Bastogne during the Battle of the Bulge. *(Public Domain US Army via Wikimedia Commons)*